'This is an original, thoughtful, well-written, and practical text for mental health professionals. Based on the authors rich and extensive clinical experience, this volume describes their novel group intervention for adults who are overcontrolled. This is a client group for whom mental health professionals often struggle to offer something therapeutically meaningful as the transdiagnostic nature of their difficulties goes unaddressed. I highly recommend it to students and experienced therapists alike.'

Gary O'Reilly, *Professor and Director, Doctoral Training Programme in Clinical Psychology, University College Dublin*

'In this fantastic new book, Rachel Egan and Richard Booth introduce their innovative approach to working with excessive self-control known as Group Radical Openness (GRO). The book outlines the origins of GRO, how and why it developed, some of the key ideas underpinning it, as well as a helpful and engaging session-by-session description of the group. This manual will be essential reading for any clinician, but more specifically, for those wanting to help people with excessive self-control.'

Chris Irons, *PhD, Director of Balanced Minds, co-author of* The Compassionate Mind Workbook

'Richard and Rachel's book sets out their humane and practical approach towards helping people whose lives are negatively affected by overcontrol. Working in a specialist personality disorder service, we have found GRO invaluable as an accessible and acceptable treatment for a highly distressed group of people. I can highly recommend this book to clinicians working with people who suffer problems related to overcontrol.'

Tim Agnew, *MBChB, FRCPsych, Consultant Psychiatrist NHS Scotland, Chair of the Scottish Personality Disorder Network*

'This book is an outstanding addition to clinical care. The sessions in GRO are thoughtful and, in many cases, highly original. The most impressive part is how Richard and Rachel structure the programme, resulting in the participants becoming more empowered as the group progresses, and taking ownership of their therapy. In my own work with Trauma, I see how GRO would be invaluable to those who are overcontrolled and embarking on a healing journey.'

Deirdre Fay, *MSW, author of* Becoming Safely Embodied *and* Attachment Based Yoga & Meditation for Trauma

'Group Radical Openness (GRO) has allowed us to provide treatment for men in our service who are overcontrolled. The personal testimonies of the men who have completed GRO showed how much they gained from participating in the programme. They found that the content increased their personal insight and resulted in many of them becoming more flexible, more open to emotion, and more connected with others. We would highly recommend Rachel and Richard's book to anyone looking for an effective way of working with overcontrol.'

GRO Clinical Team, *Westgate Personality Disorder Treatment Service, HMP Frankland*

Group Radical Openness

This innovative book introduces Group Radical Openness (GRO), a group treatment for individuals who struggle with costly and harmful overcontrol.

The book opens with the background and evolution of GRO, followed by a thorough description of how to assess overcontrol. This novel group approach draws on both Group Therapy and Polyvagal Theory and encourages an entirely different way of working with this client group. It explores the concept of overcontrol, describing a pattern of distance in relationships, rigidity, and emotional inhibition. The 27-session group treatment leads the participants on a journey where they develop trust and safety with each other, show flexibility, and become more emotionally aware and expressive. Chapters feature engaging clinical examples and strikingly original exercises.

This book is aimed at clinicians looking for ways to effectively treat disorders characterised by excessive self-control, such as mood disorders, eating disorders, and certain personality disorders. This will be an important resource in a wide range of mental health and forensic settings.

Richard Booth, PhD, is a clinical psychologist, researcher, and trainer. He is an Honorary Fellow of University College Dublin. He was Director of Psychology at St. Patrick's Mental Health Services for 25 years. He currently focuses on training and supervision for Group Radical Openness.

Rachel Egan, D.Psych., Sc., is a principal clinical psychologist in St. Patrick's Mental Health Services. She previously worked in the Irish Prison Service. Rachel is currently the clinical lead of the Group Radical Openness programme and offers trainings and supervision in this intervention.

Group Radical Openness

An Intervention for Overcontrol

Richard Booth and Rachel Egan

Routledge
Taylor & Francis Group
LONDON AND NEW YORK

Cover image: © Getty Images

First published 2023
by Informa Law from Routledge
4 Park Square, Milton Park, Abingdon, Oxon OX14 4RN

and by Informa Law from Routledge
605 Third Avenue, New York, NY 10158

Informa Law from Routledge is an imprint of the Taylor & Francis Group, an informa business

British Library Cataloguing-in-Publication Data
A catalogue record for this book is available from the British Library

Library of Congress Cataloging-in-Publication Data
Names: Booth, Richard, author. | Egan, Rachel, author.
Title: Group radical openness : an intervention for overcontrol /
Richard Booth and Rachel Egan.
Description: Abingdon, Oxon ; New York, NY : Routledge, 2023. |
Includes bibliographical references and index. | Identifiers: LCCN 2022041092 (print) |
LCCN 2022041093 (ebook) | ISBN 9781032343358 (hardback) |
ISBN 9781032343341 (paperback) | ISBN 9781003321576 (ebook)
Subjects: LCSH: Self-control–Psychological aspects.
Classification: LCC BF632 .B58 2023 (print) | LCC BF632 (ebook) |
DDC 158–dc23/eng/20221214
LC record available at https://lccn.loc.gov/2022041092
LC ebook record available at https://lccn.loc.gov/2022041093

ISBN: 9781032343358 (hbk)
ISBN: 9781032343341 (pbk)
ISBN: 9781003321576 (ebk)

DOI: 10.4324/9781003321576

Typeset in Times New Roman
by Newgen Publishing UK

It is useless to attempt to reason a man out of a thing he was never reasoned into … Reason is a very light rider and easily shook off.

Jonathon Swift (1667–1745), founder of St. Patrick's Hospital

Contents

Illustrations

Figures

Tables

Foreword by Christine Dunkley

When invited to do a foreword for this book, I initially thought I would plot the history of my involvement in this project. I would describe my initial trepidation as a visiting trainer to the renowned Department of Psychology at St. Patrick's Hospital, Dublin, to falling hopelessly in love with its staff and ethos. I yearned to recapture my early exciting meetings with Richard Booth and Rachel Egan, so that you too could *feel* their warmth and energy, and be moved by their passion and dedication to their clinical population. I wanted to describe my own experience researching and treating both undercontrolled and overcontrolled clients, perhaps to justify why Richard and Rachel would choose me for the 3 "C"s – Confidante, Cheerleader and occasional Consultant. But all of that would simply have been a backdrop to what I really long to tell you – how these two brilliant psychologists became intrigued by the concept of overcontrol, and how this led them down a path to develop this incredible therapy.

Overcontrol is a coping style that relies on predictability and personal constraint, associated with hard work, perfectionism, and often high achievement. It has the side effect of painful emotional loneliness. These are people who live slightly outside of the tribe, never quite feeling connected.

Rachel and Richard recognised the real-life suffering of overcontrolled patients in their care. They saw huge gaps in the treatment provision for this population. They devoured all they could from reading and training until they were well versed in what was out there. With the shortcoming and gaps they identified, they set forth on developing a new approach. Because of my experience with this clinical group, it was particularly fascinating to be kept up to date with their observations and thoughts as they methodically built this new model.

The pair noted that current treatments sought to teach overcontrolled patients about their style, offering lessons in how to change. The aim was to encourage the patient to apply skills in their everyday life and gradually become part of the tribe. Richard and Rachel turned this on its head. Why not form the group into a tribe and instead of teaching skills to develop closeness, have them grow it between themselves? Although this might sound like a traditional psychodynamic therapy group, they knew that would not have worked with such socially fearful clients. Enough theory, structure, and predictability had to be built in to manage their urge to flee. What a tightrope to walk – too much scaffolding and the relationships would be artificial, not enough and they would retreat fearing further social bruising. This was a complex task. To their credit, our intrepid duo stuck with the challenge and Group Radical Openness (GRO) was born. Surely the three-letter acronym was a good omen!

Rachel and Richard threw themselves into this version of therapy Jenga, carefully constructing a solid framework in the early stages, then easing out some of the 'therapist' blocks in the second, so the group would fill the void. GRO therapists are open about their own overcontrol and willing to hand over the reins. In the latter stages of the programme, the role of the therapist is much reduced and, almost imperceptibly, the shift is made so that it is the clients who challenge, support, and guide each other.

There are so many highlights I can commend to you. It gladdens my behavioural heart that the text is so clear, concise, and practical. The treatment moves far from my DBT roots, but with each divergent step being elegantly justified. Insight-building exercises abound, carefully calibrated to challenge rather than overwhelm the participants. The clinical examples in this book are so poignant they make you forget you are reading, and think you are actually there. Here is each member of the group unfolding like the petals of a peony, turning into something softer yet larger, claiming more personal space with less effort. And yes, the outcome is beautiful.

Another intervention gem is the GROhari Exercise. Yes, you read that correctly! A witty adaptation of the Johari Window that is well-paced and perfectly timed for these clients. In this activity, what has already been revealed to the group is honoured, and more is forthcoming. In the trademark Booth/Egan style, the client is invited to engage in a dialectical dance – learning more about themselves and then sharing with other people in a supported way. For a moment, I feared that what was being asked of them was too much, but that's when I forgot that GRO provides access to the gift of co-regulation. It is a masterpiece of balance, impeccably judged at every turn.

Those of you who know me will agree I like to call a spade a spade such that if you ask for feedback you had better really want it. I am seldom left with nothing to add. That is until I encountered The Tracker. This unique activity is not a one-off exercise, but a new regular practice introduced to the clients in the final third of the programme. They are invited to stand up in front of the group and map visual representations of moments where they were trying to be more radically open. It sounds too simple to be life-changing. But here, before your eyes, an epiphany takes place. The group asks a series of pre-determined questions: probing, inviting, connecting. Suddenly there is the merging of two worlds – the client is still centre-stage, but now *they are not alone.* Though they are steering the ship, there are other hands on the ropes, fresh eyes in the crow's nest, and plentiful assistance to set the sails. The team is hauling together.

This could only have been created by therapists without ego. Rachel and Richard are clinicians who understand what is needed to get an overcontrolled client to contemplate such openness. Moreover, they are willing to step aside, such that the tribe becomes the agent of change. In the book, the many examples are so rich that I defy you not to be moved. Here we have a group who feel they have never really connected, and now they can – like cochlear implant patients hearing for the very first time.

I am envious of you as you delve into this text. The author and satirist Jonathon Swift founded the hospital where Richard and Rachel work. No doubt he would be pleased that they carved out this new territory with respect, daring, and wit. He would be proud that something created in his hospital is set to have deep impact far afield. Rachel and Richard's generosity of spirit will wash over you. They will pull you gently into their tribe and there you will want to stay. You will treat your patients and your patients will treat you. It is a humbling and enlightening process.

I feel I have been an invested observer in the treatment development process, as Rachel and Richard's compassionate creativity has blossomed into this precious therapy. They have already changed lives by providing a key for many patients locked in a prison of overcontrol. Now, as this knowledge is shared with you in a "how-to" manual, they can help others further afield.

It has been an absolute privilege to accompany this pair on their journey, and now to start you off on your own. The pages await, and I will keep you no longer.

With warm affection,
Christine Dunkley, DClinP
Consultant Trainer
British Isles DBT Team

Acknowledgements

Tom and Erica Lynch introduced us to the concept of overcontrol and engaged our early interest. We had many lively discussions with them. Tom came to our hospital to train us and, memorably, sat in on one of our groups. Later, when it became clear that we were taking a very different path, we visited them in their home in France and showed them some of the novel features in the model we were developing. On this new leg of the journey, we have had many stimulating conversations with Bonnie Badenoch, Deb Dana, Kate Lucre, and Gary O'Reilly, all of whom have been hugely generous with their time and their ideas.

We are fortunate to work in a hospital where training, contact with experts in a range of areas, and innovation are all encouraged. This is personified by Tom Maher, the Director of Clinical Services, who followed the development of GRO closely. He sought feedback from service users, from the multidisciplinary teams, as well as reviewing our data with us. When he saw its impact and how well it was being received, he provided full backing. It would be hard to imagine a manager as receptive to a new treatment, or as intent on smoothing the path to make its development possible.

Over the eight years, many clinicians have worked alongside us. We would like to pay particular thanks to Katie Baird for her work in the early days, and to James McElvaney for his more recent work on our research programme. Thanks also to our colleague Clodagh Dowling, who provides ongoing support and cheerleading for GRO. We have been very fortunate in the calibre of Assistant Psychologists who worked alongside us. Claire O'Sullivan, Emer Long, and Katie Browne made significant contributions to the development of the model. We have drawn on the intellect, clinical intuition, and wisdom of our cherished colleague Violet Johnstone. Karen Looney has thoughtfully adapted the model for older adults in our service. Teams at the NHS Highland Personality Disorder Service in Inverness, and the Westgate Personality Disorder Treatment Service in HMP Frankland have shown striking innovation in their use of the model. A special thanks to our families (particularly John and Lynda) and friends for their endless support, and to Marco Booth for his wise feedback on early drafts. Along with Violet Johnstone mentioned earlier, our current team consisting of Cliona Hallissey, Muireann O'Donnell, Cian McDonough, Aideen O'Neill, Chelsea Carr, Senan Tuohy Hamill, and Georgina Heffernan have been a delight to work with.

Christine Dunkley has been our rock. She is one of the most experienced and original thinkers on the treatment of undercontrol, as witnessed by her recent book on emotional regulation. She co-authored an early seminal paper on Radically Open Dialectical Behaviour Therapy (RO DBT) and led a site on the randomised controlled trial of this approach. She took an interest in our work and sponsored our first training outside our hospital, at which she was an eager participant. Her feedback was memorably insightful. Anyone who has worked with her will know of her nourishing, validating style. She never imposed her own ideas, but sought to find ways in which we could develop our own. We awaited her edits on each chapter with excitement. In more ways than she probably realises, she did so much to keep the fire burning. There was no one else we wanted to write the foreword.

Our final thanks go to the many wonderful people who attended our groups. Working with them has been a privilege and they all hold a special place in our hearts. The words "inspiring" and "courageous" barely come close to describing their journeys. They trusted us, they taught us, and they sustained us. It is characteristic that those whose material we used were excited to contribute to GRO becoming more widely known. It is consistent with the model that their voices are prominent and carry the most powerful messages. We hope they will all feel that the book does justice to their wholehearted dedication.

Chapter 1

The Journey to Group Radical Openness (GRO)

Group Radical Openness (GRO) is a new treatment targeting a range of disorders characterised by excessive self-control. It has been successfully trialled in transdiagnostic groups with clients who experience depression, anorexia, avoidant personality disorder, and obsessive-compulsive personality disorder (OCPD). It promises to have a wider application in forensic and physical health settings. GRO started using the skills-only group of Radically Open Dialectical Behaviour Therapy (RO DBT, Lynch, 2018a). It has now developed into a distinct group therapy. The evolution of GRO is outlined in this chapter.

Living through Distress

The journey to GRO started in an unlikely way. In the Psychology Department in St. Patrick's Hospital Dublin, we were concerned about how best to respond to patients admitted with self-harm behaviour. In the first instance, we thought that if each psychologist committed two hours a week to a group intervention, we could target the immediate behaviour. Some of us had been part of Dialectical Behaviour Therapy (DBT) programmes in previous roles and we thought that we could select some skills from this model that had a proven track record. Using one element (the skills group) would not match a comprehensive DBT programme, but we felt it might still be of genuine benefit.

The doors opened on what was named the "Living through Distress" programme in June 2008. It consisted of a one-hour session four times a week. Between 10 and 16 inpatients attended who were currently or had recently been self-harming. There was no waiting list and precious few exclusion criteria. A new skill was introduced at each of the first eight sessions. These same skills were discussed in more depth over the next two weeks. For those who felt that they required more time or familiarity with the material, there was an option to repeat the 16-session programme.

DOI: 10.4324/9781003321576-1

The atmosphere was friendly, sometimes a little raucous or irreverent. Marsha Linehan's (the founder of DBT) principle of "You are doing the best you can, but you could do better" captured the emphasis on acceptance as much as change (Linehan, 1993). We spent the first half hour discussing the successes and failures of trying out what had been presented in the previous session. Then we moved to the next skill. There was a feeling of solidarity among the participants that was in marked contrast to their reported isolation on the ward. The power of the group and the capacity to learn from each other made a deep impression.

A feature of our approach from the outset was a commitment to measurement. We were well aware that we were not following an evidence-based protocol in using a skills-only group. We felt a duty to assess the outcome of our work at every point. There was a strong evidence base for DBT which includes five elements: individual therapy, telephone consult, a skills training class, structuring the environment, and a consult meeting between the therapists (Swales, 2018). The notion of replacing these with just the skills-only class was not without its critics. At one DBT conference where we presented our data, a delegate suggested that we were acting unethically in denying our patients the comprehensive evidence-based approach. We defended ourselves in three ways. First, we pointed out that if we directed all our resources towards a few patients for an extended period of time, this would mean that a much larger group of people who were actively self-harming would receive no intervention at all. We saw it therefore as a difficult but genuine dilemma: allocating a large resource to a small number of patients, or a small resource to all those who presented. Second, in having (at that time) four sessions a week, we were struck by the group dynamic that built up. Skills aside, the support the group members offered each other and the sense of relief they derived from finding others with whom they could identify was clearly very significant. Third, we knew we were deviating from standard practice and so collected data at every time point. The results were more impressive than we had dared hope from such a simple intervention. Our group intervention was having a dramatic effect on the incidence of self-harm as was shown in our first paper (Booth et al., 2014). In a second paper, this was explored further (Gibson et al., 2014). In that study, we had a waiting-list control group and we took the opportunity to study how change might be taking place. Three years later at the same conference, data was provided by leading researchers in DBT regarding the surprising impact of skills-only groups. We had been ahead of our time!

Far from being at odds with the DBT organisation, we worked closely with them to improve our own skills within an expanding format. Over time, this has developed into a comprehensive DBT programme. However, in that earlier period, we were offering a simpler model where the central aim was the replacement of self-harm with more adaptive coping strategies.

The Construct of Overcontrol

Clinicians tend to be as curious about those who do not respond to a treatment as about those who do. We certainly had a concern in the early days that there were some service users who were not benefitting from Living through Distress. In fact, they did not seem to fit in, radiating an unease rather than identifying with what others were describing. It was not clear to us why this might be, since they all had a history of self-harm.

A turning point was a talk we attended by Tom Lynch. Tom had been a senior trainer and researcher with the DBT organisation for many years. He had recently relocated to the UK and set up a research centre at the University of Southampton, focusing on the area of overcontrol. On the one hand, he acknowledged that inhibitory control is rightly valued. Superior capacities to inhibit responses, plan ahead, and delay gratification make overcontrolled individuals the doers, savers, planners, and fixers of the world. As he said, it is not just that they value honesty, fairness, and doing the right thing, but they are the reasons why trains run on time! On the other hand, he asked the crucial question as to whether it's possible to have too much of a good thing and whether there could be a cost for exerting too much control.

The construct of overcontrol, in various guises, went back over 40 years in the personality literature (Block & Block, 1980). However, Tom was a pioneer in bringing it to a wider audience of mental health practitioners. Instead of self-control, which had been the dominant clinical construct (the more the better as far as the mental health literature was concerned), he introduced us to the idea of undercontrol and overcontrol being distinct entities. He welcomed our interest and shared some of his measures. He assured us that self-harm, though less frequent, is also a common feature in those whose mental health difficulties are underpinned by overcontrol.

We were familiar with Marsha Linehan's bio-psycho-social model in relation to our emotionally dysregulated population, whom we now referred to as being undercontrolled (Linehan, 1993). We had never seen an equivalent model for overcontrol. Tom described what he thought were the biological or innate tendencies on the one hand, and the typical life experiences of overcontrol on the other. He pulled these together to highlight the coping strategies that would have understandably developed but, over time, could lead to significant mental health costs. He set out examples of his model as shown in Figure 1.1.

On the flight home from Tom's talk, we discussed how it was becoming clear that overcontrolled coping was not always problematic. However, there were certain styles of overcontrol that might incur mental health costs. Such overcontrol could be characterised by core deficits he had identified: low receptivity and openness; low flexible control; pervasive inhibited emotional expression and low emotional awareness; low social connectedness and intimacy with others. We started jotting down how Tom was suggesting that

NATURE
Low reward sensitivity
High threat sensitivity
High attention to detail
High inhibitory control

NURTURE
Self-control is imperative
Mistakes are intolerable
Always be prepared
Never reveal weakness

COPING
Mask inner feelings
Compulsive striving
Avoidance of unplanned risks
Aloof and distant social signalling style

Figure 1.1 The bio-psycho-social model of overcontrol
Source: Adapted from Lynch, 2018a, p. 47.

Table 1.1 Differences between undercontrol and overcontrol

	Undercontrol	*Overcontrol*
Core Problem	Emotional dysregulation	Emotional loneliness
Prototypical Disorder	BPD	OCPD
Behavioural Style	Impulsive	Risk averse
Emotional Style	Dysregulated	Constricted
Bio-Temperamental Predisposition	Reward sensitive	Threat sensitive
Societal Response	Attracts social disapproval	Attracts societal reward
Action	Problematic action	Problematic inaction
Thinking	Underthink (and over emote)	Overthink (and under emote)
Relationships	Crave relationships/fear abandonment	Fear relationships/cope by abandonment
Wants	Want to be understood	Want to be appreciated
Conflict	Disagreements are obvious	Disagreements are hidden

the resulting profile might differ from that typically seen in undercontrol. From memory, the distinctions to which he had referred, some directly and some inferred, went something like the one shown in Table 1.1.

Tom had given us some measures to give to our Living through Distress group that were aimed at selecting those who were likely to be overcontrolled. However, we knew the group well and it was clear to us, even before our plane touched down, that out of our group of 16, there were 4 who were clearly overcontrolled. These were also the four who were making the least progress. It was now evident as to why this was the case – they were in the wrong group. As Tom pointed out, we had made the common mistake of assuming that self-harm stemmed from a single base. This had led us to form a self-harm group in which all were being taught to inhibit their emotion. For those who were overcontrolled this made no sense at all; inhibiting their emotion was the root of their problem rather than something they needed to learn. What they required was an intervention designed to relax their inhibitory control and increase their emotional awareness and expression. We clearly needed a new group to meet their needs.

A Skills Group for Overcontrol

When we came back to the hospital, we were keen to present our ideas to our colleagues and those from other disciplines. We also needed a name for this potential new intervention. At that point Tom Lynch was calling his approach "Dialectical Behaviour Therapy for Emotional Overcontrol". We found this a bit of a mouthful and took the name of one of the constructs he had used in early drafts of his book that he had shared with us – "Radical Openness". The name stuck.

At one of our hospital academic meetings, we explained some of the core differences between standard DBT and Radical Openness (the intervention Tom was trialling). Though both groups were structured in similar ways, in Radical Openness the focus was on emotional loneliness rather than emotional dysregulation. We explained that though overcontrol has many advantages, there are many costs, one in particular. When a wall is built around emotions such that nothing is given away (often not even to oneself) and nobody is let in then, over time, a person becomes incredibly lonely. This does not refer to a loneliness for contacts (which may well be present), but a loneliness for connection. Tom was already working out ways of teaching the skills in areas he saw as likely to be deficient (such as in social signalling), which became key features of his emerging therapeutic approach, RO DBT (Lynch, 2018a). This treatment also placed an emphasis on self-enquiry and a leaning in towards uncomfortable emotions. This contrasted with DBT where the emphasis is more on external contingencies and finding ways to tolerate or regulate difficult emotions.

Our colleagues showed real interest in the construct of overcontrol and in this emerging approach. They could see the potential for Radical Openness. A transdiagnostic approach targeting an underlying common psychological difficulty made sense to them. Their doubts centred on whether we would find enough patients to fill a group, a concern we shared. They also wanted to know more about what our adapted group intervention would look like (what would the skills be, how would they be taught, how would we compensate for the lack of individual therapy). There were clearly challenges ahead.

We started the search for participants for our overcontrol group with a much closer look at those being referred to the programme for undercontrol, Living through Distress. It became apparent that, with careful assessment, about a quarter of those on the waiting list were in fact overcontrolled and would be suitable for our new group. It is interesting that this is a similar proportion to that mentioned in other studies, an alarming statistic in its own right (Hempel et al., 2018). This is a topic that is discussed in depth in Chapter 3.

Tom Lynch had worked with both an older population and those with eating disorders. His advice to us, however, was that the largest pool in which overcontrol was leading to mental health costs was likely to be with those labelled as having "refractory depression". This was the group he was targeting in his own randomised controlled study that was then under way (Lynch et al., 2020). With a slowly growing confidence about what to look for in identifying an overcontrolled population, we started to assess patients who had been categorised as having failed to respond to treatments for a mood disorder. We found a high proportion met criteria for overcontrol. We would have no difficulty filling our first group. Nevertheless, this begged a question. How had we not previously realised they were there? It seems that the stoic, reserved, and unemotional presentation of this clinical group meant that they often stayed under the radar. It was a surprise to us all that there were at least as many patients in our service meeting criteria for overcontrol as for undercontrol.

Next, we needed to plan the intervention. Tom was still working on his treatment manual, but he generously sent us early drafts as his ideas were developing. His basic structure was strongly influenced by his DBT roots and contained the same core elements: the weekly one-hour individual session; the weekly skills training class; the option of a telephone consultation between therapist and client at times of crisis; and the therapist consult meeting. In the individual sessions, the treatment priority is to address deficits in the client's social signalling with reference to the five behavioural themes. This is carried out through discussing Diary Cards that the client fills in during the week and through work in the session, such as demonstrating to the client what their social signalling looks or sounds like. The skills training class is similar in style to that in standard DBT. What differs is the content. The 20 skills taught over 30 sessions include modules on enhancing social connectedness, letting go of unhelpful envy, activating social safety, and relevant mindfulness skills that would promote openness and flexibility. Each skills training lesson lasts two and a half hours, including homework review, a brief break, and new teaching. There is an option of telephone consultation between therapist and client outside working hours, with the aim of creating a stronger sense of connection. Finally, there is a therapist consult meeting to enhance empathy in therapists, to promote their adherence to the treatment, and to provide a platform for their personal practice of Radical Openness.

For much the same rationale as we had used in setting up Living through Distress, we decided we would opt for a different structure for our Radical Openness programme. Once again, we chose to drop the individual therapy and put all our focus on half-day groups twice a week for nine weeks. The format included explaining the model and providing pertinent skills with the opportunity to practice them. It was a closed group with all participants starting and ending together. The challenge was to follow Tom's lead and promote very different skills to those we were teaching in Living through

Distress. The aim was to target what was underpinning their loneliness rather than helping them to regulate their emotion more effectively.

Even from our early hesitant trials, it was apparent that the participants welcomed a model with which they could identify, and one that moved away from a focus on psychiatric symptoms. They talked of finding this approach less stigmatising, less isolating, and it reduced their feeling of being blamed. Above all, it gave them a sense of agency – there was now a roadmap with clear steps to follow.

Our own reaction was one of excitement. The group-only approach was not only more cost-effective, but seemed to have great potential for this population (Booth et al., 2018). The core challenges of being open to interpersonal feedback, demonstrating empathy, signalling emotion, and risking intimacy seemed particularly appropriate to practice in a group setting. The participants, whose main presenting difficulty was emotional loneliness, were having the vital experience of being part of a social group. Once we had an established format, it was time to put our initial impressions to more objective review.

Our First Study – An Investigation into a Group-Only Approach to Radical Openness

Karen Keogh was one of our first assistant psychologists to work with us for a year and then go on to clinical training, returning to the department to carry out her doctoral research. This pattern has been happily repeated many times since. Her thesis was not just our first formal study of the impact of Radical Openness, it was the first study anywhere for this group-only approach. We were very curious as to what it would show.

The study was a non-randomised controlled trial (Keogh et al., 2016). Participants who met criteria for the programme started the group if a place was available (n = 58). Those referred at a time when the programme was full (n = 59) were placed on a waiting list and offered places in the next available group (on average ten weeks later). These participants continued to receive treatment as usual and acted as the control condition. All participants were, or had recently been, inpatients and met criteria for overcontrol.

Radical Openness consisted of 18 sessions, delivered over a nine-week period with participants attending two three-hour group sessions each week. On average, 12 participants attended each cycle. Sessions 1–9 included an explanation of Lynch's bio-psycho-social model and the teaching of pertinent skills. For example, "flexible mind" was a component in which participants learned to identify three overcontrolled states of mind: fixed, fatalistic, and flexible. They learned how to move between these states. "Novel behaviour" was a way of opening up to new experiences and engaging more fully with life. The skills were taught a second time to deepen the understanding, provide opportunity for more experiential learning, and to enhance generalisation.

It was a closed group format to heighten the experience of being part of a supportive tribe. Keogh specifically commented on the atmosphere of validation and cheerleading, as well as commiseration and empathic support that fostered the experience of being part of a social group.

Even from this relatively short intervention, there were a range of positive results. The Radical Openness group was associated with significant improvements in general mental health relative to the control group. Secondary analyses showed statistically significant changes on measures included to examine specific domains related to overcontrol. For example, changes on the Social Safeness and Pleasure Scale (Gilbert et al., 2008) suggested that participants experienced increased feelings of warmth and connectedness during the group. Significant change on the Personal Need for Structure Scale (PNS) (Thompson et al, 2001) suggested that participating in the group was associated with a relaxing of rigid and rule-governed behaviours. In Tom's text, Radically Open Dialectical Behavior Therapy, the opening chapter includes a review of the most significant studies to date in this field. This was one of them (Lynch, 2018a).

Our Second Study – A Comparison of Undercontrolled and Overcontrolled Group-Only Approaches

The second assistant psychologist to collaborate with us for her doctoral thesis was Rose Keane. She set out to compare our undercontrolled and overcontrolled groups. Much of her work was on assessment which is covered in Chapter 3, but she also focused on the care pathways for the respective groups and their response to treatment (Keane, 2016).

In relation to the demographics and care pathways, the undercontrol group were, on average, younger by ten years. Some had previously been seen in our adolescent service and others were referred in early adulthood. Their struggle with their environment was obvious and invited an urgent response. Their care pathway was driven by a formulation targeting their emotional dysregulation. There was little focus on any Axis I diagnosis. Instead, they were more likely to receive an Axis II diagnosis of Emotionally Unstable Personality Disorder/ Borderline Personality Disorder (EUPD/BPD) and a speedy referral to an intervention such as our Living through Distress programme.

This contrasts with the overcontrolled group who presented at a later age. They appeared to have more protective factors and a history of less psychiatric involvement. It seems that both they and their psychiatric team focused on symptoms and presenting issues from a diagnostic perspective (usually a mood disorder). This created a time lag where initial attempts at treatment tended to be medication based, commonly targeting depressive symptoms. Treatment aimed at the underlying psychological factors seemed to be considered only after these initial medication-based interventions had been deemed unsuccessful. It is striking that there was almost no mention of a concurrent Axis II disorder, though OCPD would in many cases have been a good fit. A narrow focus on Axis I disorders meant that core maintaining difficulties (such as a harmful overcontrolled coping style) were not addressed, and there was a clear risk of repeated treatment failures.

This was the first time that two interventions of similar duration, and with groups from the same hospital population, had been compared. Regarding response to treatment, there was significant clinical change in the target areas that both programmes addressed. For the overcontrol group, the skills intervention targeted interpersonal intimacy, emotional expression, and flexibility. It was therefore gratifying that the participants in this group (and not the other) reported more social connectedness, less ambivalence about emotion, and a lower requirement for order and structure by the end of the intervention.

In her discussion, Rose noted that many in the overcontrolled group referred to how they had been termed "treatment resistant" (Keane, 2016). She felt that it would be more accurate to say that, as clinicians, we had been blind to the concept of overcontrol. One effect of this shortcoming has been to rob this group of their sense of agency. Acceptance and change are basic foundation blocks of DBT. The way we have historically approached these two groups runs the risk of pushing too hard for change among those who are undercontrolled and fostering a passive acceptance in those who are overcontrolled. She concluded by saying how this is likely to be unhelpful for both.

The Evolution of Our Group Approach

We were heartened by having two studies under our belt which showed that not only were we having an impact, but this was being reflected in the areas we were targeting. It was now a time for some serious soul-searching. We were undoubtedly breaking out of the model of a skills-only group, and began to explore what was working well in our adaptation of Tom Lynch's work. Tom's manual had been completed and he had nailed his colours to the DBT mast, as was reflected in the final title for his treatment: RO DBT (Lynch, 2018a). It was evident that our treatment was diverging.

Adapting from Lynch's Original Model

When Tom was working in a standard DBT model two decades ago, it was logical that he would modify the content when he identified overcontrolled patients who were slipping into the DBT net. They required an entirely different set of skills, aimed at their very different needs. This early work helped to progress his thinking. However, the risk of adapting the treatment meant that the broader question may have been overlooked as to whether the structure of DBT was the best vehicle for treating overcontrol. We held in mind the image some use to describe the difference between undercontrol and overcontrol, that of the small figure atop a large elephant. In undercontrol, the elephant represents emotion and the rider represents reason. As long as the two are happy to be on the same path, all progresses well. But if something makes the elephant (emotion) decide to take a different path, the best the rider can do is to hang on helplessly. An undercontrolled intervention thus aims to help the rider gain more control of the emotional elephant! In overcontrol, the roles are reversed. The small rider now represents emotion and reason is represented by the powerful elephant, which is the dominant voice. The challenge of the treatment is to give emotion a bigger voice. Each of the individual elements of DBT was explored to see if they helped with this process. For example, Lynch refers to his skills training as a class (as is usual in DBT), specifically to differentiate it from group therapy. Its aim is to "educate rather than heal" and the focus is on "the material being taught, not on the individual being taught" (2018b, p. 9). The format is similar to a lecture where notes are taken, and it is made clear that this is not a forum for interpersonal feedback. We realised that with that teaching style, the amount of content, and the many acronyms, it could easily become an intellectual exercise for a group whose fundamental problem is that they are already spending too much time on their reason elephant.

In Lynch's model, the weekly individual therapy is a chance to work on personalised goals. Although this structure is helpful in slowing down someone who is undercontrolled, we thought it less well suited for those who are overcontrolled. Specifically, being asked to identify targets from all five themes demanded they identify their own skills deficits quite early in the process. We were also worried that what happens in session would be too heavily dependent on the therapist who is instructed to modify their in-session non-verbal behaviour each time ruptures take place.

Although Tom included telephone coaching in his model, we reasoned that connecting with the therapist was less valuable in a treatment where we were encouraging clients to connect with each other.

Enhancing the Group Therapy Approach

One major advantage of the hospital set-up was that we had a steady stream of overcontrolled clients from whom we could get regular feedback. With two groups running at the same time (a third concurrent group has recently been added), and ongoing assessment for the next cycle, we had unrivalled access to an overcontrolled population. This helped both to stimulate our thinking and to challenge many of our preconceived ideas.

We realised that as Lynch's model highlighted the need for clients to belong to a tribe, we would be missing an opportunity if we did not utilise the group to give a sense of what being in a tribe could feel like. The group could become the treatment agent in which participants would signal their feelings, be open to feedback, regulate and challenge each other, and walk the walk rather than talk the talk. This ready-made cohort of like-minded people would become a fledgling tribe and the role of the therapist would be less prominent.

We were also in the fortunate position of having the regular presence of a doctoral student carrying out work alongside us. This added rigour to our observations. A recent graduate, Claire O'Sullivan, has been interested in the broader question of what constitutes overcontrol. She has collected fascinating qualitative data (O'Sullivan, 2021). Though her focus has not been on the assessment of change per se, she interviewed participants at different time points, and we have been able to use her data as a further source of understanding why a group approach seems particularly apt.

The first striking point of feedback from those who have completed the programme was the significance they placed on the group format in developing awareness of their overcontrol. They reported that they never truly understood the nature and costs of their overcontrol until they met others who shared the same patterns. The group provided a particularly good platform for awareness, not only because it is easier to open up to others who understand, but sometimes it is easier to recognise what others are describing. Hearing someone else describe their overcontrol not only reduces feelings of isolation and shame, it is a stimulus to feel what resonates.

Second, participants have said that working in a group helped them develop a much deeper understanding of how their overcontrolled strategies were learned. Some grew up in families where emotional inhibition, high personal standards, and achievement were valued at the expense of emotional development. These rules ran deep. Some grew up in chaotic environments in which they learned to fear emotional expression. And some developed an overcontrolled style in the face of early traumatic, and often abusive experiences, as a desperate attempt to gain a sense of safety and control. Group members reported that it was helpful to see the different routes and to identify with those who shared a common pathway. This seemed to develop a more compassionate understanding which, in turn, supported meaningful reflection. The power of identifying with others seemed to be a critical factor on their therapeutic journey.

Third, since many started the programme with a profound sense of isolation, the impact of this new experience of connection ran very deep. The isolation they felt was not usually mitigated by the experience of being in the mental health system. Their lack of connection meant that they held on to distressing thoughts that they were alone in their struggles. Being in the group led to a sense of belonging. In particular, the connections formed in group allowed them to be regulated by others and have the opportunity to regulate others. Both roles had proved vital.

Fourth, many of them referred to how invested they were in each other's journeys and the impact this had on their own healing. They were able to express their fears and reservations together. They talked of sharing each other's pain, shedding tears together, and celebrating each other's successes.

They highlighted the significance of showing up for each other and of holding each other in mind between group sessions. Being part of a journey of such mutual support is one they treasured.

In each of these four areas, it is the experience of group that is essential. It thus made sense for us to opt for a group approach. These are people who feel lone outsiders. In a group, it is possible for them to chart where they are and understand how they got there. Together they can build the solidarity to move forward. In company, they are getting the invaluable experience of safety that could not be achieved with a therapist alone. They also have the opportunity to regulate others and this feels empowering, uplifting, and profoundly healing. We felt this provided a strong case for a more person-centred, group-led approach that would build around these four elements.

As we moved away from Lynch's model, we realised that we were no longer using a DBT approach. We dropped the DBT acronym, enabling us to call the intervention Group Radical Openness, or GRO for short. While a group therapy approach had much to offer, there were still many details that needed to be worked out.

The Specific Areas of Development

There were three specific areas that we focused on in developing our group approach: theoretical input, therapeutic style, and themes.

Theoretical Input

Porges' Polyvagal Theory is an enlightening lens that helps us see and understand our reactions to threat and our core need to connect and attach (Porges, 2011; Dana, 2021). The theory and its application will be further explored in Chapters 2 and 4, but here are some core summary points. The autonomic nervous system receives and adapts to information from inside our body, outside our body, and between us and others. This leads to the activation of one of our three nervous system pathways. These states are necessary for survival. Porges has cleverly set out how these states function (Porges, 2011). When there are more cues of safety, we find ourselves in our social safety system (ventral). Here we settle into relationship with another. We are supported by a gentle heart rate, our voice and facial expressions radiating safety. Without that sense of safety, we move into stronger arousal (sympathetic), prepared for fight or flight and transmitting a sense of danger to others. If danger seems further escalated, the third branch of our autonomic nervous system (dorsal) is activated. In this state of helplessness, we enter a type of hibernation. We may collapse and dissociate, and we convey to others that our system is closing down.

For our overcontrolled population who are constantly scanning for danger, this theory makes abundant sense. They may have a limited experience of being in ventral, but they will readily identify with sympathetic or dorsal (usually one more strongly than the other). They find an awareness of what is happening to them a stabilising influence. It helps to have words to put on the adaptive functions of their states. Even more significantly, it helps to understand that movement between these states is not volitional. This invites them to reflect on their experiences that led to such threat-focused vigilance, and to be gently curious of the experience of others in the group who hold similar levels of threat.

We have developed Polyvagal awareness exercises in each of our three themes. For example, in the first theme, we ask the group to reflect on how they relate to others when they feel in ventral safety, how they relate in sympathetic mobilisation, and how they relate in dorsal helplessness. The act of description seems genuinely useful. It is a way to come to terms with current patterns (for all three themes) and, crucially, to begin to wonder how life might be different if they could somehow spend more time in their safety system.

As the group goes on, this heightened awareness allows them to notice the power of the presence of another. They realise that what most easily moves them away from a threat-based protection focus is the sense of being accompanied. They become more conscious of how others in the group are regulating them and how they, too, are regulating others. The group slowly develops a confidence that it can navigate between the three states rather than being stuck in one. There is a growing appreciation that relentless efforts at trying to self-regulate, or recommending self-regulation to others, serve to heighten threat, not reduce it. It is the non-judgmental connection with others that moves them away from their predominant protective responses to flexible movement between the three states.

Therapeutic Style

Sessions that are heavy on content may be easier to plan and easier to implement but do not fit into the GRO model. In this therapy, the aim is that participants learn about a model for understanding their own overcontrol. It is also central that they develop relationships with each other and with the facilitators. The interaction between group members is fundamental to the process. How the sessions are structured thus requires creativity. This is an area covered in detail in Chapter 2 but, at this point, it is useful to give a flavour of the therapeutic style.

A prototypical GRO exercise (fully explained with case examples in Chapter 7) is when all of us (facilitator and participant) take our turn at the board to draw eight circles, the relative size of each being important. In distinct quadrants, we draw circles that represent the degree to which we experience four emotions: anger, sadness, fear, and joy. For example, a large anger circle would denote that we are aware of a lot of anger in our lives, and a small sadness circle would indicate that we are less aware of sadness being present in our life. In a different colour, we then return to the four quadrants and draw circles representing the degree to which we express each emotion.

This is an exercise that demonstrates some key characteristics of the way GRO is delivered. First, it is common that we, the facilitators, model an exercise showing our own vulnerability. This is partly because it is easier for the group to understand an exercise when they have seen it demonstrated. More than that, this exercise shows that none of us have equal sized circles because we are all human and we all have a history. By modelling the core exercises, we are saying that each one of us has been shaped by our experience, that we all struggle, and that we all have the resource of an intuitive wisdom best accessed when we are in a state of ventral safety. The group are invited to help each person reflect. How might they have learned to keep a particular circle so small? Is it possible that a large circle for one emotion masks a smaller circle for another? What might it mean, for example, that expressed joy is more than experienced joy? This has proved a safe way to talk about emotions. It engenders a reaction and yet it is sufficiently removed for the exercise not to become overwhelming. It demonstrates how emotion is related to the other two themes. It is also a connecting exercise. It involves some self-disclosure. The participants see each other in a more vulnerable light, and this binds them closer. It is very much a group exercise. Everyone takes their turn both revealing their circles and gently questioning others. They demonstrate and hone attunement to each other; they have the experience of supporting and being supported; they regulate others and are regulated by them. This reflects the essence of the group.

Themes

As part of our policy to simplify content where possible, we used our qualitative data to help determine the themes to be used in the programme. Although there was much overlap, three themes emerged, as opposed to the five in RO DBT (Table 1.2).

In GRO, these three themes are at the core of our work. Four sessions are spent on each one, with the purpose of building awareness and understanding.

Table 1.2 Themes in RO DBT and GRO

RO DBT	*GRO*
Aloof, distant style of relating to others	Distance in relationships
Extreme caution and excessive focus on details	Rigidity
Inhibited or disingenuous emotional expression	Emotional inhibition
Rigid, rule-governed behaviour	
Frequent use of social comparisons, along with feelings of envy and bitterness	

There is space to understand how patterns developed, to describe how each theme is currently manifest, and then gradually move to its costs. In the second half of the programme, each person works out their own targets and declares to the group what it would look like for them to be more connected, more flexible, and more emotionally aware and expressive.

In highlighting these three themes, the group provides options that are not available in skills training. There is now a forum where they can see how they connect with others, where they can demonstrate flexibility, and where they can become aware of their capacity for emotional expression. The group provides opportunities for feedback as new behaviours emerge. It is important to note that in GRO there is an expectation that social signalling will change as a result of the work, but it is not the primary target.

The Components of GRO

GRO is a transdiagnostic group intervention for a range of clinical presentations including mood disorders, eating disorders, avoidant personality disorder, and obsessive-compulsive personality disorder (OCPD). Rather than targeting symptoms associated with these difficulties, it is aimed at the underlying mechanism of costly overcontrol.

The programme is divided into two parts. The initial stage comprises the first 15 sessions in which the aims are to heighten awareness and understanding rather than target change. The first three sessions (see Chapter 4) involve small group and whole group exercises where there is opportunity to explore the three themes and how they might have developed. The different early learning experiences are shared. Participants are exposed to the "ladder" of Polyvagal Theory to understand how their overcontrol often leads them to getting stuck and unable to access the ventral vagal pathway where social connectedness is found.

Next are modules of four sessions, one for each theme (see Chapter 5 on Distance in Relationships, Chapter 6 on Rigidity, and Chapter 7 on Inhibited Emotion). Much of the work is carried out through tasks, discussions, and experiential exercises rather than formal teaching. By the end of this phase, the aim is to have formed a cohesive tribe where the participants feel a deep trust in us and each other. At this point, they are familiar with the general issues around overcontrol but, more importantly, they are aware of their personal experiences of the three themes, and how these were likely learned. They come to accept that their personal overcontrolled strategies are apparent in the group. The expectation is that they feel they are in the right place, with a group of like-minded people, in front of whom they would now be prepared to risk meaningful change.

The second stage of the programme is more focused on change. It starts with a personal statement by each individual, covering four categories (the GROhari Exercise, Chapter 8). In the first, they declare what the group are likely to have noticed about their overcontrol. Then they move to sharing what they have not yet revealed about their overcontrol to the group, perhaps as a result of shame. Third, they open themselves to the support of the group. And fourth, they set out their hopes and goals for the changes they wish to implement in the latter phase of the programme. These are explored using the Tracker (see Chapter 9), a vehicle used to highlight multiple examples of change. It differs in many ways from a chain analysis, while having an overall similar aim. One primary difference is that the Tracker requires group participation and engagement; questioning and feedback from the group are key components of the Tracker.

Fundamental to GRO is the belief that the best place to learn about connection, flexibility, and emotion is in the company of others. Not only are the participants having the experience of being in a social group, but they are with others who share their learning history and mixed feelings about giving up strategies that have, to some degree, served them well. In the second stage of the programme, they are invited to risk being more radically open within and outside the group, and to explore and respect their remaining ambivalence and its roots. The tools to help them are partly the content of the model but, to a greater degree, the connection, the shared experiences, and the sense of common humanity which are the lifeblood of the group.

Training Therapists to Deliver GRO: Feedback from Trainees

Our first presentation of GRO to a group of therapists outside our hospital was at a training we gave in New College, Oxford, in 2018. Many of those attending were RO DBT trained and some had been therapists in the RO DBT randomised controlled trial. More recently (with training online as well as in person), there has been a greater interest from those working with refractory depression, those faced with personality disorders, clinicians in forensic settings, and in eating disorder units. Although those interested in learning about GRO are a varied group, they share an intrigue in this new approach and how widely it can be applied. Each time we have delivered training, we have asked for honest and heartfelt feedback. The response has been uniformly positive, although many had not anticipated just how much personal and experiential work would be involved in the training! Their feedback on the experience of the training and the application of GRO can be distilled into four main areas.

- **The focus on co-regulation rather than self-regulation.** This has been a huge shift for therapists used to a teaching role aimed at better self-regulation. The experience of co-regulation is powerful and they highlighted the felt sense of safety that can be built from connecting with others. This change of priority is not without its challenges, since each person must be open to being regulated by others, as well as take responsibility for bringing others to a sense of ventral safety. Time and time again, the trainees would comment on this new aim of co-regulation before self-regulation.

- **Respecting ambivalence.** Trainees liked the way the GRO model respected the inevitable ambivalence to change. Participants are given the opportunity to talk to each other about how they developed an overcontrolled style and how it had often been adaptive in their lives. They are given space and support to elucidate the reasons why overcontrol strategies have worked for them, and these reasons are validated. They are also asked to count the costs. It is a balance sheet they share and work out with the group, not something they feel they are being sold by the therapist. A nervous system fixed on defence and protection is not seen as a volitional state, but rather a reflection of a wounded history. Trainees liked this perspective.
- **A group experience.** GRO fosters a journey away from a deep sense of shamed aloneness. Badenoch catches this in her phrase that the movement from "'I am alone to we are together is the foundation of healing" (Badenoch, 2018a, p. 192). Their shared history, their non-judgmental acceptance towards each other, their willingness to be vulnerable, and their capacity to take risk are deeply bonding experiences. Trainees appreciate why dropout is simply not an issue in GRO since participants come to care far too much about each other to stop coming. They comment on what it is like to consider change in their own life, even on a training course, when they experience such accepting connection.
- **Focus on generalisation.** Trainees noted that change initially occurred in group. As participants come to experience more safety, they become more intimate, more flexible, and more emotionally expressive. It is much easier to work on change outside, when new habits are being practiced repeatedly in front of trusted others. Another strength is that generalisation is easier when the group members become the agents of change, rather than a heavy reliance on a therapist who is suddenly withdrawn at the end of treatment. The more the trainees grasped the essence of GRO, the less surprised they were to learn how its impact had continued in the months after treatment (see study outlined in the section that follows).

Our Third Study – A Feasibility Study

Now that we had finalised the protocol for GRO, it was time to do a more formal investigation (Egan et al., 2021). It has been integral to our style of working to administer measures before and after treatment, as well as interview each participant at length. This provided crucial information and has, for example, informed us that the impact of our intervention has continued to become more potent as it evolved. However, that is not the same as a feasibility study that could pave the way for a large-scale Randomised Controlled

Trial (RCT) to establish GRO as an empirically supported treatment. We generated research questions focusing on the four key objectives of a feasibility study (Orsmond & Cohn, 2015). These included whether appropriate participants could be recruited; exploring if outcome measures were fit for purpose; determining whether the intervention is suitable and acceptable to participants; and exploring if GRO shows promise with the intended population. A mixed methods design was used so that quantitative outcome data could be linked with post-therapy interviews exploring client accounts of change. The qualitative data were used to corroborate outcome scores and to elaborate on and illustrate the nature and scale of change. Outcome measures were taken before and after the intervention and at six-month follow-up. The RefraMED trial that investigated RO DBT found the intervention superior to treatment as usual at the end of treatment, but there were no differences between the groups five months later (Lynch et al., 2020). We were hopeful that our intervention would show a capacity for more durable change.

OCPD is considered the prototypical disorder of overcontrol. We therefore decided to use the Five Factor Obsessive-Compulsive Inventory Short Form (FFOCI-SF) as our primary outcome measure (Samuel et al., 2012). This questionnaire measures the degree to which there is an identification with overcontrolled traits associated with OCPD. Although it is considered a trait measure, and therefore challenging to change, it catches the group characteristics so well that we felt it would be a strong fit. We noted that it had been used to explore changes in overcontrol in adolescents (Baudinet et al., 2021). We also included the Brief Symptom Inventory (BSI) as a primary measure (Derogatis & Melisaratos, 1983). This questionnaire assesses a range of psychopathological symptoms, and would allow us see if there were clinical changes in areas that were not explicitly targeted by the programme.

We included a second group of measures that were related to the three themes. The Revised Adult Attachment Scale – Close Relationship Version (RAAS) explores the extent to which a person is comfortable with closeness, and depending on others, and their level of worry about being rejected or unloved (Collins, 1996). The Personal Need for Structure Scale (PNS) looks at both an individual's desire and need for structure in addition to how they respond to lack of structure (Neuberg & Newsom, 1993). The Emotion Regulation Questionnaire (ERQ) determines if individuals alter their emotional experience using cognitive appraisal, and if they suppress the outward expression of emotion (Gross & John, 2003).

For the qualitative component of the study we used the Revised Client Interview Schedule – Version 5 (Elliott & Rogers, 2008). This was used to capture clients' experience of change during therapy and establish what they attributed as key to these changes. It included open questions about helpful and hindering aspects of the programme. The small sample meant that every participant could be interviewed. We were in a strong position to make connections between the quantitative and qualitative data.

Fourteen participants provided data at pre- and post-treatment, and at six months' follow-up (Egan et al., 2021). We had no difficulty recruiting appropriate participants. Though we chose a small sample, on the FFOCI-SF, there was a significant reduction in trait overcontrol post-treatment and this was maintained at six-month follow-up. There was also a reduction on the Global Severity Index of the BSI from pre- to post-treatment and again at six-month follow-up. This indicated that the intervention supported change in areas that were not explicitly targeted by the programme such as depression, anxiety, and low self-esteem. Statistically significant results on the three secondary measures between the first and the third time point suggest that GRO is effective in targeting the specific thematic areas set out in the treatment programme over a substantial period of time.

The qualitative interviews provided rich data on the participants' experiences of GRO. They revealed that their experience of change was not limited to overcontrol. They noted there were positive shifts in self-confidence, agency, and general well-being, which they attributed to GRO. In many cases, they cited the importance of the experience of connectedness derived from being part of a supportive group. This is consistent with the central tenet of the programme – that durable change comes from reciprocal, meaningful connections established between group members. Participants described change occurring inside the group and then, as they became more self-assured through engagement with other group members, how these changes generalised to outside the group.

This study found GRO to be a suitable intervention for individuals who are overcontrolled. The very promising results from this feasibility study put us in a strong position to apply for funding for a full-scale RCT.

This Manual

GRO has generated much interest. Word seems to be spreading and we have received many requests for training and workshops. The remainder of this book is a full description of how to implement the therapy, with our clinical insights and tips. We are passionate about sharing the potential of GRO in a variety of settings.

Chapter 2

Setting Up a GRO Programme

One of our strongest influences and mentors does not work in the area of overcontrol. Kate Lucre is one of the most knowledgeable compassion focused therapy (CFT) practitioners. She is also a skilled and highly regarded group therapist. She combines her experience of CFT and group psychotherapy in her work. We have attended her trainings and have often picked her brain when we ran into challenges because, like her, we are merging a model and a group therapy.

A third string to Kate's bow is that she is a mountaineer and this often influences her language, even her thinking. Unlike her, we prefer our mountains with roads or cable cars to the summit. However, we have discussed that if we were to do something really scary like abseiling (and the answer, Kate, is an unequivocal no – we are just talking hypothetically), we would want to go with someone like her. This has sparked many conversations as to why she would be the choice. Top of the pile is that we know that whatever the conditions might throw at us, we would have an unshakeable belief that she would get us back safely. That is not to say it would be an entirely comfortable experience (having to get out of the car and all that stuff). We know that she would go out of her way not to bring us further than our limits. We know that she would include elements and moments that would make us want more. We also know that she would leave nothing to chance. That feels containing.

If Kate were climbing a mountain on her own, she would prepare. If she were leading a group of inexperienced climbers, she would prepare more. She would not want to get caught out when she had a responsibility to others less familiar with that environment. On the mountain, she would be constantly aware of the group dynamic, and of the person who at any moment might need more attention or assistance. She would want to stretch one without overstretching another, and she would be conscious of how the group might be challenged to both lead and be led. She would have a constant eye out for deteriorating conditions inside and outside the group. We like this mountainy metaphor and we are going to stick with it for what we will be trying to cover in this chapter. We are encouraging you not to head up the mountain leading

DOI: 10.4324/9781003321576-2

others, until you both know the mountain and have made all the necessary preparations. And when you are on that mountain, we are encouraging you to remain watchful, and know what to be watchful about, so that those in the group know that you are looking out for them. This will develop their confidence to look out for each other. It is not that important whether the group reaches the summit (which as Kate would say is, after all, just another part of the mountain). What is important is that, under your Sherpa-like guidance, their interaction with their fellow intrepid GRO mountaineers will bring them to places they could never have reached on their own.

Take a Walk on the Mountain

It is best not to make plans and buy all the equipment until you have found that this style of mountaineering is an activity you are drawn to. On our practitioner level course (usually limited to 12 participants), there is suggested reading every week, but the sessions themselves are largely experiential. They present an opportunity to go through some of the essential GRO exercises, both as facilitator and participant.

In GRO, it is common for facilitators to model an exercise and then invite the participants to follow their lead. It is therefore important that facilitators carry out the exercises authentically and with vulnerability. Participants need to be clear as to what is being asked of them. When facilitators have an ease with an exercise, it invites the group to see what is required and to risk going deeper. The role of a facilitator in GRO is often to open a doorway for the group. Bonnie Badenoch, in her book on healing trauma, uses the word "companion" as a verb, which we like (Badenoch, 2018a). We companion them because what they cry out for is what we all cry out for – to feel accompanied. What distinguishes us, facilitator and participant alike, is what life happens to have served us up, and we need to have a capacity to touch on our own history so that they truly feel our presence. Does this style of companioning suit you?

As a participant on a training course, you get the feeling of what it is like when you are not sure what is going to be asked of you, what it is like to dig deeper into your own material. You feel the impact of validation and regulation from other members. You have direct experience of how being heard without judgement is a hundred times more valuable than advice. You get to find out how much can be learned when a highly prepared group does not go according to plan. In place of talking too much, taking too much control, and getting it right, there are important lessons in being present, in trusting the group, and showing flexibility.

Training also provides an early opportunity to become more aware of personal blind spots. It's OK to have them, it's OK to be working on them, but it's not OK to think that they are fine. In group, your personal values and belief systems are quickly exposed. For example, in the exercises on emotion, there is a chance to see if there is one (or more) emotion you have a less easy relationship with, as well as what might lie behind that. In the case of an emotion such as sadness, it is fine to feel that there is no point in going near it, to have little interest in its history, or to believe that it should not be expressed. It is just hard to hold such views and be a GRO therapist! There are underlying values in GRO and they relate to all three themes, not just emotion. These include that we would be better off with more intimate relationships with others than remaining distant from them, with more flexibility in place of rigidity, and with a greater capacity to feel and express emotions than keeping them inhibited. You do not need to have reached any point along such a continuum, but it would be hard to companion someone without believing that moving up the continuum of each of the three themes would be life-enhancing.

If, after the exposure that comes with an experiential training you still feel inclined to spend time there, then read on.

Selecting a Guidebook

There are many uses for a good guidebook. It can be used to explain and heighten what is around you. It can provide the wisdom of those who have previously trod the same path. It can warn of risks as well as identify beauty spots. Even in a very familiar area, it can become a dog-eared friend that highlights different points in different conditions, even after many years. A good guidebook also has a map at the back, and maps have so many uses. Perhaps most reassuringly, it gives you a chance to pinpoint where you and others are. That is always anchoring.

There are many guidebooks on the market and we have road-tested quite a few. It has been our experience that a better result is achieved if we are all using the same one, rather than some sort of mix and match. The guidebook we have opted for is Polyvagal Theory (Porges, 2011). In group, we have found that if we include too much detail, our intrepid would-be mountaineers spend more time in their heads than focusing on themselves and what is around them. What we provide them with is a bare outline of the theory to help sharpen their awareness, rather than provide a vehicle for their distraction. As their facilitators, it is helpful for us to have a broader and deeper knowledge than we intend to pass on.

At trainings for colleagues new to GRO, we often include the "Sunglasses Experiment". We had tried something similar but then came across Deb Dana's version, which is more elegant than ours (Dana, 2018, p. 161). Participants each wear a pair of sunglasses with dark lenses so that their eyes cannot be seen. They are invited to move around the room, occasionally stopping in front of others, simply looking at them with an expressionless face, an unmoving head, and without saying anything. This is carried out for a few minutes, long enough for each person to notice their autonomic responses.

Half the group take off their glasses for a further couple of minutes, and this is then reversed. Finally, all take off their glasses and connect with each other through eye gaze, smiling, and a natural tilt of the head that expresses vulnerability and a willingness to connect, adding vocal bursts (ahhh, mmmm, ohhh!) from time to time. It is an interesting experiment because, for most, it triggers powerful reactions. It is an ideal introduction to three fundamental principles of Polyvagal Theory.

Neuroception

The attendees usually have a strong desire to put words on what they noticed. Most describe their initial threat "gut reactions" through to their relief as their sense of safety was restored (although, interestingly, a few feel safer behind their sunglasses). They are surprised by the power of their own response. It is an opportunity to consider what happened through a Polyvagal lens. What set off their initial reactions? Was it that their brain made meaning of what was happening, or did the nervous system pick up signals of risk without conscious awareness? It is an interesting question and leads us to the heart of Porges' first vital insight (Porges, 2011). He coined the term "neuroception" to describe how the nervous system scans for cues of safety and danger. As he has remarked, evolution was never going to hand over the detection of risk, danger, or safety to the slow track of conscious awareness! Neuroception is a subcortical experience that happens below the realm of conscious thought (Porges, 2018a). Dana refers to it as "an internal surveillance system" constantly making autonomic adjustments, moving us towards either connection or protection as it takes in a continuous stream of information (Dana, 2021, p. 8). The Sunglasses Experiment is a good stimulus for understanding this concept: shutting off the eyes, and the area around them, and silencing any vocalisation stimulates threat in many people. It is also a good illustration that it is not necessary for people to know what their system was scanning for. This opens discussion on the difference between neuroception and perception. Further, as differences are compared between individuals, there is the chance to see that we have individual autonomic profiles shaped by our experience; we will have quite unique neuroceptive cues.

The Autonomic Hierarchy

Responses in the Sunglasses Experiment allow participants to experience movement between different levels of safety and threat. How can these be charted and described? Porges's second core contribution was to describe the risk and safety pathways that we share with other vertebrates. The most primitive defence finds its origin in early fish species. The dorsal vagal circuit protects through immobilisation and can be seen in species whose main form of protection is to remain still. Its physical target is the visceral organs.

The next stage in evolutionary development was the sympathetic nervous system that evolved with reptiles. Its function is mobilisation and enhanced action (as in fight or flight); its target in the body is the limbs. It requires the rapid accessibility of resources through the activation of the metabolically costly sympathetic nervous system.

The third and most recent system exists only in mammals, where it mediates complex social and attachment behaviours. This ventral system is linked neuroanatomically to the cranial nerves that mediate acoustic tuning, vocalisation, and facial expression. Porges has referred to this integrated function as the "social engagement system" (Porges, 2011). The development of this vagal pathway allowed mammals to convey signals of safety and danger to those of the same species using vocalisations, head gestures, and facial expression. It was helpful for mammals to recognise whether another was in a calm physiological state and safe to approach, or in an aroused physiological state when interaction would be dangerous.

Using the shorthand of "dorsal", "sympathetic", and "ventral" in GRO, we ask the participants to chart their movement on this hierarchy and to put words on their experience. They begin to have more awareness of their three states. Equally important, they start to reflect on the states of those they are working with, and what it would mean for them to be stuck in a dorsal or sympathetic state.

Co-regulation

The third organising principle of Polyvagal Theory is co-regulation. Dana writes that our autonomic nervous system "longs for connection with another system and sends signals out into the world, searching for signals in return" (Dana, 2020, p. 26). This starts from birth when we move from connection through the umbilical cord to connection through face-to-face co-regulation. In attuned parent-child relationships, parents respond their child's autonomic needs. Porges stresses that the ability to self-regulate is built on ongoing experiences of co-regulation. In the Sunglasses Experiment, the participants do not return to a state of safety on their own; they do it by smiling and vocalising to each other. This gives them a chance to reflect on sources of co-regulation in their lives, and what their lives might be like if this option was closed to them.

In summary, the Sunglasses Experiment allows us to experience what happens when the critical areas of the face that convey safe connection cannot be seen, and the soothing tone of a voice cannot be heard. This is sufficient to set off our systems of defence (neuroception) and plunge us into a state of threat that may be mapped (autonomic hierarchy), so that we see how urges and emotions change depending on which of the three states is activated. It is when the sunglasses are removed and we engage with each other that we can return to a state of safety (co-regulation).

Our overcontrolled population may be seen as having resorted to dark glasses for many years to protect themselves from the pain of misattunement and loneliness. Their social engagement system has consequently been underactivated. They misread social cues, and their own cues are not the animated ones that help regulate others. This impacts the relationships they develop, their access to flexibility and playfulness, and their emotional capacity. Their nervous system has become biased to neuroceptive cues of danger and threat, rather than cues of safety. The ability to regulate their autonomic nervous system through the reciprocity and synchronisation of face-to-face social interactions has been compromised. Their defence reactions are now frequently fired in the absence of any objective danger. They are caught in a vicious circle, interpreting and signalling threat, seldom accessing the ventral system that would change their lives.

The challenge is how to support this client group to repattern their autonomic nervous system. This has usually been attempted in individual therapy where co-regulation is achieved through working with a therapist. Our curiosity was piqued by the question of whether the members of the group could regulate each other. It might be thought that a group of dysregulated systems would just further dysregulate each other, but our experience has been quite the opposite. Not only have they been able to give and receive regulation, but having the opportunity to do this consistently, group after group, is particularly helpful in creating the pathways for durable change. It turns out that a group creates distinct opportunities for co-regulation, a view supported in a stimulating paper by Porges and one of his colleagues (Flores & Porges, 2017). It makes sense to take our overcontrolled charges up the mountain in a group, rather than one by one. This now requires us to reflect on group functioning and group therapy.

A Group on the Mountain

As clinicians, we came from different trainings in group therapy carried out with very different populations. It is not surprising that we held distinct views as to how groups best function. It has made for many reflective moments watching the other, and many stimulating exchanges outside group. To a large degree, this population challenged us to start afresh, and it became much easier as we dropped our preconceived ideas and began to see what suited and what worked. Along with a deeply held belief in the potential of the group, there were two influences we shared that gave us common ground and language. The first is the work of Irvin Yalom and the second is that of J.L. Moreno. We are not going to try and condense Yalom's 700 pages of his latest edition of "The Theory and Practice of Group Psychotherapy" into a few paragraphs (Yalom & Leszcz, 2020). It remains a masterly overview of the whole area and is gripping with its many clinical examples. However, it is worth noting three categories that underpin his work.

Irvin Yalom

Initial Therapeutic Factors

Yalom describes "initial therapeutic factors" such as hope, universality, and altruism. He breaks these down so that each can be grasped in detail. Hope, for example, is important in all psychotherapies, but it is fostered in a very particular way in a group, as the participants observe each other. They are witness to risk-taking, vulnerability, and empathy but, above all, they see improvement in others that makes a profound impression. They see that change is possible in the most direct way. Group offers hope in ways that cannot be met working one-to-one.

Universality refers to the fact that many individuals enter therapy with worrying thoughts that their history, problems, thoughts, and impulses are unique to them. Being in a group provides a powerful opportunity to find out that they are not alone and to find themselves validated and accepted by others. This is evident in many specialist groups, such as those for eating disorders and addictions. Group is the most potent medium for the resolution of shame. Shame makes us curl up and withdraw, which is why in group the sense of common humanity is so significant. It is deeply reassuring to realise that we are not alone and that others, far from being repulsed, share so many of our thoughts and our efforts to cope.

A third example of an elemental factor is altruism. Yalom details how there is something profoundly rewarding in the act of giving. This is even stronger for people who may have concluded that they have nothing of value to offer others. Rather than an exclusive focus on what is wrong, they discover positive aspects of themselves: the ability to care for another, to relate closely to others, to experience compassion. This gives a liberating sense of wholeness.

Group Cohesion

Secondly, Yalom discusses the importance of group cohesion and how it can be fostered. Cohesion is a complex area since it takes in the individual's relationship to the group facilitator, to the other group members, and to the group as a whole. What is clear is that it is built primarily through sharing one's inner world and feeling that this is accepted. It proceeds in a self-reinforcing loop with trust leading to self-disclosure, leading to empathy and acceptance, leading to further trust. This builds an increasingly strong sense of belonging, which is often reflected in low attrition. Cohesion does not always equate to comfort, however, as participants are more likely to relate to others more openly in a truly cohesive group. At times this can lead to conflict, but there is a confidence that this can be worked through. Cohesion is the foundation for other group therapeutic factors to operate. The group and the members must matter enough to each other to be willing to bear the discomfort of working through a conflict.

The Here and Now

The third and most complex factor is the way in which interpersonal interaction within the here and now can be incorporated. When participants interact freely with each other, the fundamental assumption is that they will re-create and display their general style of interaction within the group. This opens a rare chance for people to understand what may be happening, and what may be going wrong in their interactions outside the group. They have a genuine chance to better understand how those connections are made and what is interfering with the relationships becoming more intimate and more nurturing. Yalom comments that there is no need for them to describe or give a detailed history of their pathology: sooner or later they will enact it before the other group members' eyes (Yalom & Leszcz, 2020). It is relatively straightforward to enter the emotional stream of the here and now, but it is the facilitator's job to keep directing the group towards the self-reflective aspect of that process. This leads each person to risk new ways of being with others, often finding that some feared calamity does not take place. Each step along the way requires support and sometimes action by the facilitator.

J.L. Moreno

A second influence on the development of GRO was that of J.L. Moreno, the originator of psychodrama. Moreno was a Viennese psychiatrist who arrived in the United States in 1925. To put it mildly, he was no fan of psychoanalysis. He believed that since individual lives evolve from our family and society, healing should be carried out in the company of others. Though we have not followed his path on sociometry or psychodrama (two of his major contributions), there is much that can be taken from his approach and the exercises developed by his followers (see, e.g., White, 2002).

Moreno was particularly interested in individuals he referred to as "isolates". He felt that their low "sociometric status" left them especially vulnerable (see Fox, 2008). His work with people who find themselves on the periphery of social groupings has a strong resonance for us. He felt that they had been constrained by either family or society and his task was to free them so that they would be in a position to choose from a wider range of roles. He believed that this was best achieved in group therapy when the therapist was part of the group and the patients had a role as co-therapists. He wrote of how they both needed to bring their full personhood to the enterprise, and he was confident that facilitator and participant would give and receive in the process. This was a daring and innovative approach. We have been struck by how many of his exercises are sensitive to the natural anxiety of those new to groups: they are likely to fear being judged when they become the focus of attention, as well as fear what they might discover about themselves or reveal to others. Many of our exercises involving movement and embodiment stem from his work.

Know the GRO Mountain

Most mountain guides pride themselves on a special knowledge of a particular mountain or mountain range. That makes sense. They have got to know the area intimately. They know where the challenges lie, where the most spectacular viewing points are, and where danger is to be found. They are also expert on the type of climber who is suited to the mountain and should gain most from being part of the type of trek they offer. In this section, the aim is to explain how the principles of Polyvagal Theory and Group Therapy have been amalgamated into GRO, all the while accommodating what we know from working with this population.

Overcontrolled Mountain Climbers

It is almost a decade since we set up our first group targeting overcontrol. The many we have led have been great teachers and have had a profound impact on how GRO has developed. Our groups have been transdiagnostic, but there is no reason why a group could not have similar mental health presentations or diagnoses. However, what we try to avoid is any drift. This is not a treatment for depression or eating disorders, or any one of several personality disorders. It is a treatment of overcontrol which, in a high proportion of cases, underpins these and other clinical presentations.

What has emerged from our detailed interviews and qualitative feedback is that there are three sets of characteristics (referred to as themes in the programme) that are typically present in those who attend GRO. In brief, here are the core elements for each of the three themes:

Distance in Relationships

Protection is prioritised above connection.
Hypervigilance to threat inhibits signals of welcome to others.
Belongingness needs are not met. They are lonely even though there may be others in their life.

Rigidity

Specific ways of protection, adaptive early in life, are currently costly and often feel shameful.
Play and spontaneity are hard to access.
Rigid rules and standards make life hard for themselves and others.

Inhibited Emotion

Emotions are seen as a liability.

Tendency to care for or appease others, rather than express their full range of emotions.
Some emotions have been shut out for so long that they feel foreign and inaccessible.

How did these features come about? This is a key question that participants ask of themselves and of the others in the group. They find that each route is unique, but shares common ground with others. Early in life, the demands of threats were often greater than the resources available. Group members are likely to have looked for support from others but found that wanting or absent. In Polyvagal terms, they missed the soothing experiences of co-regulation, and so their ventral state of safety became unfamiliar. They developed habitual patterns of defence. Their ability to sustain nourishing relationships became compromised. In the consequent absence of social support, their autonomic nervous system moved further into a protective response and, though they may have given care to others, they did not feel it in return and were often left on their own to find ways of regulating their own physiological states.

Given what is often a lifetime of learning and habit, the challenge is considerable. This is a group that needs to engage and become social again. They need to pick up and reciprocate social signals. They need access to a ventral state, not just so that they can trust and turn to others, but so they can play, and relax, and be flexible. They need to operate a full range of emotional expression. They need to sense what it is like to feel safe and be confident that they can reach safety when it has been lost. What is required is more than learning some skills. It is repatterning a lifetime of learning. We are asking this group to remove the dark glasses they wear for protection and take the huge risk of finding out what would happen if they seek connection rather than protection. They need to do this with each other on a frequent basis and across a range of circumstances. This new style becomes evident in group and part of their life outside. To achieve this, they need to become a tribe.

The Fundamental Principles of GRO

The Group Is the Agent of Change

The first principle of GRO is that the group is the agent of change. This cannot be overemphasised. The central position of the group underpins the whole intervention. It is the time that the participants spend with each other, and the impact they have on one another, that will be the cornerstone of any durable change in this style of intervention. If they are to move from patterns of protection into new patterns of connection, it is our view that this is most effectively achieved through their interactions with each other.

It is worth reflecting on Yalom's "initial therapeutic factors". In relation to universality, a feature of the group is that they hear each other's stories.

They hear of the adverse conditions and lonely desperation under which protective strategies were sought. They hear what it has been like to live a life where such a system could never be switched off, often ruminating to a point of shutdown from either fear or exhaustion. They hear how the joys of life were rarely experienced. Though they may have portrayed something much better to those around them, the lives described in group are often lonely and despairing. They find it extraordinary to hear that they are not on their own and that they have found a home at last, where they finally feel understood. The sense of shame lifting is palpable.

Hope is the river that flows through the group process. When it is in full flow, it brings everyone along. There are times when one is struggling in group, or arrives in despair, and the others offer accompaniment. When they witness another's moment of success or joy, this lifts their morale even without any of their issues being aired. Group members often speak of having hope for others, even if in that moment, they do not have it for themselves. This gives a sense of meaning and purpose and a drive to keep going. We often do a "one word" check out to capture how people are feeling as a session comes to a close. Hope is the word that is most commonly mentioned.

In relation to altruism, they give to each other, share with each, inspire each other. They shift between caring for others and being cared for. They hear themselves credited with key moments of change. In place of despairing self-preoccupation, they become absorbed in the progress of the group and they sense their real contribution.

Cohesion is the slow-burning energy of the group. There is often laughter in the later stages of the programme when someone refers to their initial impression of others. As the group progresses, so does the signalling, not because of new skills learned, but because it naturally changes as they begin to feel safer with each other. Cohesion is particularly developed in the early work carried out in pairs. They comment a good deal on the significance of this time with just one other when they get to know another more intimately. As they report back to the group, there is a growing sense of belonging. Solidarity becomes stronger and they refer to the sense of tribe on a regular basis.

In terms of here and now experiences, when the group are in ventral (feeling safe and connected), they have ample opportunity to say things to each other with skill and respect. They will point out things to each other in a way that is more likely to be heard than if said by the facilitator. They will gently challenge each other in a manner that comes from a place of deep care and appreciation. They become each other's cheerleaders and want the best for each other, even if this means having to comment on something that might feel challenging to say. Here and now experiences become the scaffolding for the work. If someone has missed a session, they will feed back that their absence had an impact, while also communicating their appreciation for their return.

One of our most frequent observations is that, under the right conditions, participants do co-regulate. When they come back to the whole group after a pairs exercise, what they most often report is a sense of safety with the other. They felt seen, understood, accepted, and validated. As they link with each person in the group, the sense of belonging gets stronger. The world outside may not yet feel safer but, in the group, they sense something different. As one of them remarked loudly, "where have you guys been all my life!" There is a considerable literature as to why this might be the case. This will not be reviewed here, but attention is drawn to the work of James Coan and colleagues and their findings on how emotions can be regulated in a social context (Coan & Sbarra, 2015; Beckes & Coan, 2011).

Safety Is the Target

Badenoch used the memorable phrase "safety is the therapy" (Badenoch, 2018b, p. 73). There is a lot to reflect on in such a simple sentence. The participants will have had difficulty accessing the safety of ventral. As the group becomes more cohesive, they start reporting that the group is becoming their safe place. It is a felt sense of being at ease. It does not mean that all is right in their world but, in this moment in the group, they feel safe, held, and contained.

As the group progresses and safety is well established, they feel more comfortable in bringing their true selves into the room. This is not a conscious decision; it comes about as a direct result of feeling safe. They become playful, have moments of fun, and, above all, are authentic. They are not afraid to show the many versions of themselves and to set parts of themselves free that may have been hidden for years. They experience having others listening, tuning in, supporting, and identifying. There are so many ways in which contact is found to be soothing, and over time, this becomes stronger. They become more relaxed which, in turn, improves their signalling to each other. As they find it easier to return to a ventral state, moments of threat lose much of their power. They know the route back. It helps that they are working with a powerful force: the inclination to connect is a biological imperative (Dana, 2021).

Safety is also about carrying more than they think possible. The load that the group can bear should not be underestimated. At the outset, many of them feel that they are not carrying their fair share. If they cry, if they feel another contributed more, if they feel that their example was not as powerful as those of others, they feel that they have let others down. After a while, they grow in confidence that on different days, and in response to varying challenges, different members of the group come to the fore. One day they will feel that some of their pack is being carried for them; on another day, they will do more than their share of the heavy lifting. There may be natural leaders in the group but that turns out not to matter. When it comes to carrying the heavy loads, they each seem to take their turn. Coan uses the word "outsourcing" to describe how people can tolerate their distress and regulate their emotion by being in proximity to people they care about (Coan & Sbarra, 2015). This creates a view of the group as providing a collective and pooled resource from which each can draw on as they need.

Participants are likely to have a history with missing experiences of safe and predictable co-regulation. We do not see co-regulation as creating dependence, but rather building a foundation for self-regulation and resilience. GRO is set up to offer frequent, predictable opportunities to co-regulate. The task is to find ways to bring the right degree of challenge to reshape patterns of protection and connection.

The Group Is Where Change Is First Demonstrated

Contact with each other gives them the sense of being nurtured and calmed. They try out the exercises and explore what shows up and what they notice as they connect with deepening intimacy. This is change happening in the group. A common example of this is someone saying, "I just can't do this emotion" or "I don't know how to express it" and yet they become tearful or angry listening to another's story or experience. It is important to use the here and now moment to stop and reflect to this person, that while they feel they still cannot "do" the emotion outside of group, here we are seeing it live in front of us.

The journey with the group is to regain a sense of belonging. It is only when this has been achieved that change outside the group can be undertaken. In our early skills group, participants had grown to trust us (Keogh et al., 2016). Over time, in this new format, the emphasis is different; they learn to trust each other. They nourish each other, help each other, and, in turn, are supported by each other. This progression from solitary to social within the group is the powerful base of GRO. They do not talk about this experience in an abstract way, but rather, it takes place in front of our eyes.

The Framework of GRO

Group therapy is often open in its approach. GRO is more prescriptive. There are 27 sessions and each one is set out in detail in Chapters 4–10. There are also handouts for the participants that we circulate after each group, so that they can engage at all times with what is happening in the session, rather than having to take notes (see sample handout in Appendix A). A manualised group therapy may almost seem a contradiction, lacking the space for the spontaneity and flexibility that is to be fostered. We do not see it that way. We see the layout as the boundaries within which the group interactions take place.

The content has a significant role, but the key point is that the GRO exercises are opportunities for the group to connect with each other. The group can be trusted to make sense of them. If they were to get caught up in intellectual discussion, then the sessions would not be so valuable. That is why concepts and language are simple and consistent. In GRO, the group members are not told what it might be like to zip line across a ravine. We encourage them to strap each other in and push each other off. When they get to the other side, we give them space to discuss what it was like and what it brought up for them. Such exercises are chosen with care to provide contrasting cues and to be at a height they are likely to tolerate. Some need to be modelled first and, when this is required, the facilitator demonstrates what is needed and then moves away; it is not our therapy. Though we grow close to them, the relationship between group members should be considered as central.

What Is Required of the Facilitator

In this section, we outline some things that facilitators need to hold in mind so that the potential of the group can be fully realised. Safety in the group in part comes from the sense among the participants that facilitators are confident about what they are doing. If we convey that we are not sure what comes next, or we are unable to answer questions, or we are not on top of the group dynamic, then we shouldn't be surprised when the participants show hesitancy.

1 Less is More! A guiding principle for GRO therapists is to "keep it simple". The therapy is based on, and influenced by, many theories including evolutionary theory, attachment theory, social baseline theory, and developments in neuroscience. They are not elucidated here since the risk is that more theory can so easily be introduced into the programme. In group, it is more important to model that simplicity is the order of the day. Facilitators need to keep an eye out for each other so that complex material is not smuggled in. A rule of thumb is that if an idea cannot be explained so that one participant could easily explain it to another, it is ditched. The inclination can be to make explanations and models more complex. This needs to be resisted. Content must be straightforward. Further, when planning a session, it can sometimes seem as if there might be insufficient material. We must calm our fears and remind ourselves that we are not trying to fill a session; we are trying to stimulate one. The content is not supposed to fill the session, but to spark it.

   The use of the Polyvagal Theory might seem a contradiction to this principle, but it is used in a simple way. It provides a shared language to heighten awareness. It helps the participants to describe their sympathetic overcontrol (striving, perfectionistic, anxious) and compare this with their moments or periods of dorsal (withdrawn, procrastinating, dissociated). Above all, it sets out a vision of life in ventral where they could be their authentic selves: connected, flexible, and emotionally expressive. Our job is to create an atmosphere so that they experience occasional moments of life in ventral, and then learn ways of becoming more anchored there. There is work for a facilitator to ensure that all the participants get a taste of what this would be like. This work is experiential, not theoretical.

2 Gentle, slow pacing is another core principle for facilitators. This can vary from group to group as we try to attune ourselves to their needs. The general rule of thumb is that we never want to feel rushed or have the session feel packed. We need to attend to the pace and to what is happening. This can mean holding a topic or an idea until the next session. Some tasks such as Drawing the Relative Size Exercise or the GROhari Exercise take as long as they take. What is important is that the group has time and space to notice the significance of something as it is happening, rather than feel hurried. The role of the facilitator is often to contain – which means to absorb, digest, make sense of what is happening, and then ask the participants to reflect on what they have said and how they have felt. There should be time to take stock and ask the group what they need in these moments, what they need to get back to ventral. They know! If you find yourself cramming in information or not finding enough time to reflect on an exercise, then consider yourself warned.

3 A third point for facilitators to hold in mind is how to bring our authentic selves. This demands a level of self-awareness and ease with sharing. We seek to be in ventral, conscious of being knocked down into threat from time to time, and aware of taking the path back up the ladder. When we are in ventral, we can reach down to help others up, a model we hope participants will follow as they begin to feel more connected. That would not be possible if, for example, we were in driven, organised, directive sympathetic. We self-disclose our own struggles with overcontrol, while holding in mind that such openness should always be in the service of connecting with the group and de-pathologising aspects of overcontrol. As for our therapy, that is carried out elsewhere.

4 One of our reminders to each other has become a mantra: trust the group. This sounds easy, but our desire is often to jump in, to guide, to shape, when what is usually needed is to step back and let the process unfold, have faith in the wisdom of the group. This is particularly important in the second half of the programme. When we show our trust in the group, it helps them to trust each other.

Facilitator Kit Bag

Don't head up the mountain without preparation and without items that you will need. A facilitator kitbag is not a resource when things go wrong; it is something that should be with us at all times (see Lucre & Clapton, 2020). It should have elements that support, sustain, and nourish us. It is a necessity in this work, and it takes time to figure out what you need in your own personal kitbag. Kate has often cautioned us that there are places where there is no mountain rescue!

Support. The first core item in the kitbag is organisational and collegial support. Many of us work in some setting or organisation, be that a hospital, a clinic, or a prison. The intervention may therefore have to be "sold" to the service. It is helpful to feel that someone in the organisation has your back. It becomes tiring if you have to fight for every resource and keep having to justify the intervention. One of the most important things such support can provide is time. Early training, planning the intervention to suit the needs of your client group, and alerting colleagues to what you are doing all take time before you even start. They need to understand, too, that time for leave, for further training, for assessing the impact of what you are doing, and assessing for the next group all mean that the group will not be running 52 weeks a year! Early institutional buy-in is worth its weight in gold. We have found collegial support easy to build as GRO often takes clients who have not been well served by traditional treatments.

Training. Ideally, you want to fill your kitbag full of training opportunities. This isn't always possible but is certainly desirable. An initial requirement would be to attend both the introductory and practitioner level trainings in GRO so that you can develop a real competence in the model, and be part of a community exchanging ideas and supporting each other through common difficulties.

With this completed, there are many and contrasting trainings that will help enrich your practice as a GRO practitioner. In recent years, we have learned much from attending training with Deb Dana on Polyvagal Theory, Kate Lucre on Group Psychotherapy, Bonnie Badenoch on Trauma. We are not suggesting that you attend these specific trainings (although online training is making these much more accessible). What we want to illustrate here is that there are many trainings outside the strict boundaries of GRO that can help develop your practice.

Repertoire of Exercises. There is great flexibility in having a multitude of short exercises that bring calm or energy, depending on what is required. The influence of Moreno on our work can be seen here. One of his followers has a book with over 100 exercises (White, 2002). For example, to warm up, the group can stand in a broad circle. Each person takes a turn at stepping in and saying how they are or what is on their mind as the group starts. Others who share those feelings also take a step forward. It tends to be low in threat and strong on indicating commonality. A second example would be "The Matryoshka Doll Exercise" which would not be used early in the life of the group. The painted doll is pear shaped and can be pulled open across the middle to reveal a slightly smaller doll inside. There might be five layers until a tiny one is reached that cannot be split into two. You could invite each member of the group to use the dolls in any number of ways, such as what is most visible about their overcontrol (the outer doll) to what is most private (the final and most hidden doll). Alternatively, the dolls could be used as an invitation to describe how overcontrol might have looked like at different points in their life. As with any exercise in GRO, no one is under any pressure to go further than they feel comfortable, and gaps and silences are honoured as much as revelations.

The Geese Theatre Company in the UK are a team of theatre practitioners who teach and facilitate drama-based group work. They have spent many years working and providing training in forensic settings, secure hospitals, and mental health facilities (including our own). They have created compelling exercises that stimulate deep and meaningful discussions. To get a feel for their work, we will describe the Socks Game, one of many detailed in their handbook (Bain et al., 2002).

Ask the group to stand in a circle. One facilitator then produces a pair of socks rolled in a ball (of course unworn and fresh – what do you take us for?). The socks are thrown to someone at the far side of the group who throws them on to someone opposite them (rather than someone close by), and then folds their arms to indicate to everyone not to throw the socks back to them again. The person who has received the socks does the same, i.e., throws to someone else roughly across the room from them, and folds their arms. This continues until everyone in the group has thrown the socks to someone else. The facilitator who made the first throw should be the last person to receive the socks back. This is now the set order with each person receiving from the same person and throwing to the same person. Check everyone is sure about this! Throw this single pair of socks again in the same pattern until everyone is comfortable and familiar with the sequence. At this point, with one pair of socks already finding its way around the group, the facilitator introduces a second pair of socks that is thrown in the same sequence. Gradually further pairs are added (different weights, sizes, colours, textures). We often reach almost as many socks as the number of people in the group. It is a good test of tolerance of unclear rules and imperfection. If socks are dropped, they are picked up and thrown back into the sequence again, but this is a game of limited rules.

To shake it up (and to add more confusion), you may want to introduce a command to "all change" – whereby everyone reverses the order of who they were throwing the socks to, and who they were receiving them from. This can be explained just before the command. Within a short while, chaos reigns. Socks are hitting people and other socks, and there is much screaming and laughter. After a few rounds, everyone sits down and spends some time processing the exercise (a key Geese Theatre principle is not to engage in any exercise if there is insufficient time to process it). The first phase of questions relates to the experience of the exercise. For the second set of questions, each person uses the socks to answer a question pertinent to issues at that point in the group cycle. For example, "Which socks are you juggling in your life right now?" or "Which socks represent what you would like to leave behind when the group is finished?" It is fascinating to see what types of socks people combine to make different representations.

Team Supervision. Every therapist requires good supervision in their kitbag. We have found it most useful to have a supervisor who has experience in group therapy. Supervision is most sustaining when it incorporates aspects of support and building relationships with your co-facilitators, in addition to exploring reactions and responses to the clients and the work. It is also helpful to change supervisors every couple of years. We learn new things from different people. Although GRO training and supervision is the most useful at the outset, when you get on top of the model, it can be stimulating to have a supervisor from a different background who can stretch and challenge you in different ways.

Consult Group. The weekly consult group is a necessity that must line every kitbag. Coming together and having time to reflect on how the group is going, exploring ideas, and practising exercises together serves to strengthen the programme. We tend to start each consult with a check-in on where we are on our Polyvagal ladder. It is often the case that we arrive in sympathetic and then move to ventral simply by being in each other's company. We allow some time for planning sessions, but this is not the main focus of consult. We spend more of the time exploring ideas and reflecting on what we are learning from the group members and practising the exercises together. If we have attended a recent training event or read a new paper or book that is relevant to the work, we would spend time sharing this with each other. The aim is that we all leave consult feeling energised, excited, and nourished. It is also there for those times when unforeseen circumstances arise or challenging dynamics need to be addressed.

The Other End of the Rope. Perhaps the most sustaining presence in your kitbag is your co-facilitator. This relationship is such a source of strength. Building a trusting relationship is essential, because you will spend so much time with this person, experiencing the highs and lows together. As with all close relationships in your life, there will be a mixture of laughter, fun, tears, frustrations, and ruptures. It's all part and parcel of an authentic relationship. Ideally this relationship is one where you can easily lift each other to ventral and feel safe enough to share what is happening between you. The group members are always observing this relationship too and, interestingly, will pick up on little nuances between you. Make time to get to know each other properly and chat about how you would like to resolve difficulties and your own individual styles of relating. This relationship requires as much effort as you would put into any important relationship in your life.

All our GRO programmes are run twice a week by two facilitators (and an assistant psychologist). We appreciate that such an arrangement is not always possible. We have colleagues in Inverness, for example, who offered GRO once a week, run by a team of three and this worked well. What would weaken the group, we believe, is to have a larger team with any two running each session. This can work well in skills groups, but would seriously impact the cohesion of the group that is so central to GRO. Feedback from participants has repeatedly highlighted the stability and safety derived from the consistent presence of the facilitators.

The Group. Finally, your group members are also likely to be in your kitbag. You will certainly be in theirs. They teach us so much about the experience of overcontrol, about how important this journey is, and about what aspects of the group are impacting them. You know your group is running well when moments from a session linger with you long after it is over, and you find yourself grounded in ventral. A well-functioning group forms a huge part of nourishment in this work.

Ready to Set Off

At some point, you will be ready to meet in the mountain guide's hut with the rest of your team. You can check off on your list that you are trained for all weather conditions and have the necessary supports and equipment in place. You have been up and down the mountain so often that you are familiar with anything that might happen on it. You have the trails of "connection", "flexibility", and "emotion" well marked. You have the confidence and experience not just to lead a team but, in time, for the participants to take a stronger lead and go up less travelled and higher trails with you taking a more watchful role. You appreciate the level of risk this presents to them and the courage that they will require. What distinguishes this style of group is that they do not trek in silence, in single file, and for hours on end, as would many groups on a mountain. In GRO, we are stopping more often than we are walking. It is as if we are eating, poring over maps, checking out how others are doing, telling stories from our lives, sitting around a campfire, arguing about where to go, and repairing both our equipment and our relationships. A new meaning for social climbing! Actually Kate, if this is what really happened on mountains, you could certainly count us in.

If you are ready, then it is time to select your first group, and it is time for us to drop our mountainy metaphor.

Chapter 3

Assessing for GRO

The selection of the group is important. GRO is a targeted intervention. It has specific aims. If these are not consistent with a person's difficulties, then the intervention is not likely to be helpful. The group process in this style of treatment benefits from people being able to identify with each other. Including participants who can both identify with the model and the others in the group maximises its power. We would like to tell you that finding suitable participants using a short, reliable methodology is straightforward but, alas, we are not at that point. Assessment and selection can be achieved, but it is still a slow and steady undertaking. When it comes to measures, assessing overcontrol lags several decades behind assessing undercontrol. An exploration of some of the historical threads of overcontrol helps to understand why this is the case and helps to point the way forward.

Overcontrol: Two Streams of History

Ego Functioning and Overcontrol

For those of us working in the field of mental health, the construct of overcontrol may seem very recent. It may have made little impact on our training, on our work, or on our thinking. Yet it is not a recent construct. If we roll the clock back 60 years, two graduate students at Stanford were starting out on a strand of their work to which they frequently returned throughout their career (Block & Block, 1980, 2006). Jeanne and Jack Block were strongly influenced by psychoanalytic theorists such as Lewin and Fenichel, and so many of the terms they employed are no longer in common usage. They were interested in "impulses", for example, and how these can be an energising presence, as well as how they can be modulated and controlled. This led them to look at "ego-functioning" structures such as delay of gratification, inhibition of aggression, and caution in unstructured situations. It was the degree of impulse control in these areas that they referred to as "ego-control".

DOI: 10.4324/9781003321576-3

Their work suggested that ego control could be put on a continuum with "undercontrol" at one end and "overcontrol" at the other. In brief, they saw undercontrolled individuals as likely to express affect and impulses directly, even when this may be socially inappropriate. They may find delaying gratification challenging. They have fluctuating emotions, are spontaneous, easily distracted, and live life on an impromptu basis. They may be described as unpredictable, rebellious, and moody and may be less influenced by social customs.

Since our focus in this book is on overcontrol, it is worth quoting their summary description at length:

> The ego overcontroller can be expected to have a high modal threshold for response, to be constrained and inhibited, to manifest needs and impulses relatively indirectly, to delay gratification unduly, to show minimal expression of emotion, to tend to be categorical and overly exclusive in processing information, to be perseverative, non-distractible, less exploratory, relatively conforming, with narrow and unchanging interests, to be relatively planful and organised, and to be made uneasy by, and therefore avoidant of, ambiguous or inconsistent situations.
>
> (Block & Block, 1980, p. 54)

Block and Block's distinction between undercontrol and overcontrol is significant for many reasons. The prevailing thinking at the time was that high levels of control were necessarily adaptive. The Blocks opened the door to the idea that overcontrol needed as much examination as undercontrol. They also suggested that neither undercontrol nor overcontrol was necessarily adaptive or maladaptive, but rather depended on circumstances. There are times when the spontaneity, expressive emotion, and unconforming originality associated with undercontrol could help promote intimacy and creativity. However, undercontrol can also be personally costly when it leads to erratic, impulsive, even dangerous behaviours. Similarly, there are many situations, notably at work, where the disciplined and directed behaviour associated with overcontrol might be welcomed. On the other hand, in social situations, inhibited behaviours and emotions could easily lead to difficulty forming close relationships with a resulting sense of pointlessness and loneliness. Thus, the second characteristic of ego-functioning that they studied was how a person adapted to differing demands in life. This was termed "ego resiliency" and it describes the ability to respond flexibly to demands such as conflicts or uncertainty. Resilient individuals were seen as adaptive to changing circumstances. Those they described as "ego brittle" were more fixed in their responses and so might be more vulnerable to the stresses of life. Implicit in this position was that inflexible overcontrol could potentially be as problematic as inflexible undercontrol.

The Blocks' work prompted many interesting lines of research (see review by Bohane et al., 2017). To give a flavour of this work there were, for example, longitudinal enquiries such as the Dunedin study (Caspi, 2000). This study followed almost 1,000 participants from early childhood to adulthood. Three-year-old children were categorised as undercontrolled, inhibited, or well-adjusted, to see what this might predict when they were re-assessed as adults. The "inhibited" three-year-olds (this was the term used for overcontrolled) had lower levels of social support by the age of 21 and were described as cautious and lacking lively interest and engagement in their worlds. While they reported poorer conjugal relationships, they often managed to maintain healthy relationships and interpersonal adjustment at work, even when compared to those who had been classified as well-adjusted. In terms of mental health, the overcontrolled group was the most likely to be depressed and to have made suicide attempts. Far from being fatalistic, the authors described "turning points" that had improved outcomes for some. These varied depending on whether a person was undercontrolled or overcontrolled.

An example of a cross-sectional study was that set up by Miller and his colleagues (Miller et al., 2004). They identified three personality clusters in male military veterans with Post-traumatic Stress Disorder (PTSD): a low pathology group, an externalising group, and an internalising group. Their work suggests that those at either end of the control continuum experience frequent and intense negative emotions in response to trauma, but differ in essential ways with regard to the form and direction that such distress is expressed. The "externalisers" (their term for undercontrolled) tended towards impulsive sensation seeking, coupled with a propensity for labile emotions and antagonism. In contrast, the "internalisers" (their term for overcontrolled) were more likely to show apathy and inertia and had high levels of depression. In many ways, the overcontrolled subgroup were more likely to display anxiety and depression-related symptoms typically associated with PTSD. The authors suggested that treatments should not presume that PTSD is a homogenous presentation. They concluded that understanding the personality differences, such as those used in this study, might enhance our ability to treat heterogeneous populations of trauma survivors.

The final study to be cited was that carried out by Jennifer Wildes and her colleagues (Wildes et al., 2011). Over 150 patients in an eating disorder unit were classified as "undercontrol", "overcontrol", or "low pathology". They found that using these personality types had much better utility in predicting the course of treatment and clinical outcomes than a categorisation based on types of eating disorder. One suggestion from their findings was that factors that predict initial treatment response may not be the same as those associated with longer-term outcomes. For example, the overcontrolled group tended to tolerate the structured demands of an intensive treatment setting and so achieved better initial outcomes. The undercontrolled group, with a diminished ability to tolerate distress, found the structured environment of a hospital programme much more challenging. They were more likely to drop out and return for more sporadic treatment but, significantly, had a less chronic course of illness in the longer term.

What is clear is that studies that followed from the Blocks' work have consistently shown that classifying patients on the basis of personality type may have real clinical utility, and would likely improve treatment response. The research cited suggests that whether treating an eating disorder, a mood disorder, or PTSD, taking into account underlying personality type is likely to be helpful to treatment outcome. Treatment approaches have too long assumed patients to be homogeneous within these classifications, whereas there are clearly significant differences. The research reviewed here suggests that there is a convincing case to address the personality structure that underlies symptoms, and a potential for developing novel interventions on the basis of personality subtype. Using the constructs of overcontrol and undercontrol enhances our ability to grasp more about an individual's unique profile of responses. It is regrettable that the pace to turn this understanding into differing treatment options has been so slow.

Self-Control, DBT, and Overcontrol

Walter Mischel was also at Stanford from the early 1960s (we can't help but wonder did he have had some interesting conversations with the Blocks in the departmental tea room). Mischel's area of interest was self-control (Mischel, 1968; Mischel & Ebbesen, 1970; Mischel, Ebbesen, & Raskoff Zeiss, 1972). His work had two major elements. First, he was interested in how deficient self-control (both interpersonal and emotional) was associated with a broad spectrum of mental health disorders including Borderline Personality Disorder (BPD). Second, he set out to show that delaying gratification and exercising self-control could be taught and improvements made could serve as "protective buffers" against life stresses.

This work had a profound influence on Marsha Linehan. Her pioneering work on DBT was based on the premise that a difficulty controlling dysregulated emotions was a skills deficit (Linehan, 1993). Her skills-based programme ushered in an era of increased optimism, notably for those with a diagnosis of BPD for whom no previous treatment had been effective (Swales, 2018).

An unintended outcome of the influence of DBT was that low levels of self-control became synonymous with BPD. For over two decades, there was scant interest in whether there could be excessive levels of self-control that might also have mental health costs. This possibility was taken forward by Lynch revisiting this distinction between "undercontrol" and "overcontrol" (Lynch, 2018a). In the DBT groups with whom he was working, he became aware that some of those referred were in fact displaying excessive levels of overcontrol. His research showed that those deemed to be "overcontrolled" were also heavily represented in disorders that had proved difficult to treat such as resistant depression, certain eating disorders, and OCPD. Working within a DBT framework, he developed a package of skills that were directed at the needs of this very different group. His treatment manual appeared in 2018, some 25 years after Linehan's definitive manual for the treatment of undercontrol, illustrating how long it has taken to generate interest in the overcontrolled end of the continuum.

Overcontrol Assessment: Two Studies

To give a flavour of research on the assessment of overcontrol, two studies will be examined. It is not coincidental that they relate to making the distinction between overcontrol and undercontrol, because that turns out to be far from straightforward.

The First Study

The first study by Roelie Hempel and her colleagues was published in a special edition of the Behavior Therapist on RO DBT (Hempel at al., 2018). This paper has a particular focus. It provides data on the workings of the weekly consensus meeting. These meetings were set up to decide whether to include individuals for the randomised controlled trial who presented with "ambiguous symptoms". It transpired that "potential borderline symptoms" were the most common cause for discussion, with the consensus team trying to work out whether individuals easily assumed to be undercontrolled might in fact be eligible for the study on overcontrol. Of the 36 cases referred to them, 23 were deemed overcontrolled. Many of these had several borderline symptoms and two individuals had seven! This suggests a strong case for symptoms associated with undercontrol being shared by individuals with overcontrol. The authors suggest that, on the basis of their data, individuals who endorsed feelings of chronic emptiness, identity disturbance, abandonment, or suicide/self-harm might as easily be overcontrolled as undercontrolled, and these could not be the signs to make the distinction. Many with these symptoms were included in the clinical trial of RO DBT (Lynch et al., 2020).

In the second half of the paper, they proceed to recommend guidelines for researchers and clinicians interested in differentiating between overcontrol and undercontrol. We have found some of their points particularly useful and have taken four of them forward into our assessment protocol.

1 **Public versus Private.** A distinction that has relevance for assessment is that undercontrolled behaviour is more likely to be public and overt. Any mental health team will be able to name with ease those on their

caseload with clear signs of undercontrol, since the symptoms are usually readily apparent. However, suffering underpinned by overcontrol often flies below the radar. It is held stoically. It may not be shared. There are no public displays and indeed such overt signs would likely be viewed as deeply shameful. Someone who is overcontrolled may relax certain controls when they are on their own, when they might not easily be identified, or in the presence of those they trust or feel safer with (e.g., close friend or family). This of course has important implications for assessment. Assessing someone with overcontrol is going to be less clear-cut – it will be necessary to probe to find out what happens in different contexts, and with different people in their lives. They are not likely to open up readily about what is going on, and little may be apparent from what is observed.

2 **Self-injury.** Self-injury is perhaps the most common "false lead" because, for many mental health teams, this is one of the strongest indicators of undercontrol. From the DBT literature, it is clear that the impulsive undercontrolled self-injury usually has the intention of achieving regulation, particularly overdistressing emotions. Overcontrolled self-injury is different in many ways. It tends to be planned, carried out privately, and rarely requires medical attention (cuts are more likely to be neat and tended to by the individual to avoid hospitalisation). Unlike their undercontrolled counterparts, this is not typically an act that spirals out of control in the moment.

3 **Social Signalling Differences.** This is the variable to which Tom Lynch ascribes most importance (Lynch, 2018a, 2018c). He describes individuals with undercontrol as likely to be painfully aware of their inability to control their emotion and their social signalling as tending to be dramatic, disinhibited, unpredictable, and mood-dependent. Although they may try to control extreme expressions of negative emotion, they are much less likely to inhibit expressions of positive emotion. By comparison, overcontrolled social signalling tends to be understated and not mood dependent. Displays of excitement or joy are less likely. Signalling style may be flat or insincere. Overcontrolled clients may be secretly proud of their ability to control their emotions. They can appear calm and disinterested on the outside, despite feeling anxious on the inside. They are likely to downplay their personal distress with an "I am fine" response to almost any query. As a result, no one outside their immediate family may be aware of their inner distress. Deficits (not excesses) in social signalling are considered a core problem and we would agree with Tom Lynch that they are evident in many cases though they are not necessarily, in our view, the primary source of emotional loneliness.

4 **Emotional Leakage.** Emotional outbursts are associated with undercontrol, but they are an important, if much less frequent, feature of overcontrol. After lengthy periods of sitting on an emotion, there may

be lapses of self-control when bottled up emotion comes bursting out. These emotional eruptions may have greater intensity than warranted by the situation and are likely to feel shameful. Since they are seen as a sign of weakness, they can act as a further incentive to suppress emotion. Lynch has labelled these overcontrolled outbursts as "emotional leakage" (our clients have preferred the term "emotional overflow"). He sees this leakage as another distinguishing feature between undercontrol and overcontrol (Lynch, 2018a). He recommends asking about these emotional outbursts and how they are perceived, since, in overcontrol, they are not just less frequent, but are more likely to be viewed as unacceptable lapses of control.

The Second Study

The second study was carried out by one of our doctoral students, Rose Keane, whose work was cited in Chapter 1 (Keane, 2016). Rose was interested in the questionnaires that are often used when assessing for undercontrol and overcontrol. She understood that the more extreme end of undercontrol is characterised by high impulsivity, emotional lability, chaotic and intense relationships, and low distress tolerance. Thus, it was not surprising to her that measures reflecting these constructs were helpful in discriminating between undercontrol and overcontrol (a finding she replicated). However, what was not clear to her was whether some of the formal measures used to assess overcontrol would be as effective. Although they might be useful in discriminating overcontrol from a non-clinical population, she asked the more discerning question of whether they would they be as effective in discriminating between undercontrol and overcontrol.

She selected three measures commonly used in the assessment of overcontrol: the PNS (Thomson et al., 2001); the Ambivalence Over Emotional Expressiveness Questionnaire (AEQ) (King & Emmons, 1990); and the Social Connectedness Scale (SCS-R) (Lee et al., 2001). These scales did not prove effective in discriminating between undercontrol and overcontrol in her sample. The PNS looks at both desire for structure and response to lack of structure. On the first construct, the overcontrol group scored higher, indicating that they had a greater desire for structure. On the second construct, scores suggested that both groups responded poorly to a lack of structure. Thus, although there is a greater craving for structure in the overcontrolled group, the total scores on this measure did not discriminate between the undercontrolled and overcontrolled participants.

On the AEQ, which focuses on ambivalence about emotional expression, the overcontrolled group had high scores but, interestingly, so too did the undercontrolled group. Once again, there was no statistically significant difference between the two clinical samples. She suggested further research was warranted to find out the reasons for this.

Finally, on the SCS-R, a scale for "social connectedness", both groups reported a lack of social connection, a sense of being an outsider. Rose suggested a possible explanation. The overcontrol group sought social distance as a protective strategy. The undercontrolled group, on the contrary, craved social connections but found them hard to maintain. The similarity in scores thus appears to mask very different underlying processes and patterns.

Rose's research is further evidence of how far the formal measurement and understanding of overcontrol still lags behind that for undercontrol. It would certainly be advantageous to have formal measures as part of a battery when assessing for overcontrol, but her work suggests that the measures sometimes adopted at this point must be used with caution. Scales that distinguish between an overcontrolled population and the general population may not be able to distinguish between overcontrol and undercontrol. We are still some distance from a validated measure for capturing what Lynch terms "maladaptive" overcontrol. With the sometimes subtle differences between undercontrol and overcontrol, the detailed clinical interview remains the gold standard.

GRO Training in Assessment

When we are delivering GRO training, we spend time focusing on the issue of assessment, taking into account what has been discussed thus far. This is an opportunity to gain a deeper understanding of overcontrol, grasp the assessment challenges, and work out a strategy for deciding whether GRO is an appropriate fit for an individual. In GRO style, this is more experiential than didactic. Participants on our training are paired up and interview each other on the first category of the protocol before we all meet back for discussion. It is important to know what it feels like to assess and to be assessed. Most mental health practitioners are overcontrolled (now wouldn't that make for an interesting research project!) and so many are surprised as to how rapidly this can become personal. We ask them not to reveal more than they are comfortable with but equally, not to role play. These are questions they will be asking others. They feel the safety when they are met with acceptance and warm curiosity, in contrast to picking up even a hint of judgement. It is an opportunity to notice reactions when questions go deeper, even to focus on some of the costs of their own overcontrol.

Once these colleagues in training have got to air their personal reactions, we turn more widely to what they noticed and learned during the process. Our aim is that, over the course of the training session, they gradually become more skilled as they swap roles and move through the three assessment categories. In no particular order, these are some of the areas that we discuss.

1 **GRO starts when the assessment starts.** For those who join a GRO group, the assessment is the start of the intervention. This is an early opportunity for us to build a connection with them and to convey both acceptance

and hope. Our signalling, tone of voice, and validating language are all going to be helpful in building a sense of safety. Furthermore, it fosters ease if we are transparent and let them know what we are doing each step of the way. They may feel apprehensive about the process and about how they come across. We take opportunities to validate their responses and to signpost what we are looking for, even offer choice if this might be helpful ("Would this or that be more like you..."; "People in our groups tend to describe..."). We are aiming for a relaxed dialogue, where they feel more inclined to open up and help us work out whether GRO is likely to be a good fit for them at this point in time.

2 **The first response to any question is just a starting point.** As we have seen, for people who are overcontrolled, their common inclination is to under-report, to be stoic, to profess that all is well, even if they are struggling. They may also endorse undercontrolled responses, for example, viewing a few tears as uncontrollable crying. It is important that we do not move quickly from one question to another, but rather seek out a range of examples and contexts to build a fuller and more accurate picture. We have to stick patiently to each subject area, rather than accept their first response. They may not be particularly self-aware and so we take our time, patiently and warmly, because we are curious, not because we doubt what they have told us! It is helpful to allow plenty of time so that there is no sense of being hurried.

3 **Explore differences between private and public styles.** A private style does not just refer to a reluctance to disclose, but also the context in which control may be eased. Someone who is overcontrolled may relax certain constraints when they are on their own, or in the presence of their immediate family. The acid test is how they behave and how they signal in the wider world.

4 **Beware of "borderline" false leads.** For those of us who have worked on traditional mental health teams, we must acknowledge that many symptoms of borderline personality difficulties have become synonymous with undercontrol. Impulsive behaviours, emotional outbursts, and acts of self-harm may have become quick and easy indicators for a referral to the DBT team. It is useful to spend specific time exploring this area. On our training courses, we often give participants a sheet to fill out such as the one shown in Table 3.1.

These are headings for the nine criteria in the Diagnostic and Statistical Manual of Mental Disorders for BPD (DSM-5, 2022). Those with some exposure to this area, for example, having worked on DBT teams, will tick the boxes on the left-hand side readily. However, the boxes on the right-hand side tend to cause some doubt or consternation. Do those with overcontrol have some of these same symptoms? Indeed, are all of them a possibility? Those more familiar with this client group ponder how many of the nine they have actually seen in cases of overcontrol. It is good if they can be challenged to work out what

Table 3.1 DSM-5 criteria for BPD

DSM Criteria	*Undercontrol*	*Overcontrol*
Suicidality/Self-Harm		
Impulsivity		
Interpersonal Problems		
Affective Instability		
Dissociation		
Identity Disturbance		
Abandonment		
Anger		
Chronic Emptiness		

Note: Place a tick in the column if the features are commonly present.

an undercontrolled and an overcontrolled presentation would look like for each of the nine symptoms. For those new to the concept of overcontrol, there can be a dawning moment that, on the basis of even two or three of these symptoms, they may have been over-diagnosing undercontrol and underdiagnosing overcontrol for most of their careers. It can make for an animated discussion.

5 **Beware of other false leads!** A risky sport, a rebellious streak, or an isolated break with convention are examples of what might be assumed to be undercontrol. However, each can also be signs of overcontrol and are not uncommon in this population. We need to question carefully to find out more about what each represents. There are a whole range of what might initially be considered impulsive behaviours that turn out to be more compulsive in style when we dig deeper.
6 **We are not trying to persuade them whether or not they are overcontrolled.** They are experts on themselves but not necessarily on what constitutes overcontrol. They may see an infrequent display of strong emotion as indicative of undercontrol, whereas we might see it as overflow or leakage. They may be drawn to endorse words such as chaotic or overwhelming when this matches their internal experience, but this may be far from how they behave or what they signal. We look to find common ground with them on their overt patterns. While the style remains collaborative, we

hold our position on what constitutes overcontrol, an expertise we are bringing to this assessment.

7 **Overcontrolled patterns resulting from a recent crisis or trauma do not constitute overcontrol.** We sometimes assess someone whose patterns meet all the criteria for overcontrol. As we proceed, however, we may find that these have appeared only recently, often as a response to a specific set of challenges. This presentation of overcontrol does not mean that GRO is an appropriate intervention for this individual. We have found that such clients tend not to identify strongly with the other participants and can be intent on discussing the causal incident. They cannot identify with more long-held historical patterns of overcontrol.

8 **Watch carefully for what is happening when an overcontrolled system is overwhelmed.** A finding from Rose Keane's research cited earlier is that those with overcontrol tend to have far fewer previous contacts with psychiatric services than those with undercontrol. It is often only in mid-life that their resilience breaks down and a person, previously seen as always coping well, hits a wall. Their presentation at that moment of crisis may involve self-harm, suicide attempts, and high emotion. The overcontrolled system in breakdown can appear undercontrolled. As with so much of the assessment, it will take time and patience to tease out what are the core underlying features and what are signs of the current predicament.

9 **Explore the cost of overcontrol.** An important issue in the assessment of overcontrol is that of cost. This is significant to grasp as we are at pains to say we are not trying to change an overcontrolled temperament. That is neither desirable nor possible! Our hope is that in certain areas, there might be a little loosening or softening of overcontrol. For that to happen there needs to be some motivation and this comes from reflecting on cost. Once again, we think it is crucial in our training courses to have personal experience of identifying the costs and benefits. This is often a new stance for someone who is overcontrolled and who may be used to thinking that it is the rest of the world that needs to change.

Assessment for GRO

In keeping with the motto of our hospital "Festina Lente" (hurry slowly), we approach assessment with consideration, as there is no scale or standardised tool that will do the job for you. A series of closed questions is not likely to do better. The best way forward is with a patient and probing discussion. This allows the uncovering of examples that can be further explored for pattern, function, thoughts, and planning. Bear in mind that for those who go on to join the programme, this is the start of rapport building, the start of therapy. And those who do not proceed, for whatever reason, should at least be given parity of respect.

Assessment Procedure for GRO

Orientation

Run through confidentiality as per your usual protocol and orientate the individual towards the purpose of the meeting. Explain that this is an assessment for the GRO programme and not a therapy session, although we are keen to understand their history and experiences. Let them know that it is estimated that the assessment will take about one and a half hours.

Interview Style

Explain that we will be looking at three categories (connection, control, and emotion), one at a time. We don't use the titles of the three themes specifically here – distance in relationships, rigidity, and inhibited emotion – as that would be too leading at this early point. The aim is to get their sense of how each category plays out in their lives.

Assessing for GRO is not a tick box exercise. There is a great emphasis on trying to build rapport and using a relaxed style. If the person feels safe, it is much more likely they will be more open. The task of the assessor is to go to great lengths to put the person at their ease, using signalling and validating language. It is helpful to use statements such as "we often see that in people who come to GRO", "people in our groups tend to describe that", and "that makes sense given what you have said about…". Validation can play a key role in helping a person open up on what can be vulnerable ground. They are not likely to have been previously questioned about their overcontrol. It is helpful to let them know what you are doing each step of the way. Tell them what you will be covering and why. Signpost what you are looking for and offer choices if needed. We are not asking leading questions, but we do hope to provide a platform for them to explore the areas further by conveying that there are others on this similar path, and that they are not alone.

Occasionally a client responds at great length to every question, as if wanting to ensure that we have every conceivable piece of information. The more usual challenge is the person who gives very short, curt answers. Our task is not to move on to the next question but to gently persist, looking for specific examples that will provide a fuller picture. We need to build a relationship with each person so that we can be flexible in our questioning, confident in persisting with follow-up questions.

Category 1: Connection

We explain that the first category is called "connection" and is about how they relate to others. We find out about the different relationships in their life – romantic, family, friends, and work. Social events at work may be quite different from those with friends or at home. We take every opportunity for "probes", such as looking for an example of what they are saying, looking for meaning as to why they might do something, and fears or reasons as to why they might not.

Here are the main questions that we aim to cover:

- How do you find connecting with others?
- How are you with revealing personal information about yourself to others?
- What would others say about their connections with you?
- Do you feel lonely? (Probe for feelings of loneliness even when with other people).
- How do your relationships tend to end? For example, would there be a blow up or do you walk away silently? (Probing for rupture and repair versus abandoning relationships without ever dealing with an issue).
- Do you ever feel wronged, neglected, or passed over? Tell me more about this.
- Do you feel you give more than you get in a relationship? If so, how is that for you?
- How are you in social situations? (Explore differences in social situations with familiar and unfamiliar people, probing for over-rehearsing conversations and overpreparation).
- What standards do you have for yourself and others in relationships? Give me examples.
- You have referred to (list some of the points they have mentioned). How have these things cost you in your life?
- Is closer attachment to others something you want? Tell me more about that.

Category 2: Control

We explain that the second category is called "control". This may have negative associations for some, but in fact all of us like to have a measure of agency, predictability, and consistency in our lives. We normalise that when we introduce this area. This category is about how much control they like to exert. It is to do with many things including standards, rules and spontaneity, and the degree of rigidity or flexibility with which they feel comfortable. It also includes more compulsive and life-interfering strategies such as self-punishment (self-harm, restricting eating until it is "earned", excessive exercise, etc.). Check whether they punish themselves if they break or breach a personal rule. If these come up, explore the function of these strategies.

These are the general areas we look to cover.

- How are you with uncertainty (check need for planning)?
- How are you with spontaneity?

- How do you feel about rules and structure?
- How are you with getting feedback from others?
- Can you tell me about standards or rules you have for yourself? And others? For example, how you "should" behave or act in certain situations.
- What would others notice or say about your need for control/predictability/consistency?
- What about play and playfulness (explain concepts)? Are there any times you engage in activities just for fun that are non-productive?
- What is your work ethic like (check for perfectionism and/or procrastination)?
- In terms of needing structure and control, what are the costs of this in your life?
- What might you like to work on that would make life a little easier?

Category 3: Emotion

The third and final category is about their relationship with their emotions. It is important not to focus on only one or two emotions, since it is likely that they will have different relationships with different ones. There are points to hold in mind, such as anger can be directed towards self rather than others. Discussing emotions can be a gentle entry point for exploring self-harm, suicidal ideation, eating difficulties, and addictions. In relation to emotional overflow, it is important to check how often such events occur, and if they occur in public or private. These are the general questions we look to cover.

- How would you describe your relationship with your emotions?
- More specifically, how are you with each of these four emotions: anger, sadness, fear, joy? Explore both the *experience* and the *expression* of each emotion.
- Do your emotions occasionally spill out? If so, what happens and what does that look like? Does this occur in public or private?
- How do you express your emotions to others?
- What have others said about your expression of emotion?
- What emotions are you comfortable with/uncomfortable with?
- Where do you feel emotions in your body (check for physical manifestations of emotions)?
- What do you do when you are really distressed by your emotions?
- When you think about how you feel and express emotion (list some of the points they have mentioned), how has this cost you in your life?
- Is experiencing and expressing your emotions something you would like to work on?

EXAMPLE:

Here is an example of a relatively straightforward assessment.

Sheila's Assessment:

Category 1: Connection

This first category is about how you relate to others. I am interested in how you find connecting with others and whether you let people get close to you.
No, I don't feel comfortable letting people too close.

Tell me more.
I keep myself apart in relationships, just one step removed. I have this sense that the more others know, the more they could hurt me. I know that doesn't make any sense.

How are you with revealing personal information about yourself to others?
On a casual level, I can engage in conversation, but I wouldn't be revealing anything about how I'm feeling or anything like that. Friends would say getting information out of me would be like pulling teeth (laughter). I don't talk to them about anything other than chit chat. None of them would know I was in hospital last year. With my husband, I really struggle to know what's OK to share with him and what isn't. I don't want to burden him or worry him, and I just find it really awkward having intimate conversations. I think I don't know how to do them.

What would others say about their connections with you?
They would say that I am a solid, practical friend. I think they would also say that I am the quiet one. I tend to listen rather than be the talker in the group. Like I said, I can do chit chat, but I never let it get much deeper than that.

Do you feel lonely?
It's a funny thing because I am around people all the time in the office and at home. I have a husband and two kids, and yet I do feel lonely.

Tell me more about that.
I have felt lonely all my life. I remember feeling very alone as a kid. I don't like to acknowledge it and perhaps don't want to feel it. I am so used to it. It's always there, like a part of me.

Yes, that makes sense. Loneliness is a word that resonates with many people who come to GRO.

I am interested in how your relationships tend to end. For example, would there be a blow-up or do you walk away silently?
Well, I am terrible at keeping up contact with some friends. I will let it go months before replying to a text message, then I feel guilty and feel it is too late. As a result, friendships just tend to fizzle out. Endings tend not to be dramatic as I never commit enough for that to happen.

How about in intimate relationships?
In romantic relationships, I have just ended them abruptly. I would decide I can't do this any longer and essentially just disappear. I put it down to fear of commitment, but I think it is more than that. Even with my husband, I can still feel "get me out of this".

Have you ever felt wronged, neglected, or passed over?
No, I don't think so. I never let relationships get to that point. If someone screwed me over, I would tend to blame myself and think it was something I did.

How about at work?
Yes, perhaps, if someone really wronged me. There are some things I have ruminated on for years and got quite fixated on. Those people have never been forgiven. So perhaps the answer is a bit of a yes!

Do you feel you give more than you get in a relationship?
In work, I feel that I give more than others and that frustrates me at times. But then again I take on more, because I know it won't be done right unless I do it. People will often come to me there looking for my advice or my thoughts on things, and that way I give more than I get.

What about in friendships?
In a way, I do give more than I get, but I set it up that way. I am the "go to" friend. Recently, one of our neighbours had a tragic death in the family and I was the one they called on to help with all the arrangements. I went into organisation mode and sorted things for them. They knew I would stay calm and that I could be counted on. I don't think I would call on anyone to do that for me. I don't feel close enough to anyone for that.

How about in your marriage?
That's different again. I do more, but I don't give more if that makes sense. I know my husband wishes I would give more of me, but I am just not able. I make up for that by having a beautiful home that is always tidy and clean, and ensuring we are always organised and on top of things.

How does that feel?
It's funny because I quite like people coming to me, and yet there are times I really resent that so much is left on my plate. I don't seem to be able to approach anyone for the same sort of things.

How are you in social situations?
On a one-to-one level, I can come across as warm and connecting to a point. Then my anxiety starts to go up and I need to get out of the situation. People would generally describe me as shy, I think, or maybe a little cold. If things get tricky in a social situation, I will bow out at the first sign of problems.

My husband told me that I am often awkward and strange when we are with his friends. I guess that is quite noticeable. I am always conscious how others perceive me. I just find I am wary and cautious around them. It's really uncomfortable. I put pressure on myself thinking that I must have something interesting to say and end up saying nothing at all. I'm somewhat easier on a one-to-one basis. I could chat a bit more spontaneously then, but it would be about superficial stuff. I would never talk about how I feel or what I am struggling with.

What standards do you have for yourself and others in relationships? Give me examples.
That's a hard one. I didn't think I had standards but, thinking about it now, I probably do. I expect people to be polite and respectful. If they are not, I can slip into victim mode. I suppose I also expect people to be loyal, which is ironic considering I don't really commit whole-heartedly in any relationship. If I send an email or a message to someone, I would expect a response and yet I often don't respond myself. In a way, I guess you could say my standards are a bit screwed up.

You have referred to feeling lonely, being disconnected from your husband, and not having really close relationships. How have these things cost you in your life?
The cost has been huge. It has cost me the opportunity to have more meaningful engagement with life and to have relationships that I own – if that makes sense. I yearn to sit with someone and be myself and not feel so uncomfortable and shut down all the time. It has definitely cost me in my marriage too. I know my husband is burdened by my distance and I know, deep down, that I am missing out on a lot.

Is closer attachment to others something you want? Tell me about that.
I do and I don't. I mean a huge part of me wants closer attachment to my husband especially, and then another part of me wonders how will I ever change – I have been like this all my life you know. The idea of closer attachment scares me a lot, and yet I would like to try.

Category 2: Control

I am really curious to know how you are with uncertainty.
On the surface I can appear easy-going. Or at least I try to appear that way. I tell myself I will go with the flow. But I think that's a defence because I actually hate uncertainty. I try to create predictability and consistency no matter where I am. I don't like not knowing. It leaves me feeling unsafe.

And spontaneity?
My husband is great for planning things last minute and trying to be romantic. But when things come out of the blue for me, I don't handle them well. It's like warning bells go off. My general reaction to spontaneity is that I try to manage it and control it. I am a planner.

How do you feel about rules and structure?
I like rules I make myself and I like structure, but I have a thing about authority figures imposing rules on me. I don't like rules that I don't agree with. So the best rules are mine!

How are you with getting feedback from others?
I will act like I am OK with it, but inside I am telling them to sod off. In work, I get quite defensive but no one would know that. I won't defend myself in the moment. I will end up stewing on what the person has said, and I try to think up of ways I can get one over on them. Like I might bad-mouth them to others, or withdraw completely from them and punish them with silence. I know this sounds awful.

And with your husband?
I am definitely defensive with my husband and he would know for sure when I am annoyed with his feedback. I think it is almost automatic in me to want to defend myself. It brings up stuff from my childhood and being accused in the wrong, or always having to defend myself against my mother.

Can you tell me about any standards or rules you have for yourself? And others? For example, how you "should" behave or act in certain situations.
Like I said earlier, I expect people to be respectful and polite, that's important to me. But then again, I will never let them know that, and people generally don't know if they have pissed me off. I have standards around my work and needing to achieve and accomplish, but it's pointless really because no one ever says thanks, and sometimes I really wonder what is it all for. I suppose I also have standards about how I should look. I will never leave the house without make-up and I always try to dress appropriately.

Have others noticed or commented on your need for control?
My husband finds it very frustrating that I always need to know exactly what we are doing. For example, when I get up on a Saturday morning, I have a list of the things I want to get through that day. I don't tell him what they are, so when he suggests we do something different, I feel that he is interfering with my schedule. In work, colleagues would say I am very organised. I have a reputation for getting things done. But I often set completely unrealistic standards for myself. I could spend hours on end on one task and then question why I left so little time for anything else. I don't let others help me because I know they won't do it to the standard that I feel is good enough.

What about play and playfulness? Are there any times you engage in activities just for fun that are non-productive?
No, that's not great at all. I would never dance at a wedding or a night out. I hate that stuff. I am awkward as hell. I will sometimes play with our dog but, even with her, I am always thinking I should be teaching her a new trick or making

sure she has had a proper walk. It's like I make it a chore. I don't have much patience at all. I'll sometimes play board games with my husband, but he says I tend to become very competitive which takes the fun out of it.

What is your work ethic like?
When I was younger, I was much worse than I am now. I was always striving and believed I should work really hard. It was important to be seen to be effective and get that recognition. My parents praised me for achieving and that was the only time I got attention from them. It was built into my DNA to work hard. I think I have eased up a little in recent years, but anyone would say I still invest far too much in work.

In terms of needing structure and control, what are the costs of this in your life? What might you like to work on that would make life a little easier?
On the one hand, I am not that uncomfortable with being rule-based and a perfectionist. On the other hand, I do feel I have wasted so much time and energy trying to get everything right. I am exhausted. I think the costs have really been felt at home. I worry that someday my husband is going to stop trying to plan things for us to make life more enjoyable because of how badly I react when he does. I guess I would like to be a bit more playful too, and not feel so inhibited and awkward in myself.

Category 3: Emotion

The third category is to do with emotions. I am going to be asking you about your experience of emotions and how you tend to express them. I am interested to know what is your first reaction to this category.
I think it is fair to say that I work hard to numb and shut down my emotions.

How would you describe your relationship with your emotions?
I am not comfortable with them at all. I don't like feeling them or showing them. It's too vulnerable, and being vulnerable always meant weakness to me. For a lot of my life, I wasn't feeling anything at all. For years, I didn't know what a feeling was. I would ask myself is that a feeling, or is that just a pain in my stomach. Since my hospitalisation, I feel some emotions inside. I don't ever show them, but they scare me. I can sometimes feel out of my depth with them and I'm not sure what to do with them. I try hard to block them out because I don't want to end up back in hospital again.

I am going to ask you now about your experience of four different emotions if that's OK. First how are you with anger?
I definitely feel anger. I think I repress it most of the time. My husband says that I can be passive-aggressive at times. Sometimes it will all just explode, usually directed at the wrong person, such as my husband or the poor dog.

Tell me more about these "explosions".
I say explode but I would never be physically aggressive or anything like that. I might slam a door but nothing more serious.

And would other people see this?
Well no. My husband, maybe, but I would usually be on my own. And I would never express anything like that in front of anyone else. That would be awful.

And what about sadness? Do you feel and express much sadness?
I do feel quite a bit of sadness inside, but I try not to dwell on it. I would describe it more as heaviness or a muted sadness. I honestly don't know how to show it. I haven't cried since I was a child.

And how about fear?
I think there is a lot of fear in me – it is probably the main driving force for all the other stuff but I wouldn't have recognised it as fear before. I had constant fear growing up. I was wired to be afraid at home as a kid, but I would never have shown it because to show fear was weak. I definitely feel fear in social situations and that's what makes me come across as awkward and cold to others.

How about joy or happiness?
I often think I should be feeling more joy in a situation. I will frequently pretend that I am happier than I am. On those rare occasions when I do feel some actual joy, fear comes in immediately and I worry that something bad is going to come along, or I will be punished for this. My fear robs me of any joy. Overall, I prefer not to feel joy.

Do your emotions occasionally spill out? If so, what happens and what does that look like?
As I said, my anger sometimes spills out when I am alone or maybe in front of my husband. Otherwise I keep everything very much under control and that includes my emotions.

How do you express your emotions to others?
I pretty much just don't show them. Even when I had my breakdown, no one knew I had been struggling at all. It came as a complete shock to the extended family.

What have others said about your expression of emotion?
I think they would say I am the calm, stoic one. They say that I never show my emotions to them. Like I said earlier, I will be the person someone calls to deliver terrible news because they know I won't cry. I guess they would say I am pragmatic. My husband just sees my silence when I am upset. I know he hates that I can't or won't show my emotions to him.

What emotions are you comfortable and uncomfortable with?
I think I am getting a bit more comfortable with my anger. But I hate fear and the sadness just feels like a lump of lead in me. I don't think I would use the word comfortable really to describe how I feel about either of those. But I would like to get a bit more familiar with joy.

Where do you feel your emotions in your body?
I feel them mostly in my chest or my head, and sometimes in my stomach. I know that may sound silly but I will get bad headaches and then, hours later I realise that I have been feeling something. I might not know what the feeling is, but I know it's there in my body.

What do you do when you are really distressed by your emotions?
I try to distract myself from them by throwing myself into work, or doing chores or something active, or I would try to numb them.

When you say numb them, what kind of things would you do?
I would scroll on my phone for hours or watch stupid TV programmes. I would only do that after I have exhausted myself with work or chores. Sometimes, I might turn to a glass or two of wine, but that doesn't happen often.

When you think about how you feel and express emotion, and what you have described to me in terms of your relationship with emotions, how has this cost you in your life?
By always living in my head, I have missed out so much in life. When I look back, I feel I have lost so many opportunities. I really regret that. I know I have a problematic relationship with my emotions and I don't know how I would go about changing that. I suppose I am willing to try. That's something isn't it?

Yes, absolutely, and that pretty much answers my next question which is whether experiencing and expressing your emotions is something you would like to work on?
I would be interested, mostly because I don't want to end up back in hospital. I know that keeping everything bottled up led me there, but I don't know how to prevent that happening again. So, when I think about that, I know I want to work on my emotions. I just haven't a clue how to do that.

Group Suitability

Is GRO the right intervention for Sheila at this time? The answer is an emphatic yes. She is clearly overcontrolled and she identifies with all three themes. Her overcontrol is personally costly and appears to underpin the difficulties that have led to her recent hospitalisation. She acknowledges these costs, and she has expressed some willingness to work on these areas.

The question of group readiness is a tricky one. For most interventions, some sense of committed motivation is required. In GRO, on the contrary, those that fit criteria are expected to have a level of ambivalence and uncertainty. The three words of the intervention (Group – Radical – Openness) tend to trigger a variety of reactions. For many, the prospect of a group is unappealing or unsettling. Radical may seem, well, radical for a population who are more likely to value caution. As for openness, they have been selected because they aren't open! But, if they can identify with some costs and some sense of wanting things to be different, then this is a promising sign. This is why in training we run through a range of scenarios, not just of ambiguous responses, but also tailored to working out whether the intervention is an appropriate fit for the person. It is a process that is constantly being updated. Training also provides the opportunity to get into more detailed points such as the sometimes subtle differences between impulsive and compulsive behaviour, and broader issues such as whether it is possible to be undercontrolled at one stage in life and overcontrolled in another.

One point that is worth stating here is that a critical way of avoiding a deluge of unsuitable referrals is to educate the referrer. This will save much time. If your referrals are likely to come from many sources, it is worth considering having an information leaflet, or information sessions for referrers to learn more about overcontrol and GRO. In our service, we are fortunate in that the individual will have met with their team psychologist prior to being referred to GRO. The psychologist must complete a GRO pre-assessment form with the person, in which the three themes are explored. This information then accompanies the referral. We cannot emphasise enough that referrals should not be made on the basis of a particular diagnosis, or simply because other interventions have not been helpful. GRO is specifically aimed at individuals whose difficulties are underpinned by overcontrol.

It is now time to see how the 27 sessions are conducted.

Chapter 4

Cues of Safety, Cues of Danger

There was a moment in GRO several years ago that we often think back to. More accurately, it occurred during a coffee break. We were at the far side of the canteen and saw the group seated around two tables they had pulled together (against the canteen rules, we noted proudly!). One had gone out for a smoke but, as he passed by, the others gestured for him to come and join them. They had a chair ready and there was a coffee just arriving. He was clearly touched. A minute later, the entire group erupted in laughter. We never found out what was the trigger for the outbreak of merriment (was it at our expense, we wondered!). It was a contagiously joyous sight.

We were observing individuals who, on the basis of a rigorous assessment, tended towards distance in relationships. In the few sessions of the programme to this point, they had demonstrated their difficulties with both social cues and emotional expression. Yet here they were displaying inclusion, warmth, and openness; they were signalling with feeling. It needs some explaining.

One way of understanding what might be going on is through Porges' Polyvagal Theory (Porges, 2011). Deb Dana has visualised the hierarchy of Porges' three states by putting them on a ladder (Dana, 2018). This has become a key means of understanding a number of constructs in GRO.

The first use of the ladder is that it helps to promote awareness (Figure 4.1). It invites a person to use their own words to describe what they are experiencing on whatever rung of the ladder they find themselves. This encourages noticing threat when it arises, but safety too. The description broadens from a few words covering urges, thoughts, and emotions to whole phrases or specific examples. Each of the three states can be recognised from a distinctive sense of self and of the world, reserved for just that state. Familiarity with the distinctions between the states provides a step to noticing movement on the ladder and what might be triggering it. Many in our groups are intimately acquainted with their sympathetic system, striving towards accomplishment, mobilised against threat. However, the Polyvagal ladder gives equal attention to the shutdown, collapse, and dissociation of the dorsal system, on which

DOI: 10.4324/9781003321576-4

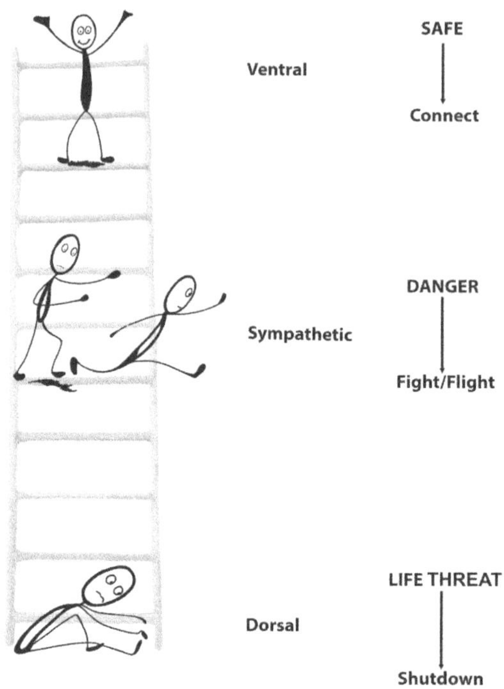

Figure 4.1 The Polyvagal Ladder
Source: Image drawn by Gary O' Reilly, with permission from Deb Dana.

focus is less common. It turns out that this is an important area in overcontrol and it often provides relief when it is described.

Second, the ladder is a way of digging deeper into the three themes of GRO. It provides a map for each one. It gives a fascinating perspective on how relationships, control, and emotion can be experienced in quite different ways, depending on which part of the nervous system is being activated. It provides a fresh lens through which participants can discuss their experience, allowing them to see the areas of common ground, as well as how their personal experience has shaped unique patterns.

A third aspect of the theory is that it highlights that movement down the ladder is not volitional. The nervous system is wired to be vigilant. It senses what is going on within the body, outside the body, and between others without conscious awareness. This concept of "neuroception" is helpful for us to hold in mind. It moves us away from judging someone who drops down the ladder as wilful or resistant. It heightens our responsibility to help each person find a pathway back to a safer state. It also heightens the importance of our own self-awareness as facilitators, both in what we bring to the group and what might be triggered in us during a session. The potential of the group is to some degree dependent on the extent to which we can show up with a regulated presence.

The fourth and final point of relevance is the principle of co-regulation. This touches the essence of GRO. A key way to go up the ladder is through regulating with another. It turns out that this is much easier than finding the way on our own. In the canteen on that day, the group had managed to co-regulate. Through each other they had come to feel safe and connected and, in that state, they were relaxed and able to let their hair down. It may only have been for a short time but it was, nevertheless, a shared pathway to ventral. A principle of GRO is that the more frequently co-regulation is experienced in group, the more easily it can be accessed in daily life. If the group members can have a ready access to the experience of co-regulation, then this is something they can bring to their lives outside the group.

Apart from referencing Polyvagal Theory, there is another important issue that is explored in this chapter: how the costly patterns of each person's overcontrol developed. In characteristic GRO fashion, this is not approached theoretically but through curiosity and self-discovery. The group provides an opportunity for each person to reflect on their own journey and to hear about the journeys of others. This comes after some initial housekeeping and a potted history of GRO, so the participants have some context for the approach.

GRO starts at a relaxed pace. Participants should not feel a sense of being pushed or of being drowned in information. The tempo is steady and gentle. There are challenges, moments when they will find themselves going down the ladder. If the group find a way of bringing each other back up, perhaps even to that state they found in the canteen, that would be truly significant. The prospect fires the imagination. Theirs and ours. This chapter will introduce and describe the plan for the first three sessions.

Sessions 1–3: Introduction to GRO and Polyvagal Theory

Session 1: Introduction to GRO

This first group may feel challenging not just for the participants but for us too, the facilitators. There is much to cover. There is apprehension in the air. The faces are unfamiliar. We all register threat starting a new group. It is usually a relief to get started.

In subsequent sessions, the first half is devoted to hearing their self-enquiry since the previous session. In its absence, this opening session can seem a daunting length. As facilitators, we meet for an hour beforehand. We want to be a regulating presence for the group. It is a chance to check in with each other and to remind ourselves what is most important. The risk is that we will talk too much (one of us in particular!). We remind ourselves that there will be opportunity to hear important information time and again throughout the programme. We can labour under the illusion that if we add more content, it will all be retained and useful. In fact, this is unlikely. What participants are likely to hold on to is how they felt, their impressions of us, and whether they believe they are in the right group. We try our best in this session to create a sense of containment and build hope. We do this by getting everyone involved as much as possible right from the start.

The aims (as in all subsequent chapters) are for the participants.

Aims of Session 1

- Grasp the practical arrangements of the group
- Take part in establishing group agreements
- Understand the concept of overcontrol and the history of GRO
- Reflect on how their overcontrol developed

Session Plan: Session 1

INTRODUCTION AND ICEBREAKER

At the start of the first session, we welcome everyone by introducing ourselves and orienting participants to the programme. We outline the practical arrangements for the group, such as the times and dates of sessions, the length of the mid-session break, and the fact that handouts will be provided so they don't have to take notes. We talk of the importance of building a group in which they feel truly safe.

As an icebreaker, we ask each group member to spend a few moments talking to us about their first names. For example, they might tell us about the origin of their name, whether they like it or not, and any other information they wish to share. The exercise allows us to hear from everyone right from the beginning. It turns out that each member has something to say about their name, and we find out if there is some variant they would prefer us to use. This icebreaker fosters connection right from the start, often generating some welcome laughter.

GROUP AGREEMENTS

Following the icebreaker, we draft up a set of group agreements. We ask the group to consider what is particularly important for them and explore any concerns or issues. The group agreements can be edited and amended as the group progresses. It is helpful to have them as reminders throughout the programme.

The aim of group agreements (we don't like the word rules) is to state together what everyone needs and expects for the group to feel contained and for it to work. Overcontrolled individuals may well like rules, but this is not about being told what to do, but collaboratively drafting up a set of agreements. This starts us off on the journey of it being "our" group in which we are all active participants. Typically, they discuss confidentiality, the value of each member, the importance of hearing and respecting all views. It is important to start punctually, but we prefer people to come late than not at all. We encourage them to switch phones off or at least to silent. As facilitators, we have some agreements that we must include such as limits of confidentiality and the commitment (in our service) to report back to each individual's referring agent at the end of the programme. We also ask them to agree to come and talk to one of us if they are considering dropping out.

PUTTING OVERCONTROL AND GRO IN CONTEXT

In general, we do not talk for too long a stretch but, in the early groups, it does take some heat off group members to sit and listen to us, and there is important information to convey. At this point, we spend about 15 minutes giving some background to GRO, as they may well wonder why they have not heard much about it up until now.

This can be achieved in various ways. We tend to start with the undercontrol – overcontrol distinction, which is part of our journey. Most of this group will likely have heard of our DBT programme in the hospital. We explain that those who attend DBT could be described as undercontrolled. We elaborate on five key features of undercontrol, such as the challenges of dealing with emotions that fire so easily and resolve so slowly, and how this can often lead to a life of distressing chaos (Table 4.1).

We explain how DBT evolved to provide skills to help regulate emotions and tolerate distress. It is only in more recent years that clinicians have asked the question as to whether a person could have too much control. We then compare the profiles of undercontrol and overcontrol and invite discussion (Table 4.2).

Table 4.1 How undercontrol presents in five areas

	Undercontrol
Core Problem	Emotional underregulation (chaos)
Behavioural Style	Impulsive
Societal Response	Attracts disapproval
Thinking	Underthink (and over-emote)
Relationships	Crave intimacy/fear abandonment

Table 4.2 How undercontrol and overcontrol present in five areas

	Undercontrol	*Overcontrol*
Core Problem	Emotional underregulation (chaos)	Emotional overregulation (loneliness)
Behavioural Style	Impulsive	Risk-averse
Societal Response	Attracts disapproval	Attracts reward
Thinking	Underthink (and over-emote)	Overthink (and under-emote)
Relationships	Crave intimacy/fear abandonment	Fear intimacy/cope by abandonment

It resonates when they hear that the core problem of overcontrol is not chaos but loneliness. They identify with the notion of being cautious or risk averse and they see how, from early years, their willingness to follow rules, work hard, put others first, and not draw attention to themselves may have been encouraged and appreciated. However, it tends to touch home that inhibiting their emotional life and keeping others at arm's length may have been costly. They often find it intriguing that strategies they developed at one point in life have turned out not to serve them well at another. This is a good opportunity to explain emotional "overflow" or "leakage" (sudden, intense outbursts of an emotion that may feel disproportionate to the current situation), and how this is a feature of overcontrol, a result of holding down all that emotion for so long. It is important that they appreciate that these infrequent outbursts are not to be confused with undercontrol.

We explain that there are two different approaches to working with those who feel that their overcontrol is costly. The first is RO DBT, which consists of individual sessions alongside skills classes (very much in the style of DBT). The second is GRO which is a group therapeutic approach. They are attending the latter!

HOW PERSONAL PATTERNS OF OVERCONTROL DEVELOP (AND HOW THESE CAN BECOME COSTLY)

We ask the group members to reflect and tell us about their life experiences that may have influenced their overcontrol. On the one hand, their accounts are likely to be highly personal. On the other hand, there is substantial overlap, providing a chance for people to identify with others in the group. It is important to note that we give scant reference to biology. It is acknowledged, but its contribution is less known and so could open the sort of debate that we are trying to avoid. In contrast, when they talk about their life experiences, they are sharing something personal with the group to which others can relate. They are learning through discovery, rather than theoretical models.

As facilitators, we would typically lead the way on a task like this. It is easier to follow when there has been a model, and the group often comment on how much they appreciate us sharing our experiences. This is not a life story or a revelation of the most intimate events of our early life. It is simply making links between what happened (usually early in life) and the way in which overcontrol now manifests itself. It must be totally honest and authentic.

Facilitator 1:
I would say that there was an emotionally stifling atmosphere at home. I don't remember rows or traumas. You got up and got on. Being stoic was admired. "Letting ourselves down" referred to us being visibly upset. There was a worry about what other people might think, so it was all smiley faces to the world. Academic success was very highly valued. All this fostered a not very rounded individual. I was smart for my age but naïve and nerdy. I backed away from relationships and was wary of different ideas or views. I had standards, whatever they were. In relationships, partners said they had difficulty getting to know me, getting behind the façade. All of this has softened, but yet is still there. I find myself reverting to it unless I am watchful.

Facilitator 2:
My childhood was a bit different. It was chaotic and emotions were everywhere. I learned very quickly that I had to be the "good kid". There was no more room for my emotions or my needs. I also learned that in order to get attention and love, I had to be calm and not create any fuss. I learned to depend on me and me alone. I actually remember one day in school deciding I am going to make a life for myself and emotions and people would not be part of that. I believed from a young age that connecting with others would only hurt me, and I developed unrelenting standards for myself and others.

It is important to highlight that life messages are learned in our early environments. They may be consistent with the overall family dynamic or they may be reactive to the family environment. They can be statements or rules that have been given directly or picked up indirectly. They may come from home, school, or peers. It is from these early experiences that we develop strategies that in time become our overcontrolled ways.

The group is then split into pairs for 15 or 20 minutes so that everyone can start this personal exploration before coming back to the main group. Some give reactions to what they discussed; others relay their example in more detail.

I filled the vacuum left by my parents to bring up my younger siblings. By the age of 10, I had the responsibility of any adult. Neighbours would probably be screaming for social services these days, but the truth was that at the time,

I saw it as having real upsides. It gave me status. It gave me purpose. I wasn't complaining. It did mean that I was an outsider at school and that led to some vicious bullying that had a lasting impact. I ended up a fragile ship, focused on work and duties and caring for others. I was detached from myself, I didn't have a friend in the world. I learned to hide my sadness and loneliness behind a mask. Everyone but me was astonished when the whole façade came crashing down. I find it quite emotional to make the links between what was happening growing up and what we have been discussing about overcontrol. I certainly developed ways of cutting off from myself and others around me. I had learned it was safer not to feel, not to participate, not to connect.

The aim here is to de-shame and move away from pathologising overcontrol. In fact, it is important to talk about how some areas of overcontrol were functional and necessary in life and may still have uses now.

OUTLINE OF THREE THEMES

Participants very often request a roadmap or some means of having an overview of what we will be doing. One way in which we achieve this is by talking a little about the three themes. Group members will have been introduced to these during their assessment session, but it is important to remind them of the key areas that are the focus of GRO. We draw a horizontal line across the board, marking "distant" at one end and "connected to self and others" at the other end. This is a time to talk about how they may have learned that distance in relationships was safer, but the cost is likely to have been disconnection, not just with others but also with themselves. We are looking to encourage them to explore this (e.g., there might be many people in their lives and yet not much deep connection; they may wear a mask to try and please others to the extent that they have lost the sense of who they are).

The second line has "rigid" at one end and "flexible" at the other end. If they can generate examples as to what this conjures up, this is the best way to go (but always good to have a few personal examples up our sleeves, if they go quiet on you!).

For the third line, we write "emotionally inhibited" at one end and "emotionally aware and expressive" at the other end. Again, this is a rich area for discussion (e.g., for some the whole area of emotion may be completely foreign, while for others they may be very aware of emotion but never express it). Some may say that they express certain emotions, while others are a "no-go" area.

Talking about the three themes gives a clear road map of the areas to be explored. This is an opportunity to discuss that we do not use diagnostic categories. This is a transdiagnostic group in which costly overcontrol is the common underlying factor.

CHECK OUT AND SELF-ENQUIRY

As the first session comes to a close, ask each member to spend a moment checking in with themselves to see what has landed and how they are feeling. We ask each person to give a short response. It is at this point they often declare that they are in the right group or that it has been revealing to hear a model that resonates with their experience. They frequently say how reassuring it is to be seen and understood by others who "get" them.

Finally, we explain about the self-enquiry exercises between sessions, which will be discussed with the group in the following session. This first self-enquiry invites them to think about the life experiences that have shaped their overcontrol. This is an extension of what they have already been doing in this session and so should be easily grasped. We end by encouraging everyone to go gently with the work, and highlight that we look forward to seeing them in session two.

Self-Enquiry 1: How Overcontrol Develops

Reflect on your life experiences that have influenced your overcontrol. At the start of the next session, we will invite you to discuss examples that you are comfortable sharing with the group.

It is helpful to give an introduction prior to the first self-enquiry. In the group agreements, it is likely they will have talked about respect for others. This is an opportunity to highlight the importance of respect for self. It is common in overcontrol to want to get everything right or to compare their contributions to that of others. The challenge is to notice these urges and judgements if they occur. They will gradually see that there is value in each contribution. The aim in this self-enquiry is that they would honour their own life experiences and develop respect for how their current coping strategies and ways of living were formed, often at very difficult times in their lives.

The first self-enquiry is usually powerful and emotive. Many make clear links that had not previously been apparent. One facilitator leads the exercise, letting the process unfold gently, avoiding jumping in with questions and inhibiting others from offering advice, however well-intentioned. The aim here is for the participant to state their own insights. One task for the second facilitator is to keep an eye on the clock, having divided the length of time scheduled for the first half by the number of participants. The length of time for each person does not have to be exact, yet we must ensure we hear from everyone. A common phrase we use is that "we want to ensure we hear from everybody today in the self-enquiry" as we quietly keep up a momentum.

As the group goes on, they are likely to comment on emerging similarities. The self-enquiry also helps build on the group's language. We hear how one group member spends her life "building a wall around her", while another had a smile "nailed to his face". It is such evocative phrases that help the group develop its unique character. By the end, it will be apparent that many personal patterns of overcontrol may have once been adaptive and therefore need to be honoured. The costs are not initially clear and, indeed, may not be apparent until much later in life.

Here are two examples:

I knew some of the stuff that was happening in my family was dreadfully wrong from an early point. There was no-one I could go to, no-one I could tell. All I really knew was that I was utterly on my own. I knew that nobody could ever find out. I couldn't be hurt more if no one knew. I became a master at pretending that everything was just fine. I learned to convey I wasn't upset, to smile through my anger, to laugh through my hurt. "Rein it in" was one of the things I kept telling myself if I felt the slightest emotion. There was no way I would risk doing or saying anything that might make things any worse. I became overcontrolled and overcontrolling in what I did, even in what I thought. I got very good at it. I developed very regimented ways of doing things. I developed overcontrol because I had to. Now I am not sure I can do anything else.

I have had a heavy sense of responsibility for as long as I can remember. I was always trying to make everything OK for everyone else. I was the strong one, the problem solver, nothing was too much trouble. I had no needs. I came to believe this myself. More and more was foisted on me. To this day, I have no idea how to ask for help. I push through. I am the model employee who will work every hour in a day to get a job done. It exhausts me, but I can't see another way. I had so many unspoken rules growing up. I played my part in shaping what has developed, and yet I feel so resentful that is how I lead my life. But there's no room for me to say so or to touch my anger. No-one would have had any idea how to react when I was a child, and I have no idea how to express any of this now.

Session 2: Introduction to Polyvagal Theory

Aims of Session 2

- Become familiar with the Polyvagal ladder
- Put personal words and phrases to ventral, sympathetic, and dorsal
- Grasp that moving between states is not a choice
- Understand that there are stronger and milder versions of each state

Session Plan: Session 2

The intention is that the participants will be able to know where they are on the Polyvagal ladder and be able to describe what they feel and how they react in each of the three states. This session is not about explaining Polyvagal

Theory in depth. Learning should be through discovery and discussion, rather than lecturing, which should be kept to a minimum.

THE POLYVAGAL LADDER

We start by showing them the ladder (see Figure 4.1). It is important to use the same graphic again and again so that it becomes familiar. We briefly set out the stall of the three nervous system states. We would usually explain this from an evolutionary point of view. One of the most primitive defences (still evident in certain animals) is to stay still in the face of threat – freeze, and hope not to be noticed. A more evolved survival strategy is fight or flight – taking on a hairy mammoth or making a speedy escape. The third state, the most recent to develop, is where we connect. This social engagement system is essential to how a tribe survives. We use the graphics for the three states. What we must do is describe how these three states operate in our lives. In overcontrol, we tend towards vigilance to threat and so the ventral state may prove more difficult to access.

We then show the "Hearts Aligned" video (www.youtube.com/watch?v= INzhUviglgs). It makes for an ideal reference point. It is touching and many in the group will rise a rung or two on their ladder simply by watching it (discussion point right away). Heart rate is an objective measure and it is monitored in this demonstration. We want to draw out a series of points. We ask about the heart rate of the three people as they were sitting on the couch because it is referenced. Then there is the rapid return to baseline. We encourage a wide-ranging discussion as to what might have put their heart rate up and whether this was likely to be the identical trigger for all three of them. We won't use the term here but this is "neuroception", the pre-conscious scanning of the environment that is happening all the time. The key point here is that they do not choose to change their heart rate any more than they choose to move down their ladders. This is important for a group which may think that rational effort will cure anything. It is easy for them to see how all three people in the video are regulated by being reunited with their dogs. They often find it interesting to discuss the finer points, such as the moment near the end of the clip when Glen is crying and is unsure as to what emotion he is feeling. We ask them where they would put him on the ladder (in our view he is in ventral).

DESCRIBING THE THREE STATES

The facilitators write up a few words or phrases that would work as generic descriptions for each of the three states. For example, safe, connected, and calm in ventral; agitated, uneasy, restless in sympathetic; numb, shutdown, disconnected in dorsal. The group are then broken up into pairs and continue the task. When they come back, this is the time to introduce that there could be milder or stronger versions for each state (mild worry at one end of sympathetic could be blind panic at the other, but it's all sympathetic). Some examples are unique to an individual.

OUR CURRENT LIVES DESCRIBED WITHIN THE THREE STATES

At this point, we become more personal in our description of the three states. It is best if we, the facilitators, initiate the discussion. We give "a glimpse into our lives" using the language of the three states. We try and give a sense of all three, even if one is less familiar to us.

I have recently retired. There used to be far more movement in my nervous system. There were many demands in work which had me in threat most of the time. But there were many more ventral moments too. I would bump into colleagues, have lunch with them, discuss creative ideas with them, laugh with them. Now that I am home and since my dog has just died, it is a much flatter line stuck in the higher end of sympathetic. I have converted a bedroom into an office which makes for more productivity. But it can also mean drifting into undisturbed dorsal at times.

Sympathetic is my "home away from home". Work is the primary source of this, feeling like I can never keep up with all of the demands, feeling agitated and angry that others are perhaps not seeing how hard I work and wanting to scream "back off!!!" Home demands also fall into my sympathetic. I find myself coming towards the weekend worrying and feeling restless about all I have to do. When I am deep in my sympathetic, then dorsal starts to creep in. This is a cold, bleak place but it can also feel like a relief sometimes. I am really disconnected and numb and just want to sink into that dark hole and stay there. Thankfully, this doesn't happen too often and I am back in sympathetic telling myself to suck it up and get a move on. Moments of ventral are sadly less at the moment because of the global pandemic. I am actually quite the social butterfly (even if no-one truly knows the real me). I love meeting up with friends, having a nice dinner out, and having a giggle. That's me fully in my ventral. Spending time with animals also brings me straight into ventral.

Self-Enquiry 2: A Glimpse into My Life Using Polyvagal

For self-enquiry, we are asking you to give us a glimpse into your life using the three Polyvagal states. Describe how it feels when your sympathetic state kicks in, when your dorsal state takes hold, and when your ventral state comes alive. Give some examples.

The priority here is getting them used to describing the three states. If we get a glimpse into their lives, so much the better. We go gently if they describe how they used to be, or where they should be, and we encourage moving away from that to simply noticing, observing, and describing how it is now. If they describe only one of the states, we ask them to be curious about and put words on the other two, even if those are only rare visits. Recent examples can be particularly illuminating. One group member said that, after the last group, she found herself in dorsal: "I refused to feel anything when I got home, I just didn't think". Another found himself in sympathetic – "I felt so irritable, I could feel myself radiating 'keep away from me'". It is so helpful to have such specific examples.

Sympathetic

In sympathetic, I am restless. I should be doing things. If I'm at home, it is cleaning, ironing. There is a pressure on me to DO something. There is a list in my head, far too long to get through but that is what I have to strive for. At times, I feel overwhelmed and exhausted. I may slow for a bit, but this is just not good enough. I am like a rat in a cage on one of these wheels, always running. I would likely be defensive and irritated with others. I push them away and then feel angry I am left to do everything on my own.

In my sympathetic, I just want to scream and run away. In meetings in work, I want to tell everyone to sod off. I feel so tense and my shoulders and chest start to ache. Then I worry there is something physically wrong with me. Everyone is irritating me and I start to think about all the ways I want to get back at them.

Dorsal

I have a chair I slump into when I am in dorsal. It may be a relief to be out of relentless sympathetic, but this is not ventral. It's a relief because it's nothing, but it is a disconnect. Time doesn't matter. It is cut off. Inevitably, I slip a little lower and it is hopelessness, blackness, despair. I find it hard to get out of that chair. It can feel like I am at the bottom of a hole. I am aware of a chink of light, but it is a long, long way away and seems impossible to get to. I may as well stay where I am.

I used to think dorsal was easy, safe. I cut everyone out and that kept me protected. But thinking about this now, I know it is a dark place. In dorsal, I am alone. It can get scary and it starts to become really painful. My wife knows when I am slipping and she has tried to communicate to me how hurt she is when I shut her out. I know that I am hurting her, the one person whom I love the most and, yet, when I am there, I cannot pull myself out. It feels awful.

Ventral

The simplest way for me to reach ventral is to go for a swim in the sea. I come out and I am calm, hopeful. People seem friendly. Just lovely. There is a kiosk and I get myself a coffee and, even on the coldest day, I drink it slowly and I am at one with the world.

When I am up on a stage playing a gig, I am in ventral. I am connected to the audience and to myself and to my instrument. It is a high like no other. Planting stuff is another way. My whole body eases. I love the feeling and sensation of the clay and dirt in my fingers. I feel a deep sense of gratitude watching little seeds grow into something beautiful.

It can be hard for people to become more aware without drifting into self-blame. "What is wrong with me that I can't get into ventral more?" "How do others make it seem so easy?" We remind them of the biological nature of our states and our lack of choice in what triggers and pushes us further down the ladder. However, this self-enquiry can also engender hope. We explain that just as the autonomic nervous system is shaped by early experience, it can be reshaped with ongoing experience. The autonomic pathways that support moving out of protection into connection can be strengthened.

Session 3: Triggers and Glimmers

Aims of Session 3

- Recognise "Triggers" and "Glimmers"
- Reflect on how life would be different if it was lived "a few rungs higher"
- Understand that co-regulation is easier than self-regulation

Session Plan: Session 3

INTRODUCTION

We congratulate them for their work on noticing and putting words on their three states. This is likely to be a new way for them to look at their experience. We all tend to think of our brains making all the decisions, when in fact our nervous system is at work at a much earlier point. This surveillance system is always on duty, looking for cues of safety to urge connection, or cues of danger, which would lead to mobilisation or shutdown. They are beginning to step back and notice this. This isn't easy, because most will have grown up in environments where there was no encouragement (or it might not have felt safe) to tune in to their emotions or their internal experiences (such as changes in heartbeat, urges to act).

TRIGGERS

Tuning in to their nervous system, they may very well have noticed jumps down the ladder. We use the term "triggers" (cues of danger) for what brings us from safety into states of protection. We might ask them to think of a moment when they felt a distinct shift from safety into threat ("When it was proposed that we break into pairs, I felt my heart thumping and a hollow feeling in my stomach"). This is a chance to see where they were pushed (mobilised for action or overwhelmed into shutdown) and ask is this the protective state that is most familiar to them. It is often easier to start noticing the bigger jumps, which helps develop awareness of the more subtle changes. It is important that they start to get to know the ways in which their nervous system sends them information.

Some triggers feel grounded in the present moment (such as when they realise that it is their turn for self-enquiry and they feel a bit anxious). At other times, their response can feel out of proportion. This points to a cue from the past that is being activated in the present. For example, feeling overwhelming anger at someone coming back late from break, or feeling numb when someone tells them they appreciate what they just said, usually points to an experience from the past coming alive in the present. They need to recognise that the nervous system simply takes in cues and enacts the response it deems necessary to ensure survival. We encourage them to note the connecting threads and to observe the patterns.

GLIMMERS

Deb Dana describes those micro-moments when we feel a spark of ventral energy as "glimmers" (Dana, 2021). Glimmers tend to pass by easily because we are wired to react more intensely to negative experiences. Once the group have noticed one or two glimmers, they can become curious about finding more. With increasing awareness, glimmers often start to show up more frequently outside group.

We give examples of some of our own triggers and glimmers from group. This is the best place to start as they appreciate that our regulation is also constantly in flux. They are surprised to learn, as we relate examples, that they are often unwittingly offering us glimmers of connection. They are encouraged to begin recognising their own triggers and glimmers, while listening carefully to those of others. This is what they now do in pairs.

When we come back for discussion, we ask them to set the intention of noticing at least one personal glimmer in every group.

LOOPS

Sometimes movement is just not possible. A person may find themselves trapped in either dorsal or sympathetic. The technical term is a dorsal or sympathetic "loop". We ask them what it would look like if someone was stuck in dorsal (looking away, zoned out, not hearing what is going on, detached, drifting, appearing hopeless or abandoned). And what would a sympathetic loop look like? They might mention being agitated, restless, on edge, high heart rate and high energy, perhaps more driven in their interaction with others, or stuck in a particular emotional state. These two states look very different, but they are both examples of being stuck. It is easier to recognise when someone else is in a loop!

CO-REGULATION

We are not in the business of proposing change at this point. However, there is one consideration to hold in mind. Regulation is the term used to go up the ladder towards ventral. Co-regulation (regulating another or being regulated by another) is much easier than self-regulation (trying to do it on your own). It is clear from Polyvagal Theory that co-regulation is the basis for self-regulation. An essential principle of GRO is that we create opportunities to feel what it is like to be regulated by others, and to develop the attunement and trust to let them regulate us. Self-regulation is not seen as a viable option until co-regulation is in place.

One of the main ways we co-regulate is through connection. There may have been moments in group when someone has said or done something that soothed others, resonated with them, amused them, moved them, made them feel safe, or even made them feel sad. These moments are the most common ways of moving back up the ladder. This is why connection is the first of the three themes that we will be exploring.

We also become more sensitive to the glimmers of others in the group. Should the opportunity arise, it would be a lovely gift to offer another group member something that might help them regulate. How can we make co-regulation more available is a question we need to be asking.

LIFE A FEW RUNGS HIGHER

An interesting question to ask is how their lives would be different if lived a few rungs higher on the Polyvagal ladder. It would not be desirable or possible to be in ventral all the time, but, for many reasons, their lives are likely to feel easier, safer, more connected, and full of possibility if they could get into their ventral state more often. This is not an exercise about how to climb up the ladder. It is about imagining what it might look like and feel like if they were living just a few rungs higher.

Facilitators first ask each other: "What would life be like if you lived a few rungs higher?"

I think I would be more open with my partner.
I would be more present with things I enjoy, not thinking this has to end.
I would appreciate the blue sky without wondering if there are rain clouds on the horizon.
I would feel a greater sense of freedom, less of the chains of worry holding me down.

Then we ask the group to respond to this question. We highlight that life a few rungs higher may be more about approaching than avoiding. If there is time, it is well worth having another pairs exercise here, since this question can be a strong foundation of hope.

I would throw my head back and enjoy myself.
I would find peace without constant scanning and dissection and analysis.
People might finally get me.
I would feel equal (not an underling).
I would drop the mask.
I would feel happiness rather than peer in on the happiness of others.
I might get to know what I like and who I am.
I would sleep better.
I would do what I want to do rather than what I should do.
I would commit.
I would be expressing my emotions.

CHECK OUT

We usually keep this short. Even a one-word check out gives a good insight into where they are. By this point, we find they are more authentic and their guard is down a little. They are more open about being lost or down if that is where they find themselves, and less reticent to express hope if they are seeing some light.

Self-Enquiry 3: Triggers and Glimmers

Think about your own triggers and glimmers and track the cues that bring you up and down your ladder. Are they different inside and outside of group? Think of the glimmering possibilities from smells, images, memories, and music, as well as some co-regulating moments with others.

I walk the dog at more or less the same time every day. Yesterday I was in deep sympathetic and I was irritated with every person I met, every dog I met. Why couldn't they allow me a bit more space? Why couldn't they keep a closer eye on their dog? The triggers were everywhere. Random things just bugged the hell out of me. People too close to me, people hogging the pavement, owners behaving like their pets. The previous day, I was in ventral and I couldn't get enough of everyone! So, if I can head off higher up my ladder, it will feel as if nothing would bother me.

Most of my triggers start in my head. I generate them. I worry about what others are thinking and not thinking. I keep myself in threat. Glimmers don't seem nearly as powerful and they seem more external. I would have to go and seek them out or set them up, while the triggers are just pouring in. Doesn't feel like an even battle. It's a massacre. Do others feel like that?

I am conscious of avoiding certain people because they are such reliable triggers. I know they will pepper me with triggering questions: Did I hear you were in hospital? Are you back at work yet? I would cross the street to avoid them and to avoid being triggered by them.

We try and allow some time for them to look back before starting the first theme. It is interesting to hear what they have taken from the sessions so far, and what they notice about the developing group dynamic. If it does not come up spontaneously, we draw particular attention to examples of co-regulation that they have already observed.

Chapter 5

Distance in Relationships

We went to the Dalkey Book Festival several years ago. There were 50 people crammed into a small pub to hear Northern Irish novelist Nick Laird and American writer Sebastian Junger discuss what the word "tribe" meant to them. Nick Laird's observations were pessimistic, founded in his childhood growing up during the Troubles. His experience had cautioned him about tribal behaviour, and he had seen tribes define themselves by how much they feared or hated other tribes. The word had almost entirely negative connotations for him.

Sebastian Junger, on the other hand, took an entirely different view. In his late teens, as a self-imposed rite of passage, he set off to hitchhike across the United States. He describes the start of this journey in the opening chapter of his book "Tribe" (Junger, 2016). In one touching episode, he explains how a homeless person took responsibility for him. He was somehow viewed as part of this man's tribe which made a deep impact. Later in his life, this inspired him to live with various groups who were bound together because of the extreme circumstances in which they found themselves. This included living in Sarajevo when it was under siege, and living alongside US Marines in frontline combat. He also became interested in what he could learn from tribal societies. In particular, he researched the differences between the North American Tribes who lived a consistent life for some 15,000 years and the society in which he grew up. His short and inspiring book details what we can learn from tribal societies. He has some interesting thoughts as to "why war feels better than peace … and disasters are sometimes remembered more fondly than wedding or tropical vacations. Humans don't mind hardship. In fact, they thrive on it, what they mind is not feeling necessary" (Junger, 2016, p. xxi).

In the best traditions of the festival, as the evening wore on, we found ourselves walking around the small town engaging in lively discussion with the authors and others who had attended. There were many and wildly differing experiences of tribes. It became clear that our training and experience in group therapy put us firmly in Sebastian's camp. Time and time again, we had seen the beauty of the human spirit in groups. Group therapy provides the

DOI: 10.4324/9781003321576-5

chance to act selflessly, to feel some of the solidarity that is at the core of what it means to be human. However, it encouraged us to reflect on the continuing erosion of these tribal capacities. Those who attend our groups struggle with connecting. In fact, they are experts on how to stay on the edge of tribes or any social grouping. Their primary aim is to stay safe and, in interpersonal terms, this usually means keeping others at arm's length.

The four sessions in this section form the first theme of distance in relationships. In these sessions, participants become aware of their style of distancing. They also have the corrective experience of a feeling of solidarity, of feeling necessary, and of knowing that the group is genuinely better because of their presence. These four sessions are not just the start of increasing awareness but, more importantly, they offer the experience of what the trauma writer Deirdre Fay calls "belongingness" (Fay, 2021). This is more important than any knowledge we could impart.

Sessions 4–7: Distance in Relationships

Session 4: Introduction to Distance in Relationships and "Swords and Shields"

Aims of Session 4

- Reflect on the advantages and disadvantages of connecting
- Consider the impact of disconnection on self and others
- Identify their protective "swords and shields"

Session Plan: Session 4

This is our first theme: Distance in Relationships. We draw out the line below so that they have a visual reference for our discussion.

Distant in Relationships ________________Connected to Self and Others

The aim is to become aware of how they relate to others and themselves, and to explore the reasons why they may have adopted a distant style. It is also a chance to experience connection and belonging in this group, and begin to see how some flexibility in connecting could be enriching. Relating to others in ventral may be a new experience. It's good to make it clear that we are not pushing for change, but for curiosity and awareness.

ADVANTAGES AND DISADVANTAGES OF CONNECTING

Our starting point is to consider the advantages and disadvantages of connecting. We split the group into smaller sub-groups of three or four. We ask them to think about and explore the advantages and disadvantages of connecting with others, and then gather them back for discussion. We write up the advantages and disadvantages on the whiteboard, using their language and phrasing. We ask each person to reflect on what it is like to see these words and what it brings up for them.

We find it best to start with the disadvantages. The ideas come pouring out! There are many reasons why a person might choose not to connect (such as losing independence, having social shortcomings exposed, being disappointing or disappointed, or fears of rejection, hurt, even betrayal), and these need to be respected. Let them give it full vent! When they turn to the advantages of connection, the pace and energy usually slow. This gives space for our irreverence – maybe we should pack up and go home and live a disconnected life!

We cannot overestimate that we really welcome their ambivalence. We want to hear why they do not want to let go of their overcontrolled strategies and how terrifying this might be. It is important these views are genuinely validated. It must not feel as if we are trying to sell something, or that we are arguing with them. Allowing uncertainty to be present in the room generates further respect for their experiences and the challenges of this work.

IMPACT OF DISCONNECTING ON SELF AND OTHERS

Discussing the impact of disconnecting on self and others is potentially a deeper, more personal conversation. For this reason, we split the group into pairs to explore this, and then invite them back to the whole group.

For some this can be highly emotive. It may be upsetting to reflect on how distancing has impacted themselves and those they care about. Here are some examples.

I feel cut off, misunderstood, not tuned in. There is a constant pressure – I like to be liked and yet I spend time worrying that my friends probably hate me. I would love to be known, but there is no way I could let that happen.

If I don't give anything away, I can't get hurt. And if somebody does then let me down, I can always say that I wasn't expecting anything anyway. The result is that I never fully give of myself. I am always holding something back. I signal "go away" when I want to say "I need you". The cost is that my life can become painfully lonely. I carry the weight of so much sadness and regret.

I remember a friend's parent calling me aloof. When I looked it up, I realised that does catch me pretty well. I hold myself back. I size people up and then try to work out what's required. I would like to be open, but it just doesn't come out. It's quite new for me to consider the impact of this on others. I think they don't get the best of me and they end up puzzled and sometimes hurt. They never get to know me.

I have felt lost and lonely and misplaced in the world. I keep my guard up. I have a fear of giving others ammo! I am always hovering on the outside, though I would dearly love to be on the inside. I never give myself fully to anything, and in return, no one ever gives themselves to me.

THE TRIBE

After the detailed discussion on advantages and disadvantages of connecting and the impact of disconnection on self and others, we briefly introduce the concept of a tribe. We tend to present the evolutionary and biological context, that is, that we have evolved to function and survive by depending on others. We do not spend too long on this, but highlight the key message that we are innately wired to function in social groups, and we do not get to choose this. Ask the group to reflect on this and encourage them to name any thoughts, queries, or judgements.

Before bringing the session to a close, we tell the group the story of a woman with her swords and shields (which is included here).

SWORDS AND SHIELDS

Swords and Shields Story (adapted from Lynch, 2018b p. 88):

> Back in the days of Ireland's ancient past, there was a farmer who lived all alone, tending to her cows on the Hill of Tara. When she was younger, she had enough bad experiences with people to be wary of them. She had come to believe that no-one would truly ever like her, which left her feeling lonely and isolated. One day, she explained her struggles to a passing trader. He suggested she head to the nearby marketplace that was thronged with people. He was sure she would find out that people would want to get to know her. Despite her doubts, she followed his suggestion. A few weeks later, he passed by her farm and enquired how it had worked out. She explained how she had prepared by strapping her sword to her back and her shield on her arm – you can never be too careful in a crowd. She went to the marketplace and sat on a bench, waiting for people to approach her, the sword and shield glinting ominously in the sun. Nobody came near her and everyone avoided making eye contact with her. She declared to the trader: "see, I told you people wouldn't like me!"

This story stimulates discussion on the ways they have kept others at a distance and what their swords and shields might be. We invite the group to give initial reactions. Examples of swords (more attacking) could include a sharp tongue, blaming others, using silence as a weapon, or over-intellectualising. Shields are more defensive and somewhat more passive, but can be equally powerful.

Common shields are flat facial expressions or fake smiles, or behaviours such as withdrawal, avoidance, deflecting, or appeasing.

CHECK OUT

At the end of group, we ask everyone to take a moment for some self-reflection. We check out the emotional temperature in the room by asking each person to say briefly how they are feeling or what is staying with them as they leave the session. As a signal of the GRO style, we tend to steer away from reassurance or advice, and we validate what they are saying. We explain that the self-enquiry asks them to reflect on their own swords and shields, and wish them well until the next session.

Self-Enquiry 4: Swords and Shields

We all have our own "swords and shields" to stop others getting too close. What are your ways of keeping people at a distance?

In this self-enquiry, we encourage each person to discuss what are some of their swords and shields that inhibit connection. Some people see a difference between a sword and a shield, while others see it as a collective term for a defence. Either is fine. Here are some examples to give a flavour of what to expect.

When people get close to me, they are more likely to see my sword. I'll be a bit sharp in how I talk to them. I think I do it when I'm feeling exposed or vulnerable. I think my shield is never being the real me around people. I'll just act or talk in a way that I think people want to hear, even if it's not me at all. I don't think people ever really connect with me, because I am not real. I'm just this version of myself that's always changing. Then I end up feeling misunderstood or confused about how others respond to me.

My wife says that I can be passive-aggressive. I think that's my main sword: I'll just be passive-aggressive in what I say and what I don't say. I'll be irritable with people around me and just isolate myself from them. To be honest, I think people avoid me when I'm like that so I don't even have to try too hard at disconnecting. They do the work for me.

I'm not really sure I have a sword. I think I'm hiding under my shield so much that I never really have to use it. I'll just straight out avoid people, especially if they want to come close to me.

I've built a wall up around me so that people don't even get close to seeing what's beyond it. I think, at this point people have given up trying to climb it or knock it down. I don't think I do anything that hurts others to keep them away. If anything, I'm more inclined to use my sword on myself. I'll feel angry or lonely and I'll just turn it inwards and stab myself with it until I've caused myself enough pain.

Session 5: Connect + 1

Aims of Session 5

- Increase attunement to each other
- Share personal information
- Notice blocks to connecting
- Cultivate a willingness to disclose more

Session Plan: Session 5

To start off session five, ask each person to tell the group one thing about themselves that the group do not know or might not expect. This could be anything such as hobby, a place they have visited, an unusual interest, an exciting experience. We usually start with one of our own examples. This warm-up is a chance to tell everyone a nuanced (or not so nuanced) fact about themselves. This is all part of connecting, allowing others "in" and sharing some private information. This can be interesting, surprising, and sometimes hilarious, which makes for a good start.

CONNECT + 1

In the second half of session five, we introduce "Connect + 1". This is one of the original skills from the RO DBT programme called Match + 1 and we have adapted it in GRO (see Lynch, 2018b, p. 436). It provides a chance to practice some of the steps necessary for real and authentic connecting. It highlights how group members may engage on a surface level with friends and loved ones to avoid going deeper and to keep themselves safe. Connect + 1 is a way to become more aware of how true intimacy and connection with others are often avoided, for example, by peppering the other person with questions or deflecting. Some find this exercise threatening and risky. It is important to pay heed to this and to acknowledge what it brings up.

We start by building a "Closeness Scale" with the group. We explain that while we do not want to get caught up in exact numbers, the scale provides a visual aid for different levels of intimacy. We draw a horizontal line titled "Closeness Scale" and explain to the group that our task is to build a rough idea of what each point on a 10-point scale might look like. At lower levels of disclosure, nothing is given away (e.g., talking about the weather). A 3 or a 4 starts to become more personal, but may still be relatively safe. A 5 suggests a higher degree of revelation, often with or about emotion. A 7 or 8 indicates more vulnerability, with a 9 or 10 being the type of information they would only share with one or two others. The scale can be refined as the exercise continues.

The facilitators then model Connect + 1. We often share what we did the previous weekend. Such a topic generally offers enough scope to allow both surface level description and deeper disclosure about our emotional reactions to what occurred. It is important to be prepared to model this and have your examples ready. The exercise can feel inauthentic or incongruent when first trying it out, because Connect + 1 involves talking in turn, without commenting or questioning the other. This can feel (and indeed is) unnatural. It may be useful to explain what the exercise tries to highlight by modelling how *not* to do it first. The group recognises that, as overcontrolled individuals, they may avoid connecting by peppering others with questions or shutting down conversations. In this exercise, they do not question, they only disclose, so that there is a series of short exchanges.

Guidelines for Connect + 1

1 Choose something you are going to discuss, such as a hobby or a recent event.
2 Begin Connect +1 by telling the other person something that is at the lower end of the closeness scale.
3 Listen to how the other person responds and see if they meet your level of self-disclosure. If they do, consider going one level higher by revealing more information about yourself, your opinions, or your emotions. You can choose what to reveal, but keep it honest and genuine. Connect +1 is not only an exercise in self-disclosure, but also an exercise in attunement.
4 As Connect +1 progresses, try and resist the urge to ask the other person questions.
5 Remember, it's not a race to the top! When doing Connect +1, it is fine if one or both of you choose to stay at a lower level. It is important not to rush up the closeness scale, as so much depends on timing, and the relationship itself.

We instruct the group to pair up and spend a few minutes trying this out, after which everyone has the opportunity to reflect on how it went. The aim is to be aware of the level of intimacy in the conversation and to make a considered choice to go up a level or not. We talk about how hard it is not to ask questions or to jump in with validating comments. While the intention is coming from a good place, doing this is often about our own needs and can take away from what the person is saying. Ask them to notice urges to intervene, problem solve, appease, or ask further questions.

The initial impact can be quite variable. Some get so excited that they race up the Closeness Scale, blurting out whatever comes to their mind. They soon realise that disclosing too much too quick (what we call a Connect + 8) serves to block connection. Some acknowledge that their apparent level 5 or above is actually a scripted response with which they have little emotional connection. For example, it might look vulnerable to hear someone describing their struggles with their mental health, but these may have been described many times before. They could be part of a set of standard responses that are a more subtle way of keeping others at a distance. Others find themselves locked in at the lower end, realising that they are very unfamiliar with what drifting up the scale might involve. The common response is just how hard it is not to ask questions. This often feels selfish but, after a while, it can be surprising how another person's emotion is felt without having to ask questions or respond directly. It turns out that nodding, eye contact, and physical presence work well for attunement.

Reflections on Connect + 1:

I found we were really empathic with each other without having to ask questions. That surprised me. It felt like we were truly listening to each other and giving each other permission to just talk without the interruptions of questions.

I found it interesting that even when our time was up, there was much more I wanted say. It was like I was on a roll. That is really unusual for me. I was surprised at how much I enjoyed it. If you had explained at the start what we were doing, I would have thought this will never work!

This was challenging. It pulled me out of my comfort zone. I would normally go to a 3 or 4 and stop there, but this time I went further. I don't think we expected it to go the level it did. We got to a 6 or 7 for sure. We had said before we even started that we wanted to cap it at 5, but we kept going.

I think I went in too fast and then found myself dropping down quickly. I kept judging myself on where I was on the closeness scale. It was hard, but it has highlighted to me what I normally do in conversations.

We explain that over time, they can phase out the strict boundaries of this exercise in favour of its lessons. For most, this is a chance to listen with more attunement and to take their space in relation with others. Having spent years working hard not to share of themselves or be vulnerable, the challenges are learned gradually and remain a work in progress. For their self-enquiry, they are invited to try this out with other people in their lives.

Self-Enquiry 5: Connect + 1

Practice Connect + 1 a few times between now and our next session. Reflect on how it went and what you noticed.

Session six starts by breaking into pairs and carrying out a further Connect + 1. Apart from the opportunity to work with a different person, this ensures that everyone will have something for their self-enquiry. If they have had the opportunity to do Connect + 1 outside the group, all the better.

In reflecting on the exercise inside or outside of group, ask how it was for them and how the other person reacted. We want to hear what they noticed. It is fine if they stayed at a level of "trading facts", but we are pushing for a sense of their reactions and thoughts at different points. What did it feel like to spend an equal amount of time talking about themselves? What did it feel like going up the Closeness Scale?

I did Connect + 1 at home with my partner, and I really noticed how it flowed. It was a nice, natural conversation. I had explained it to him before we started and I think that helped. I really enjoyed the fact that I wasn't asking questions. It was different. The conversation ended in tears in a good way. We went up gently and felt very connected to each other.

I learned a lot from this. Before doing this exercise, I would never have noticed or known how much I ask questions to avoid talking about myself. Sometimes others might not even have the chance to answer a question before I am onto the next one. I realised why I do it, it's purely to avoid having to talk about myself on a deeper level.

I found I was really eager to do the exercise. I learned that I am OK going up higher on the scale about things in the past, because the past doesn't impact me as much. I don't have the emotional attachment to it anymore and I am removed from it. Whereas I find it much harder to go up the scale with present issues or present things that might be emotional for me, because my reaction is more spontaneous.

I became very aware of what I don't share. I would always have said that I was open but often I am making light of things. It's time to change that. I want to acknowledge with others when I am in pain. I tried Connect + 1 with a friend and instead of using humour, I answered her truthfully when she asked how I was. Then we naturally just moved up the scale. It felt so connecting.

It is helpful when people notice their struggles with this exercise, for example, staying at a 2 and then jumping to a 7. Encourage these insights. It may be a difficulty in finding the middle ground or it may be a protective strategy – lying low for a while and then scaring the other away with a 7, thereby derailing them and ensuring that they do not go any further.

Always be on the lookout for the language of the group, such as one describing himself as having the demeanour of a news presenter, staying calm and collected, revealing nothing. This can be referred to at a later point, particularly when you notice them no longer doing this.

Session 6: Signalling and Listening

Aims of Session 6

- Understand the importance of signalling
- Explore how signalling and listening are different in the three states (dorsal, sympathetic, and ventral)
- Practice authentic listening
- Experience being listened to

Session Plan: Session 6

We open this session with a warm-up exercise such as inviting each person to let the group know what animal energy they are bringing to group today. We start off and then invite them to take their turn. We may hear how one person is feeling like a Labrador puppy, full of energy, while another might be feeling like a bear ready to hibernate! We encourage them to add some relevant movement. This is a gentle start into our discussion on signalling.

SIGNALLING

We explain that we are going to be talking about signalling and listening, and how they are important avenues to building connections with others. There are a range of video clips to choose from, but we feel the Tronic's "Still Face" experiment has the most impact (www.youtube.com/watch?v=apzXGEbZht0). The image of the baby becoming distressed at the mother's flat face brings home the power of signalling. We invite discussion on their reaction to watching the clip. Sometimes they speak about how they have been told by others that they often appear disinterested or aloof. Others bring up memories of how they were attended to in early life. We stress the importance of approaching this topic with a gentle curiosity. We reiterate our mantra that much of our style of interacting developed as a means to adapt and cope with very difficult situations.

We explain how humans, from an early age, are drawn to look at the upper third of the face of anyone they meet. This is where the autonomic nervous system first scans to see if someone is a friend or a foe. No species has as many muscles around the eyes, and we have this extraordinary social signalling system that communicates our emotions and intentions. We are not limited to scanning the facial expression of others; we are also drawn to any slight tilt of the head, or non-language sounds such as "aaaah" and "mmmm". However, the facial expressions remain key. Our nervous system works on a "better safe than sorry" principle and so, if the signals are not clear, they tend to be interpreted as disapproving. A neutral look or flat face is not perceived as harmless, but generally read as threatening.

We describe how easily they can find themselves in a vicious cycle. They have talked about spending much of their time operating from a sympathetic or dorsal state. They appreciate that in such a chronically active defence system, they are likely to send out signals of threat that push others away. The resulting lack of social support arouses further threat, and so they are caught in a spiral towards loneliness. The group is the place to find out more about how their threat system impacts their capacity to connect.

We sometimes show them an in-vivo example of how powerful signalling can be. One of us describes something important and meaningful, perhaps a recent event that brought up some emotion, to the other. The facilitator listening holds a flat, motionless, and neutral expression. We do this for a few minutes and then invite discussion from the group as to what they noticed. Many comment on how uncomfortable it was to watch one of us bearing our soul, while the other showed no reaction. They speak about how upsetting it is for the person talking not to be met with any welcoming signalling. Their emotional responses to this brief exercise further capture the strength of the impact of signalling.

LISTENING ON THE POLYVAGAL LADDER

Signalling and attuned listening go hand in hand. Our capacity to listen depends on our own autonomic state. We invite the group to think about what listening looks and feels like in the different nervous system states. In dorsal, we may be aware that something is being said, but we may find it hard to truly connect with what the person is saying. We are likely to feel removed, disconnected, or numb, and our signalling may be flat and distant. We may be going through the motions of listening. When we are in our sympathetic state, we will likely have urges to jump in, to offer advice, to be thinking what we "should" say, and how we "should" respond. In this state, we often intrude on the space of the other and our signalling is likely to be more active. In ventral, it is usually easier to listen without an agenda. We can listen without imposing our own ideas or beliefs onto the person. We remind the group that this is the essence of safety. In ventral, we don't have to think about our signalling as it is naturally responsive and inviting. We listen with our eyes as well as our ears, and maybe with our touch or heart if we feel moved. It is helpful to get the group thinking about how they listen in their most familiar state.

LISTENING EXERCISE

We ask the group to pair up and try out being a listener and being listened to. The person speaking is invited to talk about their overcontrol at an earlier point in their life. This could be a specific event or something more general about how their overcontrol presented at a certain age. Ask them to spend a moment thinking about a certain time in their lives, for example, at age 5, 15, or 25 and bring to mind what their overcontrol was like for them at that age. We remind them that it doesn't matter how coherent their account is. This is not so much about the content of what they are saying, but having the experience of being listened to.

We explain the exercise and inform them that the listener is being asked to just listen and not to respond verbally. They can signal with their eyes, a head nod or tilt, or a vocalisation (mmm), but they are asked not to make comments or ask questions as far as possible. The speaker will be invited to speak for a few minutes.

Before sending them off into their pairs, we model it once so that they get to observe and witness what it is like for the person speaking to be listened to. We invite comment on what they notice. Many will speak about the signalling of the listener and how this comes across. They reflect on how difficult it can be not to say something or respond to the speaker, and we talk about how this can be more about the listener's need (usually from a sympathetic place). We remind them to keep an eye on time and to ensure to swap over.

When they come back to the main group, they are usually buzzing with reactions. It is agreed that it is both powerful and unusual to have someone truly listen to you. It can also bring up sadness and a realisation of how they often felt unseen and unheard. The listeners, too, have an important perspective. It might have been hard to be fully present, so it is helpful to understand how they remained authentic and what they were signalling.

Examples:

That was really powerful. I feel quite emotional after that. It was amazing to be listened to and I could really feel Maggie's warmth and care, even though she said nothing. I thought I would find it really hard to speak, but it was just like a stream of consciousness. I ended up saying things I had never said aloud before. Then when I was listening to Maggie, I felt really privileged that she trusted me.

I felt very listened to and at ease. It was comforting to feel listened to. Perhaps the people I live with don't generally listen or at least don't listen with great intensity. I loved having the space to feel heard. I hope my signalling was OK. I was conscious of it initially but then kind of forgot about it.

I was in my sympathetic for both the listening part and when I was talking. I could feel a lot of tension in my body. I noticed my negative self-talk coming in, telling me I am not signalling right, or I am not listening properly, and what I am saying is nonsense and boring. I found it very hard to be in the moment. I was tempted at times to come in and say certain things. I had to resist that urge. I hope I gave the signal that I acknowledged her story. I felt so held when she was listening to me.

FINAL DISCUSSION

Listening is not just hearing the words of another. It is also an exercise in attunement, which is a huge part of our work on the theme of distance in relationships. We can tune in to how autonomically regulated or dysregulated the other person is. We can ask what might their nervous system need in this moment to move them up a rung on their ladder. We can try to sense if we can be that regulating presence.

We end this session with a brief check out to capture how they are feeling as they leave the group.

Self-Enquiry 6: Signalling and Listening

For this self-enquiry, look out for opportunities to listen to others in your life and to be listened to. Notice where you are on your ladder and whether this affects how you listen.

Take some time over the coming days to notice your signalling and that of others.

I tried out my listening and signalling with my 17-year-old son. Teenagers aren't great for talking or listening so it felt like a good challenge (laughs). We were walking into a shop and I just asked him how he was and how school was going. I was conscious of keeping eye contact and wanting to be at ease with him. I think he noticed this. He started talking and I just listened. I realised he's not my little boy anymore, he is growing into a man, and I felt really proud. It was a lovely moment. It didn't last too long but, in that moment, we were really attuned to each other.

I found this really hard. I realised I don't listen to people. I'm always so worried about what I'm going to say next that I'm not present. I tried it with my mum and my sister and I think I was just in sympathetic all the time. I think they picked up on my signalling too. This is definitely one I want to try out more, but it is hard.

I tried to notice my listening and signalling at a work training event. I was paired up with a new colleague. It was nice to be with her and I actually opened up a little more than I would normally. I caught myself frowning once or twice and tried to soften it. When she was listening to me, I was uneasy. I definitely find it easier to be the listener than being listened to.

I told my husband about this self-enquiry and he said that he often feels I am not listening to him by my body language. This really surprised me. He said that I often sit tilted away from him and look disinterested. I was so sad to hear this, but it really helped because then we had a good chat about it and we both really heard each other, probably for the first time in years.

Session 7: Styles of Relating to Self

Aims of Session 7

- Become more aware of how their self-talk impacts relating
- Introduce language for two styles of relating: "unacceptable outsider" and "secret pride"
- Make the link between self-talk and associated behaviours in the group
- Participate in an exercise to further understand unacceptable outsider or secret pride

Session Plan: Session 7

UNACCEPTABLE OUTSIDER AND SECRET PRIDE

We start by talking about how, up to this point, we have focused on their relationship with others. In this session, we now ask them to reflect on the way they relate to themselves. It will be important that they slow down and notice how they treat and speak to themselves, even the tone they use. When they become better acquainted with that voice (and some of them may know it well), they see its potential impact on their ability to connect with others. In particular, we are focusing here on two forms of self-relating that can inhibit connection.

We start by asking people to think of times when they might not feel part of this group and, at those moments, what they might be saying to themselves. Their examples typically fall into the category of putting themselves down or doubting themselves in some way. When we get a collection of similar statements, we say that a term sometimes used to describe these sentiments is "unacceptable outsider". This is a message that comes up in many variants, such as "I am not good enough" or "others will find out that I am not good enough". It catches the idea that some may be giving themselves strong messages that their contribution is likely to be of little or no value, or that the group would not accept them if their true self were to emerge. The impact of such beliefs may keep them at the edge of, or even a little outside, the group. We ask them to give further examples of what one group member labelled his "inner saboteur".

On the whiteboard under the heading of "Unacceptable Outsider", we draw a line and invite their thoughts and beliefs, which we write in their language. Common examples are "I'm too weird", "I'm flaky", "If they got to know the real me…". Then on the other side of the vertical line, we write up related actions or behaviours ("I won't fully engage", "I will give the illusion of participating", "I will stay under the radar"). What they tend to describe is how their negative view of themselves inhibits their participation. They may find themselves risking less, saying less, following others, or trying to be overly agreeable and appeasing. At times, they may stay silent or disconnect. As one of them said, when that voice kicks in, "I zip it".

A direct contrast to Unacceptable Outsider is "Secret Pride", a term used by Lynch (Lynch, 2018a, p. 217). This self-relating style can be harder to see and harder to admit to. It is a sense of being special, perhaps somewhat better than others, or at least different from them in some way. The primary thought is that others don't and won't really "get" me. The "secret" is that the belief is not usually openly declared. It is certainly more socially acceptable to devalue self rather than devalue others, which can be a feature of Secret Pride. This is one reason these thoughts are generally kept private. Often, those with Secret Pride see themselves as an enigma as they look (with that touch of smugness) at others around them – but there's no way they would want others to know!

There are variants to look out for. Sometimes it comes across as stoicism, "no matter what the physical or mental cost, I can do this", seeing oneself as particularly strong while at the same time blaming or looking down on all around. Others have described it as a badge of honour ("You think you have suffered … you have no idea of what suffering is"). It may also be a feeling of having nothing in common with others and so not having an interest in connection.

We have an initial discussion on whether they identify more strongly with one or with both. We generally find that there are many more in the former category (unacceptable outsider). However, for the smaller number in the second category (secret pride), it can be such an important realisation. Some will endorse both sides, depending on context, which is perceptive because most of us have elements of both in our make-up (see Figure 5.1).

Figure 5.1 Unacceptable outsider and secret pride

"TAKING THE ROLE OF" EXERCISE (FACILITATORS)

Following a discussion on the two styles of self-relating, the facilitators then interview each other. Or more precisely, we interview that part of each other. One facilitator volunteers to opt for unacceptable outsider and the other takes secret pride. The facilitator is invited to recall a recent time when this voice would have been evident. This helps step into this style, and embody it, before responding to the five questions below (which are distributed to the group).

This interview style is called the "Taking the role of" which we learned from Kate Lucre. It is a particularly evocative therapeutic technique since, rather than talking about a part of us, we are talking from this part. It is worth saying this a second time – we will not be talking **about** this part of ourselves, we will be talking **from** this part of ourselves. Thus, the interview is not of the facilitator, but of their unacceptable outsider or secret pride.

Interview Questions

How long have you been in X's life?
This is a good opening question as it provides some context. This could be a lifelong style, one that arrived later in life, or one that arose through a particular circumstance.

What do you do that is helpful for X?
This is consistent with our overall approach. Of course there are advantages to this style. Let's hear them!

What do you do that is unhelpful for X?
This is the opportunity to put words on some of the downsides.

What are the costs of you being in X's life?
This sounds as if it might be the same question as the previous one, but it generates more specific responses and is often the lightbulb moment.

How would X's life be better if you softened your hold on them or you were less present?
This is the clincher. We are not looking for personality change. We are saying that with a little softening of this style, life might be more connected and less painful.

It is useful to model coming out of role. We usually do this with a few deep breaths and a series of physical shakes, as if to shake off the role we have been holding and coming back to our whole selves.

Here is an example of one facilitator's Unacceptable Outsider

How long have you been in Emily's life?
I have been in Emily's life for a long time, but I probably made myself really known when she was in primary school. That's when I came to the fore and I have stayed ever since.

What do you do that might be helpful for Emily?
I keep her on her toes. I tell her when she is being pathetic and weak, which is quite often. I tell her to work harder, do more, prove herself, or otherwise people will see how awful she is and they will hurt her. I am trying to protect her.

What do you do that might be unhelpful for Emily?
Well, I guess I can be quite nasty at times and I definitely keep her stuck. She is afraid of a lot of things because of what I tell her. I stop her doing lots of things she wants to do. I also keep her quiet and discourage her from expressing her needs. I suppose she has regrets over lost opportunities because of me.

What are the costs from you being in Emily's life?
Loneliness and regret. These can lead to her feeling angry and resentful too.

How would Emily's life be better if you softened your hold or her or you were less present?
She would be freer, and have more confidence in her abilities. She wouldn't be so focused or worried about others and how others see her. She would probably do more things for herself that are good for her. She would throw her head back and be herself.

Here is an example of the other facilitator's Secret Pride

How long have you been in Toby's life?
I have been there most of his life.

What do you do that might be helpful for Toby?
I give him confidence. I get him to go for things he might not otherwise. I get him to express his needs and not to doubt himself.

What do you do that might be unhelpful for Toby?
I think I make him judgemental. It becomes important that he does things better than others, which is a slippery slope. I can keep him apart from others. There are times he would do better to listen, to consult, to consider others rather than roll on regardless. I think I make him resentful.

What are the costs from you being in Toby's life?
He gets lonely in his righteous ivory tower.

How would Toby's life be better if you softened your hold on him or you were less present?
I think he would be kinder. Have a more peopled life. Be a better listener. Be more present with those dear to him. Generally a better human!

The group are then asked to comment on what they have observed. What does it bring up? What did they notice? This is likely to have been a deeply impactful exercise as they get a feel for what this part of us is like, how it communicates to us, and the impact it has on our lives and our connections.

The facilitators interviewing each other is another important moment in the group. This is something we will have practised in consult, pushing each other to reveal more, rather than practicing to see what can be omitted in the interests of safety. Authenticity and vulnerability are contagious. If we get personal, it will help them. And, of course, we are showing ourselves to be on the same continuum, not in any patronising way, but meaningfully struggling with similar issues. This is genuinely de-shaming.

"TAKING THE ROLE OF" EXERCISE (PARTICIPANTS)

In pairs, we ask them to interview **either** the Secret Pride **or** the Unacceptable Outsider part of the other. They then swap roles. We ask them to stick to the questions on the printed list. When they have finished, it is important to have time to process the experience.

Group members often comment on how helpful it is to separate out these parts of themselves and to give them a voice. It is validating to know that, though they are present, these parts are not all of their identity. They are surprised by the emotion it brings up both as interviewer and interviewee. Even in those who see their unacceptable outsider or secret pride as having played an important role earlier in their life, there is usually regret at what they have lost out on as a result of these styles. The secret pride is often putting words on something that is very familiar but that they had never quite described. There can be laughter and relief. One said that she often says to herself that she is more depressed than anyone else and can feel weirdly proud of that badge of honour. Secret Pride may also be a compensatory response to Unacceptable Outsider. It may protect feeling like an outsider at all costs. Another person said that in his desperate shame, he would clutch at anything to look down on somebody. It is liberating to talk about these things.

Self-Enquiry 7: Unacceptable Outsider/Secret Pride

Reflect on your relationship with yourself. Explore if either or both terms Unacceptable Outsider or Secret Pride ring true for you.

Catch examples of the impact of these styles on your connection with others (in the group and outside the group).

What would it look like if you were to soften this view of yourself?

- What would you be doing differently in relation to others?
- What might others notice?

My unacceptable outsider stops me from doing so much socially. "They wouldn't want to know me" or "I'll make a fool of myself". It's all about holding myself back, toning back the real me, often deciding to pull out of things at the last moment. If I do go into a situation, then the unacceptable outsider can come alive again afterwards. I ruminate for hours on whether I caused offence, whether they were irritated by me, whether they judged me for not saying much or leaving early. Everything goes under the microscope and is replayed through my unacceptable lens. If I were to soften this view, I think I would feel much more confident and at ease in myself. I almost can't imagine what that would feel like.

When we first discussed this in group, I thought I am definitely in the unacceptable outsider category. I relate to that with certain friends, work colleagues, and any social event really. I just never feel I fit in. I thought I didn't have any secret pride and then I was thinking about work. I usually only talk to and go for lunch there with people who are similar to me, like on the same intellectual level. I love having intellectual conversations. I often find myself thinking that I have the potential to be better than others at certain tasks and strategic problems and solutions, especially in the workplace setting. I hadn't really thought of that as impacting my connections with others, but it does. It stops me connecting with people I might feel I have less in common with and I guess I am cutting out a whole range of possible connections. I guess if I were to soften that, I would be more open to those other types of connection.

I have massive secret pride about my mental health difficulties. I feel like no one gets it. They don't understand how hard this is. I crave to connect and yet I feel I am so damaged that even if people allow me in, they will reject me once they see how flawed I am. I guess my secret pride is trying to lessen the awful feelings that come with unacceptable outsider.

As a child, it was primarily unacceptable outsider for me. I blamed myself for everything bad that happened to me. Then as a teenager, I think my secret pride came to the fore. I used my intelligence and high school grades to stop feeling so awful. Whilst this gave me some sense of self-esteem it did not change my sense of loneliness or help in connecting to others. The loneliness and feeling different wasn't going to go. So instead of saying it was all my fault, I went to the other extreme blaming or rejecting everyone else and further distancing myself.

In the discussion on what softening this voice would look like, some feel that the idea of changing is futile and hopeless. One group member said that this voice was "woven into her tapestry". However, they tend to like the word "softening" as it offers hope. Softening this talk would include allowing space to acknowledge it, bringing acceptance and understanding to the functions of these styles, and respecting and validating them, while trying a gentler approach. It might also include noticing comparisons and pausing for reflection. It is important they build the sense that even a small, stumbling effort towards softening is of value, since a deeply held view of self and others is not going to be turned easily.

Chapter 6

Rigidity

In the movie *As Good as It Gets* (Brooks, 1997), Jack Nicholson portrays Melvin Udall, a misanthropic author who displays a range of life-interfering rigidities. The film is classed as a romantic comedy. He is obnoxious and lacking in empathy (not characteristics of overcontrol) and overly focused on his work (62 books to his name). We are invited to laugh at his various rituals (centring on his fear of contamination) and routines (he demands the same waitress serving him the same breakfast at the same diner every day), and his wide range of unattractive quirks. We do not get to know the history of his state or the torment behind it, and so it is easy to join in laughing at his rudeness and dismiss his behaviours as eccentricities. He is not keen to count the costs for himself or for others, and so we are drawn to identify more with those he upsets along the way. His rigidities only soften when he falls in love with the waitress. Change happens as that relationship develops. If only life were so easy!

Our experience in GRO is that this theme is about as far from amusing as one could imagine. For one thing, rigidity may be more hidden than distance in relationships, and so there may not be the reassuring sense that there are others in the same boat. Rigidity can be a deeply lonely state. Participants may start with lighter examples such as an overreliance on lists, an acknowledgement of a lack of spontaneity, a preference for taking on tasks that others cannot be trusted to complete. However, it usually does not take long before examples are shared that arouse deep shame. There may be genuine worry that revelation of certain habits could elicit harsh judgement, even in this group. The detail of eating habits, the overwhelming nature of obsessive practices, the wish that harm may befall those who have done them wrong, or the severity of self-punishment for not achieving standards (cutting, burning, starving themselves) can be truly hard to share. Once the revelations start, though, there is often a torrent of relief.

Our challenge is to foster a sharing of these rigid strategies and yet provide a sense of containment. The latter is vital since some of their rigidity may have brought their life to a standstill, even to the point of wanting to end

DOI: 10.4324/9781003321576-6

it completely. We need to tread delicately. Our approach is to start by using a checklist to identify rigid patterns. This makes for a gentle start in which participants share common ground. They are invited to use the Polyvagal ladder to explore how their rigidity may differ, depending on whether they are in sympathetic or dorsal, and to think of what their occasional forays into ventral flexibility might look like. This is a good grounding for the deeper second session where we explore their more compulsive rigid patterns.

In the third session, we explore the concept of "seeking". When fostered, seeking can promote our growth-enhancing engagement with the world. This is a chance to see that the connection they feel with the group could be a stepping stone to re-awakening their seeking system and to regain familiarity with what delights them. The fourth and final session on this theme is play. With a set of carefully chosen games, it becomes clear that when they feel secure and connected, the group find play hugely enjoyable. However, play is a fragile state and some may easily find themselves plunged into threat with strong urges to leave or shut down. In this theme, we are opening the door to possibility, both in softening rigidity and in engaging with ventral flexibility.

Sessions 8–11: Rigidity

Session 8: Becoming Aware of Rigidity

Aims of Session 8

- Reflect on some of the benefits of rigidity in their lives
- Discuss some of their rigid patterns
- Map rigidity on their Polyvagal ladder

RIGIDITY AND ITS BENEFITS

We explain that we are leaving the first theme (Distance in Relationships) and moving to Rigidity. We ask them to tell us some of the benefits of rigidity. This is an opportunity for some to talk about how standards and a strong work ethic have led to great productivity. For example, it can be a source of pride to have gone "above and beyond" at work. It is a chance for others to talk about the satisfaction they get from providing order. Their position may come with strong views that their ways represent how life should be lived and, indeed, one that is highly rewarded in society. It is also important that they have the chance to say how hard it would be to live without rigidity.

We set out both ends of a continuum for this theme so that they have a visual representation in their head. The word "flexibility" tends not to trigger threat, as long as their rigidity is recognised as being adaptive and often useful.

Rigidity ____ Flexibility

THE RIGIDITY CHECKLIST

We give them each two copies of the Rigidity Checklist, one blank and one filled in with our scores for each item. The purpose of the list is to broaden their understanding of what rigidity looks like. We explain the scoring system and then discuss a few of our 2s (which represent "strongly applies") (see Figure 6.1).

0	1	2
Does not Apply	Applies	Strongly Applies

Hyper-perfectionism or procrastination	
Little flexibility in standards for self and others	
Delay gratification to a punishing degree (e.g. resist temptation altogether or only allow rewards after they have been 'earned')	
Insistence on appreciation and recognition for achievements	
Strong preference for situations where there are rules and prescribed roles	
Avoidance of taking unplanned risks	
Lack of spontaneity and play (often leading to regret over lost opportunities)	
Struggling to see others' perspectives	
Believing there is a right and a wrong way to behave (high moral certitude) and there is only one correct answer	
Tendency to hold grudges and ruminate on them	

Notice your 2's in particular – use them to start working out what the costs of this theme might be (for yourself and others).

Figure 6.1 The Rigidity Checklist

Facilitator Examples:

I am definitely a 2 when it comes to inflexibility in standards for myself. It is interesting that I am OK with others having lower standards – it is the ones I hold for myself that I cannot budge on. I will berate and shame myself when I feel I have let my standards drop, or others might see that I am not living up to my standards. Another 2 for me is delaying gratification. I strongly believe any time off must be earned and deserved. I find it very hard to allow myself to enjoy something if I feel other tasks are waiting. It feeds into my belief that if I am relaxing or taking time out, then I am lazy. I avoid taking unplanned risks (another strong 2!). This one impacts me and those around me in equal measure. My partner will often express his frustration that I will not do anything unless it has been pre-planned. I am sure it feels a little suffocating for him at times.

I am a 2 when it comes to appreciation and recognition for achievements. I have a deep need for my hard work to be recognised by those around me. My parents praised me for being a hard worker and for achieving. However, there was implicit criticism when they weren't praising me. I think I came to equate an absence of praise with being unloved or unseen. Even now, I crave recognition and reassurance, as otherwise I can be caught in a loop of worry of what people might really be thinking.

After we have gone through a few of our 2s, we invite them to question us on our responses. It is really helpful for them to see and observe our own struggles with rigidity and how these standards manifest in our lives. We are also gently alluding to the impact on others. We may discuss items on the list that have not arisen so that they are clear what each means. For example, we explain that in relation to the first item (perfectionism or procrastination), it is common to work until things are absolutely perfect, to a standard far above what most would achieve. Some people, however, may feel that they can't reach such a standard and so choose to opt out. In this case, they may put tasks on the long finger. The reasoning behind this is that if something is not started, then it cannot fail. Thus, procrastination and perfectionism can be two sides of the same coin.

When we are satisfied that they understand the concepts, we split them into pairs, filling out and discussing their responses to the checklist. There is no overall score, rather it is a way of encouraging them to reflect on some of the constructs we will be focusing on. Both members of the pair can opt to discuss one item at the same time, or for one to go down the whole list before reversing roles. Either way, this is a good means of seeing what this theme might encompass. It touches on standards, on rules, on harsh views of the self and others, and how imprisoned they may be by their rigidity. Their task is to talk specifically about the statements they marked themselves as scoring a 2, the areas they felt had strong application. We include a further question for those who have the time: are their responses obvious to others or would they tend to be well hidden?

Participant Examples:

I didn't think I was overly rigid until I went through this checklist. I am a 2 for many and a 1.5 on most of the others! This surprised me.

I never thought about how much I delay gratification. That is a strong 2 for me. I will often go for hours without eating or not "allowing" myself to meet up with friends if I feel I haven't completed a certain number of tasks. Others don't get it and think I am too uptight, but it feels so indulgent to treat myself.

I never take unplanned risks. I have been stuck in a job that I hate because I fear I will get into trouble if I leave. I don't know who or what I will be in trouble for! I know I am miserable in work, and it definitely impacts my family. They see me struggling and cannot understand why I won't make changes.

The resulting discussion tends to be very connecting. It is helpful to hear a wide range of experiences. It is often easier to recognise examples from others than to generate them themselves. When one member takes the risk of giving a vulnerable example, there is great comfort as others follow through the door of disclosure. There are some light-hearted moments at this point, as if there is some conspiratorial glee in thinking what harm is there in being a little rigid.

RIGIDITY AND THE POLYVAGAL LADDER

The Polyvagal ladder is a good vehicle for developing this theme further. It allows people to understand that their rigidity is not a simple construct. It can appear differently depending on a range of factors and contexts. We encourage them initially to think about their rigidity across the three states. What is their rigidity like in sympathetic as opposed to dorsal? What would ventral flexibility look like and feel like? They are then asked to describe what they notice in their body as they explore rigidity in each state, their urges and emotions, and what they are likely to think and say. Specific examples are best for seeing and truly understanding this theme. If there is sufficient time, there is the option of a second pairs exercise here. It is more likely that the whole group will discuss this, and it is the subject of their self-enquiry. Deeper reflection on this topic is encouraged over the coming days.

Self-Enquiry 8: Mapping Rigidity onto my Polyvagal Ladder

Start to map your Rigidity and Flexibility on to the Polyvagal ladder. It is often best to start in sympathetic. Think of a specific time when your rigidity was apparent in sympathetic.

- **What was happening in your body?**
- **What did you do or what urges did you have?**
- **How did you feel?**
- **What did you think and say?**

Ask the same questions using an example in dorsal.

Finally, start to think about what your ventral flexibility looks like or would feel like if you could access it more easily.

Hearing others is not just about deepening the felt sense of common humanity, but it is also a trigger for further awareness. Here is a flavour of the three states from one participant (note we ask them to start in sympathetic and then go to dorsal, so that they can finish in ventral). Some may not be able to identify much with ventral flexibility. However, it is important to hear it described, even in more hypothetical terms, so that its pathway can be charted. Even those who can identify with it somewhat describe it as almost baffling that such a state could survive in their rigid world.

My Sympathetic Rigidity*: It is black and white. It starts with lists so I can work out what needs to be done. Then I go into drive. I can be very productive, but at a huge cost. Nothing is ever good enough. My head is buzzing with thoughts that I don't share with anyone – Are others meeting my standards? Am I meeting theirs? If it goes deeper into sympathetic, there is a sense of barely hanging in, with threat always looming. I am on edge and entrenched, which is a lethal combo. In this state, I feel like I am blinkered to life and to those around me. I really can't cope if anyone goes off script. It's just push, push, push throughout the day. Zero enjoyment. Unrelenting. Very draining mentally.*

My Dorsal Rigidity*: I am not bothered. My standards go out the window. I just procrastinate. I crouch away from life. I zone out. It may look like I am listening, but really I am saying in my head, "you are doing it wrong, you are doing it wrong, you are doing it wrong". I call it irritable hibernation. I don't want anyone making any demand and I would love them all to just go away. I don't make calls. I don't return calls. My life is put on hold. There is this awful sense of not being able to break out of my rigid enclosure.*

My Ventral Flexibility*: There is an ease rather than a sense of right and wrong. I can go with the flow. Decisions are easy and I take on others' perspectives. I may still want to be organised or productive, but it doesn't matter so much how things turn out or what anyone thinks. I can see the fun and lightness in things. I am patient, present, free, and can let myself go. My outlook on life is "bring it on" rather than "what could go wrong". I can adapt, even if things go belly* *up. The days seem longer and I can see the pleasure in things. My body is not in threat, heart rate is low, breathing is calm. It no longer really matters how the dishwasher is loaded.*

Session 9: Protectors

Aims of Session 9

- Understand the concept of "protectors" and identify personal examples
- Appreciate that protectors arose at times of great challenge in their lives
- Listen to their own and to others' experiences of protectors
- Understand the initial function of their protectors

NEUROPLASTICITY

The "Sentis" two-minute clip on YouTube is a good introduction to the power of neuroplasticity and how we all have the capacity for change, including our entrenched habits and strategies (www.youtube.com/watch?v=ELpfYCZa87g). Some group members highlight that it makes change appear easy, which is not their experience. We flag the key words that it takes "repeated" and "directed" practice to change our pathways. We are not saying that finding ventral or moving to flexibility is easy, but just that it is possible. We agree that pursuing change in sympathetic can be disheartening. The images from the video are helpful to hold in mind during this session.

EXPLORING PROTECTORS

We remind them that something they have all talked about are their high levels of threat and vigilance. It is not surprising that they have come to rely on more extreme strategies than we have discussed so far to help them deal with this. Earlier in their lives, they might have wanted to turn to others when they didn't feel safe, but, at certain times, they may have found themselves alone and unaccompanied. Avoidance and dissociative strategies may have formed part of their protection. At other times, their efforts to try to gain control over their environment, themselves, or others may have been more visible. They may have been desperate to find something that would have provided some sense of agency and safety. We highlight that it can feel particularly challenging to work more deeply on this theme.

We use the word "protectors" to describe what involves a lot more than a preference for tidiness and order. A protector is something they developed that may hold back, or block out emotions or pain that would be hard to face. We stress that our aim is not that they should rush to drop these strategies, but rather heighten awareness of how they may be present. They become easier to discuss when the group embraces the fact that the strength and extent of their protectors reflect the magnitude of pain they need to hide. Often when we can't control the pain that is going on inside, we will seek to control what is going on outside. The likelihood is that protectors will have served an important purpose.

We provide a picture of the areas that often come up, such as those related to eating, extreme over-working, misuse of alcohol and drugs, and suicidal ideation and self-harm. This helps to oil the initial revelations. We throw the floor open to hear some of their preliminary thoughts and examples. It is common to feel a heaviness in the room as shame and secrecy are often so strongly associated with these areas. We provide examples from our own lives of some of our protectors that arise at times of stress. Our protectors are not likely to be as ingrained or as compulsive, but we seek to describe them, modelling our own vulnerability. It also gives them time to start reflecting on the costs of their protectors. These may not emerge easily, as they may not have faced the hurt they have caused others or the loss they have felt themselves.

PROTECTORS EXERCISE

We pair them off to discuss examples of protectors in more depth that they then bring back to the group.

Just as I was thinking that this was about a little harmless cleaning and tidying! I have a level of rituals, including self-harm, that trigger a lot of shame. This is hard stuff to talk about. Even when I turn to technology, it's not for fun, but to move my mind away. I need so much distraction in my life.

I think my protectors changed at every point in my life. I remember lining up my teddies as a small child or having to have certain lights on as I got a bit older. As a teenager, it moved to my body image and I became obsessive about my eating. I think it's been the same underlying thought process and avoidance, trying to feel something other than the emotions that are trying to push out. It just seems to come out in different ways at different stages in my life.

A habit that I have developed is that I overwork. I would often go non-stop from 6 am to midnight and then straight to sleep with no down time. I often spend weekends working. My life has revolved around work. It gives me control and validation, both of which I craved at home and at school.

The one I am thinking about comes up when I am really stressed. I think I have always used exercise as a way to distract myself from criticism. When I am under pressure, I set myself exercise goals I have to achieve. If these aren't met, and they would usually be impossible to meet, I punish myself by saying that I don't deserve to eat food I would like, or that I don't deserve to go out. This can become quite extreme.

SELF-ENQUIRY

For the self-enquiry, we invite them to further reflect on their protectors and link them to specific life experiences that might have led to their development.

Self-Enquiry 9: Protectors

Think of some of your current "protectors" (compulsive and life-interfering) and decide which ones you might share with us.

What life experiences might have led to their development?

My dad was very ill when I was growing up. When I was nine, he took his own life. He had depression. I didn't understand what had happened. Things didn't feel right or safe. Over time, I started to feel that I hadn't been good enough to have kept him here and that I needed to try harder. However, no matter what I did, it never felt that I was doing things right or being the way I was supposed to be. Even now I am obsessed with trying to make my environment better or safer. I am always trying to improve myself. I am very rigid about work and exercise. I never go to bed later than 9:30 pm. Other people will say that I am crazily inflexible, but what's hard for me is not doing these things, not sticking to my schedule. If I don't do them, I feel like such a failure. That's the core: protectors are there to keep thoughts of my failure and my dad at bay. But they never last, they work for such a short while and yet I can't give them up. There are times I throw in the towel and everything goes out the window. I eat loads of ice cream, don't exercise or clean, and watch all the TV I have missed. My whole life falls apart and I just succumb to everything I don't usually allow myself. That is when I am at most risk of self-harm. There is no middle ground.

My father was an alcoholic. It was not safe for me to be seen, to be noticed. I would hide in a cupboard as a child. It was not just to avoid attention. It was also a way I could shut everything out. I would just disappear. That became a way I lived my life so that even when I got to school, I tried to be as invisible as possible. I had this expression "hiding in plain sight" and I got satisfaction from that, although it was a very lonely existence. I meandered along, putting things off as much as I could. When I was at the point of being found out, there would be this intense rush to get things done. But outside of those moments, I have learned to live a life unseen. That is why my rigidity has been so dorsal, so avoidant.

This theme has felt like being hit by a bus. There is something here that I need to start looking at but that is hard when there is so much shame. I find it difficult to talk about my protectors even now. At work, I constantly try to prove myself. The hours I work are completely ridiculous and obsession with that has become my number one protector. I have control there and it gives me validation. When I am not working, I don't know what to do, and I find myself getting stressed which drives me back there. My protector is a destroyer as compulsive and as blind as any addiction. I can see now that it has all been about numbing, about not dealing with my emotions.

Responding to protectors often poses particular challenges for facilitators. Our urge may be to push for their removal. In our trainings (and in our own attitudes), we can see less tolerance in this theme, reflected in more advice-giving and less active listening. This is where co-facilitators support each other and present a more gentle approach. It is vital that we view protectors as a seawall against inner pain to which we are not privy. We want to offer our presence, our acceptance, and our care, not our views and tips on how to get rid of them. If certain protectors feel unreasonable and disproportional to us, this should be a reminder as to how little we know about a participant's history and inner life, rather than seen as an obstacle to progress.

Session 10: Seeking

Aims of Session 10

- Grasp the concept of seeking
- Explore how seeking was both encouraged and discouraged in their lives
- Understand the importance of being in ventral for novel seeking

SEEKING

Having just discussed protectors, this session makes for a lighter contrast. We return to the Polyvagal ladder (see Figure 4.1) and briefly summarise what they have learned about how rigidity may present in sympathetic or dorsal, using some of their examples. The focus now turns to ventral flexibility. We ask them what this might look like. "Open", "creative", "spontaneous" are some of the words that often come up. A key question is how such an outlook can be fostered. In this session, we use the construct of "seeking" as a way of promoting a more open engagement with the world. We introduce the concept by giving examples from our own lives. We invite them to explore how their own seeking may have been discouraged or inhibited, before asking them to look back to times when it was in full flow. The hope is that if they can be drawn away from their rigid patterns to what might excite them, to what is out there in life waiting to be discovered, they could access their ventral flexibility more easily.

WHAT IS SEEKING

"Seeking" is a term used by Jaap Panksepp and Lucy Biven (Panksepp & Biven, 2012). They describe seeking as a system that invigorates our excited engagement with the world and leads us to be inquisitive and curious. It energises us to look forward – to meet, to explore, to play, to discover. Rather than dwelling on a formal definition, we describe it by giving some of our own early examples.

My first memories of school are of Fridays. I presume I would have been four or five years of age. We had this fabulously creative teacher, and for a few hours before lunch on Fridays, we would do what would now be termed Arts and Crafts. We made things, stuck things, modelled things. I can still feel the various materials we used and I can see, in my mind's eye, the boat I made to float in the bath or the collage of leaves I stuck up in the kitchen. I can feel the excitement I used to feel going to school on a Friday morning, wondering what she would have us doing next.

WHEN SEEKING WAS DISCOURAGED

It is helpful to give them space to express how seeking was absent or robbed from them. We find that letting them talk about how this valued system was shut down is an important step. It allows them to then throw themselves more fully into exploring their own warm memories of excited engagement. They talk about this in pairs and then reflect with the whole group.

Examples:

I think I was carefree as a kid and my parents' expectations killed that. When I got excited about music, they sent me to piano lessons. When I was in awe of the computer, they sent me to a class called "computer kids". They were so focused on achievement that they took the fun out of anything I showed an interest in. They were both such anxious people, always wondering what could go wrong. They saw life as a chore, rather than an adventure. I think, in the end, I became scared of trying. I can still see myself desperately wanting to climb a tree, but just standing there at the bottom, unable to take the first step. I find that such a sad image.

I think I have stopped my own seeking more than anyone else. For anything I do, I have to have a checklist. Where's the joy in that? I started learning to knit recently but it was because I wanted to be sustainable, rather than feeling excited about it.

I think seeking was lost when I was abused. It was all part of that innocence that was torn away. That vulnerability or playfulness now seemed a risk when it had cost me so dearly.

MEMORIES OF SEEKING

We then turn to what they remember about seeking. We explain further how our seeking ranges freely when we feel connected. This is a discussion among the whole group so that they can help each other generate examples. It also serves to lighten the energy for those who feel they had limited seeking opportunities. As one group member stated, listening to others, and seeing their faces light up, brought them straight to ventral.

Examples:

My neighbours had a farm. I loved going over there to play because there was always a new adventure to be had. It was a total escape and while I was there running through the fields, playing with the animals, I was free and totally at ease.

Going on little trips to the shop with my granny, that was my seeking. She would encourage me to sing songs and pretend we were heading off somewhere exciting on our little walk. I loved it. I felt so safe and we were excited at what we would conjure up next.

DRAWING WITH THE NON-DOMINANT HAND

We ask them to draw the memories they have just been describing. We invite them to do this with their non-dominant hand. There is usually some apprehension about drawing with their "bad" hand but once they get started, they realise it is easier to summon images and representations without thinking about how good or bad a drawing will be. The lower expectations that come from using their non-dominant hand allow for a better route to what lies there. The results are uplifting.

Examples:

There was a playground near my home where I grew up. I remember many evenings clambering over the locked gate with one particular friend, so we could play there on our own. I drew a swing and there's little me on it. We used to have such a great time there, playing and laughing, often until it got dark. Going high on the swing produced such a rush of endorphins. It felt amazing, the two of us laughing and shouting. Such simple joy. I was trying to draw the whoosh of the swing.

I loved doing this drawing, although it won't make any sense to you. I drew a scene from when I was younger. Foraging around the city to find things to make carts, and ride them down the hill. It was all about building something and going fast. You can see the bits and pieces of wheels and wood in the drawing. It was really satisfying, even when things went belly up. It's so long since I thought of some of this stuff and I have loved re-creating it. Those are feelings I miss so much.

There's a lot of elements in my drawing. That is the sun up here at the top because things felt lighter and brighter and happier when I was seeking as a child. Not a care in the world. It almost shocked me to recall that I did have such fun and that I did look forward to stuff. These four figures here are my band. We had cardboard instruments and we would turn the music up high and mime away. We were instant rock stars, changing group every week. I have particular fondness for our Pink Floyd era. We weren't just carefree, we were invincible.

Occasionally the discussion expands and questions arise as to whether the seeking system is confined to ventral flexibility. In fact, the seeking system also operates further down the Polyvagal ladder. Seeking in sympathetic is a constant striving and never feeling satisfied. For example, seeking in sympathetic can lead them to overeat, overwork, or move towards the protectors they described in the previous session. However, our focus here in this session is exploring seeking as a means of accessing ventral flexibility. The excited engagement with the world we have been describing requires us to be secure and connected, and allows us to savour moments of ventral energy.

NOVEL SEEKING

Finally, we turn to "Novel Seeking". This is not just moving towards tried and tested ways of seeking in the world, but specifically aiming for areas that are unfamiliar. In a ventral state, can they see new options and open new doors? Novel seeking should always add something to life. It may be something a person does to improve their relationships with themselves or with others. It may also be something that, up to this point, has been avoided out of fear. The aim is that it should not be a challenge leading to inevitable sympathetic, but rather offers a gateway into ventral. Moving away from the familiar and predictable can be demanding and does involve some risk, but the results are generally rewarding. This becomes the self-enquiry.

Self-Enquiry 10: Novel Seeking

We are inviting you to try out something new that feels like seeking for you. Ideally, this would be something that elicits ventral anticipation and delight. Remember to aim small.

I took advantage of a moment that arose with my six-year-old goddaughter. She has some new video game where you dance along to the songs. I would normally baulk at the idea, but she asked me to play. I agreed to join her for one song. Two hours later, I was still dancing. It was so much fun, although I can hardly walk today! I think I could learn to throw myself into things without thinking so much.

I never, ever go to a café on my own. I have admired people who do that, but never could myself. I would feel that I hadn't earned it or that it would be indulgent. But yesterday I went to a café and just sat there having a lovely coffee, reading my book. I had moments of thinking that I really shouldn't be here but, overall, it felt great. I was elated after it.

I never spend money on myself. I save and save and save. I am rigid about that because I am thinking that someday I will be old and feeble and likely still alone, so I will need the money to maintain any quality of life and ensure future medical care. But I went online and booked a small weekend trip away. It was hard to do, I have to admit, but now I am really excited for it.

I went to the local art shop and bought myself some paints and blank canvases. I always want to tap into my creative side but never let myself because of the lengthy "to do" lists. But yesterday, I said damn it, I am going to give myself some time and paint. I totally lost myself in it and it was true ventral.

Session 11: Play

Aims of Session 11

- Explore the concept of play in GRO
- Understand the conditions that make play safe
- Experience moments of fun and lighter ways of belonging
- Use play to exercise the pathways from protection to connection

PLAY

Play is our second vehicle for learning more about ventral flexibility. Play provides particular opportunities for fun, lightness, and enjoyment. Just as the group can accompany each other in their tears, they also need to be able to throw back their heads and laugh together. This allows them to continue developing their signalling to each other and deepens their connection. Play and playfulness can provide a joyous sense of belonging.

Play presents the group with many opportunities for learning about themselves but it is a fragile state (Geller & Porges, 2014). In Polyvagal terms, play is in that overlap space between ventral and sympathetic, and the connection with ventral is easily lost. In just a moment, anyone can find themselves plunged into feeling uncomfortable and awkward. Part of this session involves playing games, but most value comes from the subsequent reflections. Participants describe times of fun and, in contrast, times when they are thrown from playfulness into excruciating self-consciousness. It is a chance for real awareness about how their nervous system changes across a range of conditions. It is also an opportunity to try and find a way back to connection, rather than staying in a state of resigned helplessness when threat has taken hold.

LET THE GAMES BEGIN

If a group of children are offered the opportunity for play or games, most will jump excitedly at the prospect. For a group of adults sharing features of marked overcontrol, the prospect is more likely to elicit dread and an urge to head for the door. It is important that we do not set this up as a session in which they are all supposed to be having fun. We are suggesting games as a further chance for reflection. Whatever comes up, comes up. We certainly do not want them to have to feign enjoying themselves. The insights as to what it feels like to be on the outside as others are having fun are as significant as those moments when they find themselves lost in enjoyment.

We start off by asking them to reflect on memories of laughter or playfulness in the programme to date. Even in the heavier sessions, there will have been lighter times that the group shared together. Thinking back to these times helps to set the tone and mood for delving into play.

We need to choose the games carefully. What we are aiming for is social play with the right degree of challenge. Deb Dana always advises to stretch rather than stress. Examples of games that have more social elements include "Heads Up", "Equidistant", and "Giant Jenga". Heads Up is similar to, but much less threatening, than a game of charades. One person places the phone or device facing outwards on their forehead. This person must guess which word the other group members are miming or acting out. The words pop up on the phone and the person gets 60 seconds to guess as many as possible, based on the clues given to them by the other participants. Equidistant involves movement around the room. The group are instructed to choose two people, without naming them. The objective is they must move into a position that is equal distance between these two people within 60 seconds. This is not as easy as it sounds! Most people are familiar with Jenga, but not many have seen the scale of our giant Jenga set, which starts off two feet high. In Giant Jenga they must remove a block from a large tower and attempt to place it on the top of the tower without the whole thing coming crashing down. These games provide multiple opportunities for laughter, fun, but also for discomfort.

What is as important as each game is the opportunity for reflection after each one. Some questions we invite them to think about include:

- What was it like to participate in this game?
- Did they experience having fun and, if so, what did that feel like?
- Did anyone find themselves in threat? What was that like?
- What urges came up if they found themselves going down their ladders? And what history is that tapping into?
- Are people becoming more aware of what their nervous system needs as threat takes a hold?
- Did they notice any of the other group members move to a state of threat? If so, did they think of reaching out to them in any way? How did they work out what might be helpful?

We highlight any examples of looking out for themselves or looking out for each other. Rather than looking to leave the game, or indeed the room, they develop a tolerance for moving up and down their Polyvagal ladder – and helping others do the same. The act of looking around for anyone who may be being left miserably behind is profound. If they are watching out for each other, then they are truly becoming a tribe.

We want them to realise that it is possible to go from threat back to safety again, because they may easily believe that avoidance or escape are the only options. Their attempts at co-regulation are likely to be well received – it feels good when a group show such thoughtful caring. It is particularly helpful if the signals of welcome are accompanied by offers of choice (Would it help if you stayed seated? How would it be if one of us took your turn? Would you like to sit this one out and just join in when you felt like it?).

SELF-ENQUIRY

We encourage them to notice moments of play and playfulness going forward. However, this self-enquiry is not focused specifically on play, but on the whole theme of Rigidity.

Self-Enquiry 11: Reflections on the Theme of Rigidity

For this self-enquiry, we are asking you to reflect on the theme of Rigidity. We have seen how rigidity presents itself when you are in threat, and we have discussed the importance of your protectors. We have also discussed how accessing ventral makes it easier to engage with life from a curious, playful, and excited perspective. In the next session, we will carry out an exercise to further explore your reflections on this theme.

In the spirit of the theme, when they come back at the next session, this self-enquiry is carried out in a different way. We get them to imagine a diagonal line across the room, with rigidity at one end and flexibility at the other. We split them into two teams (so that no one is left standing on their own). The first team stand on the line and the second, staying seated, ask the questions. The latter start with three questions (written on the board).

- Where were you on the line at the beginning of the programme?
- Where are you now?
- Where would you like to be?

In turn, the first team move on the line in response to each question. The questioners bring a gentle curiosity. This is a more embodied exercise and so further questions are suggested such as: What does it feel like here? And here? What would it be like to inch a step further? The teams then swap roles. Discussion follows as they describe how moving up and down the continuum gives a deeper sense of the costs of rigidity and the possibilities that might come from softening rigid patterns.

Chapter 7

Inhibited Emotion

Leaving emotions until the third and final theme has distinct benefits. The group cohesion is stronger, the participants are more prepared to risk being vulnerable, and there is a firmer sense that ruptures can be repaired. All of these are significant as this is the theme that, in prospect, often holds the most dread. This may be because they have had or witnessed negative experiences with one or more emotions. They may be aware that their emotions are bubbling away, but they have had to keep sitting on them for fear that all hell will break loose if they are accessed. For others, emotion has been shut out for so long that it seems a foreign concept. It is only vaguely related to and is not sufficiently present to be frightening.

Whatever their emotional history, our challenge has been to develop a way to discuss emotion that is experiential, but without the risk of driving everyone underground. One principle is to start small and slow. We limit our early discussions to just four emotions – anger, sadness, fear, and joy. It seems more manageable to confine the choice and steer clear of an emotion such as shame at an early point.

Our first exercise uses Polyvagal Theory as an entry point to emotions. We ask the group to consider how an emotion such as sadness might be experienced in each of the three nervous system pathways. It turns out that some are intimately acquainted with their sympathetic sadness, a tearful and often uncontrollable outpouring that they may find themselves locked into. They may be surprised to reflect on the concept of ventral sadness where they could be present with it and not feel controlled by it. This could be an experience they might choose to lean into and learn from. This would be so much better than the unremitting grief of dorsal, in which they can feel disconnected and lost. This is a good start as it opens the door to the possibility of constructive emotion without contradicting their own emotional experience.

We make a clear distinction between experiencing an emotion and expressing it. People may feel sadness but inhibit its expression, or they may not feel it in the first place. The distinction is a good way to get them to

DOI: 10.4324/9781003321576-7

question others about their emotional life and to reflect on their own. It allows for moments of emotional contagion and experiencing emotion for others. The vehicle for discussion here is the "Relative Size" exercise. This provides further preparation for the remainder of the programme, where the expression of emotion plays a much larger part. They also take turns as questioner and guide for one another. This is the first formal experience of them taking agency and responsibility for each other. This experience is strengthened in the final exercise of this theme.

There can be a plaintive hope that the solution is to try and build a life in which there would be greatly reduced amounts of fear, anger, and sadness and an abundance of joy. This is not realistic and would set them up for a fall. What we are proposing is not decreasing the first three, but rather having more balance in each, and more experiences of the ebb and flow of these emotions in ventral. That is something within the power of the group.

Sessions 12–15: Inhibited Emotion

Session 12: Introduction to Emotion

Aims of Session 12

- Begin to explore emotions
- Give voice to fears around experiencing emotion
- Map emotions on to their ladders
- Celebrate their emotional lives

Session Plan: Session 12

INITIAL DISCUSSION ON EMOTIONS

We signal that we are moving on to the third theme, Inhibited Emotion. We check on their reactions even to the title of the theme. Early discussion helps us to grasp how they understand and view emotions. We cannot assume that everyone has a similar response to emotions, or even a similar understanding of their function; they certainly will not have a uniform history. We have found that some in the group may experience quite intense emotions, but spend a great deal of energy actively suppressing them. For others, they describe not feeling anything – like an alexithymic state of numbness – and so are not aware of any active suppression. It is important to explore and highlight such differences, as the idea of moving towards emotions can trigger a range of threats depending on their starting point.

Our initial focus is on four emotions: anger, sadness, fear, and joy. We aim to lead a lively debate rather than set out the formal functions of emotions. Our starting question is whether we can make a case for experiencing each of them (or did evolution get it wrong!). The responses are often dubious, and it is good to hear them say why they might be better off without emotions (joy is indulgent, anger is dangerous, sadness is pathetic, fear is weak, and so on). What they are faced with, however, is that they are feeling increasingly connected to the group and one of the acknowledged reasons for this is that emotion is becoming more apparent.

Rather than discussing emotions in general, we find it often helps to revert back to specific incidences of emotion we have seen in the group. Moments of sadness have been acutely felt by us all. When a group member has become upset about a recent or a distant loss, we have been drawn to care for them, to offer support. Expressing sadness has this effect. Anger may not have been expressed towards each other but, typically, group members will have felt angry on behalf of others, outraged, for example, as to how another was mistreated or neglected. Anger, too, may have been expressed at external sources (noise of the air-conditioning, chairs removed from room, etc.). Fear is the emotion most commonly felt, as there are many triggers of threat from the social demands of a group. Fight or flight is well known in this group and there should be no shortage of examples. The opportunity could be taken to explain how emotions prepare the body for action. In the case of fear, it shuts down digestion, expands the visual field, takes in more air, all of which are preparations for fight or flight. There are now moments of joy, too, in the group. We can think back to points of great laughter and fun. We all appreciate what these emotions bring and how we are drawn to more of whatever sparked them.

We also discuss how they may have a "go to" or default emotion that feels easier to access and may come more naturally to them. If this is the case, this emotion may be masking or protecting other emotions that they find more difficult to experience or express. Perhaps their anger blocks out their sadness, or their sadness blocks out their anger, or perhaps fear may block all the other emotions. There may also be a "nothing" emotional state, an experience built up over years that they resort to when under significant pressure or threat.

We acknowledge that locking up emotions may be the best choice if the only other option is letting them loose. We encourage them to respect and understand their own emotional history. We want them to learn more about their emotions – slowly, safely, and in ways that they retain agency in how they respond to them. We hope that they will see that emotions bring depth, colour, and life to this group, and they deepen the relationships between us. The same could happen outside group.

POLYVAGAL AND EMOTION

The Polyvagal ladder is a good way of stimulating curiosity by encouraging a view of emotion in each of the three states. This is something we start and they then continue in pairs. This will also be the focus of their self-enquiry.

We typically discuss two emotions to get them started. We usually choose sadness and anger. We discuss them both in general and with some specific examples. Sympathetic sadness may feel uncontrollable, a seemingly unending cycle of tears. This sadness is not helping, it is overpowering. Dorsal sadness may lead to feeling consumed by grief, lost in despair, abandoned to a place of utter loneliness. In ventral, it is possible to lean into sadness and be present with it. It can be communicated to others in a way that elicits comfort and support. The sense is that though our heart may be aching, we learn from it.

We might give an example of ventral sadness:

It was the anniversary of my grandmother's death recently. She died many years ago and I don't often allow myself time to sit and think about her. She was such a special person in my life. I went for a walk on my own and purposely allowed myself time to remember her, such as memories of baking soda bread with her. The tears gently fell down my face. While I miss her so much, it was lovely to allow myself that moment to think about her and feel the sadness and how much she meant to me.

In terms of anger, sympathetic anger will likely include aggressive behaviours. We may shout, scream, lash out, and it could develop into a fit of rage in deep sympathetic. We may also harm and punish ourselves, hit, burn, slice, starve, etc. In dorsal anger, it is more like "white rage". Here we are seething, it is not active externally, but we may have distinct vengeance fantasies and ruminate on these for hours. Ventral anger is asserting our needs. It is saying that I matter. It is highlighting to ourselves and another that a boundary has been crossed and this is not OK. Ventral anger is delivered in a respectful way, respectful to both the self and the other.

Here is an example of ventral anger:

I have a work colleague that I get on great with. He is charming and funny, and really generous and kind. We have known each other for years. However, he has a tendency to tease me in front of others in a manner that I can find humiliating. I used to put up with it and would often shut him out for a few days if I was feeling quite hurt and angry afterwards, but would never tell him. He was clueless to the impact. One day, he popped into my office after lunch – he had made a stupid joke about me over lunch that day and said stuff that was not OK. Instead of laughing it off, in my efforts to be cool and "easy-going", I told him I was pissed at him and he had really hurt me. I also told him that I wanted him to stop doing making jokes about me in front of others and to think about why he was doing it. I felt so empowered and relieved afterwards, and it made our friendship much stronger. He still occasionally attempts jokes at my expense, but all it takes now is a knowing look and he will not to go any further!

Self-Enquiry 12: Mapping My Emotions on the Polyvagal Ladder

Before the next session bring your awareness to your emotions. Look out for moments of joy, even if they are fleeting.

Map anger, sadness, and fear on to your Polyvagal ladder. Take one emotion at a time and go in the order sympathetic, dorsal, ventral. Think of your experience of that emotion in each of the states. Do you have some specific examples?

In this self-enquiry, it's important to let the discussion flow. We are not concerned about getting each emotion perfectly mapped, or considering if one element actually belongs in a different state. We want them to start making distinctions about the different possible presentations of each emotion. What they hear from others offers so much value. There is no universal profile, but here are some typical responses.

Anger (Sympathetic – Dorsal – Ventral)

Anger seems like such an inappropriate emotion to me. I would never let myself act on it. I am scared of my sympathetic anger. I experienced it a couple of times in my life and it was explosive. That scarred me. I hate the way I behaved – shouting at people and so on – and I decided that I wouldn't get angry again. I have been pretty successful at sitting on it.

I think dorsal is where I go with my anger. A silent resentment. Quietly angry and seething, but nothing expressed. I may be a little snappy and irritated, like a grumpy bear. I won't forgive or forget, but I would never let anyone know this. In this state, I don't care enough even to feel the anger towards myself. I haven't the energy.

I can't think of an example of ventral anger. I could imagine that it is being rightfully angry at someone when they have done something that annoyed me. I just couldn't imagine that conversation ever happening. I always turn it back on myself. No matter what the circumstance, I would claim responsibility, because any strong assertion about my needs or wants would be off limits. I would rather die than say something angry towards someone. The only thing I could do would be to advocate for someone else or, easier still, for some cause. I could get angry about oppression or climate change – but it would just be way too hard to be angry for myself.

Fear (Sympathetic – Dorsal – Ventral)

Sympathetic fear is so familiar to me. I am tense and on edge. I feel butterflies in my stomach and tension in my chest. My poor system is asked to churn out the adrenaline. Fear controls me in so many situations. There are moments of sheer panic, and then there are everyday fears about so many situations. Endless fears of judgement or needing to explain myself. I can be jittery for long periods. It is like my brain is rattling around dreaming up fears to torment me with.

In dorsal, fear is still consuming but I am now isolated. At one level, it's like taking myself away somewhere safe, but my fear hasn't gone away and I know that. I may be shut down but fear is out there, knocking at the window.

I found it hard to think about ventral fear, but I suppose it is like nervous excitement. I remember going into hospital to have my baby. I was terrified and excited in equal measure. It was an excited fear, if that makes sense. I think it's the same when I put myself forward for something that is important to me, and yet I am nervous about the outcome.

Sadness (Sympathetic – Dorsal – Ventral)

In sympathetic, my sadness feels like overflow. Literally. Snotty nose running, eyes streaming, make-up down my cheeks. It is not pretty. I think my family can find it a bit scary. I cry as if I'm heartbroken and I feel so fragile.

If the sadness becomes overwhelming, I go into dorsal. I am numb and depressed, and I can't feel anything at all. It feels as if it could be permanent. It is deep and inactive. I am helpless and hopeless. It seems that no one else is carrying this much sadness, and no one could understand it.

In ventral, it's like a soft sadness. I feel sad for others and will cry with friends if they tell me something sad. I can comfort them, although I sometimes worry that my crying would take over. I kind of know that this sadness will be temporary, it won't last forever. Just very rarely I have been comforted in my sadness and this felt very, very good. I think that's what ventral sadness must be like.

This self-enquiry often leads to interesting insights about signalling and emotional contagion. For example, one person said that he realised that while he is feeling a great deal of emotion, his facial expression is often signalling that he is fine. Others around him will not ask or know what is going on. Another talked about how witnessing emotions in others in the group allowed her to touch her own emotion. This can be surprising for some, and is usually a welcome revelation.

Sessions 13 and 14: Drawing the Relative Size

Aims of Sessions 13 and 14

- Visually represent the experience and expression of emotions
- Explore the impact of seeing the differences between the experience and expression of certain emotions

Session Plan: Session 13

DRAWING THE RELATIVE SIZE

A key distinction we endorse in the group is between experiencing and expressing emotions. The exercise we developed for this task is called "drawing the relative size". In our characteristic style, we model this without too much preamble. The board is divided into quadrants, each representing one of the four emotions (anger, sadness, fear, and joy). There are two elements to the task. The first is to draw circles whose relative size represents the **experience** of each of the four emotions. In a different colour, the second part of the task is to draw circles (again in relative size) that represent the **expression** of each emotion. The facilitator who models this exercise needs to be fully prepared. We set the tone. Our examples must be authentic and we need to be open to some gentle questioning. When we give evocative examples, the group picks up on the power and meaning of this exercise (see Figure 7.1).

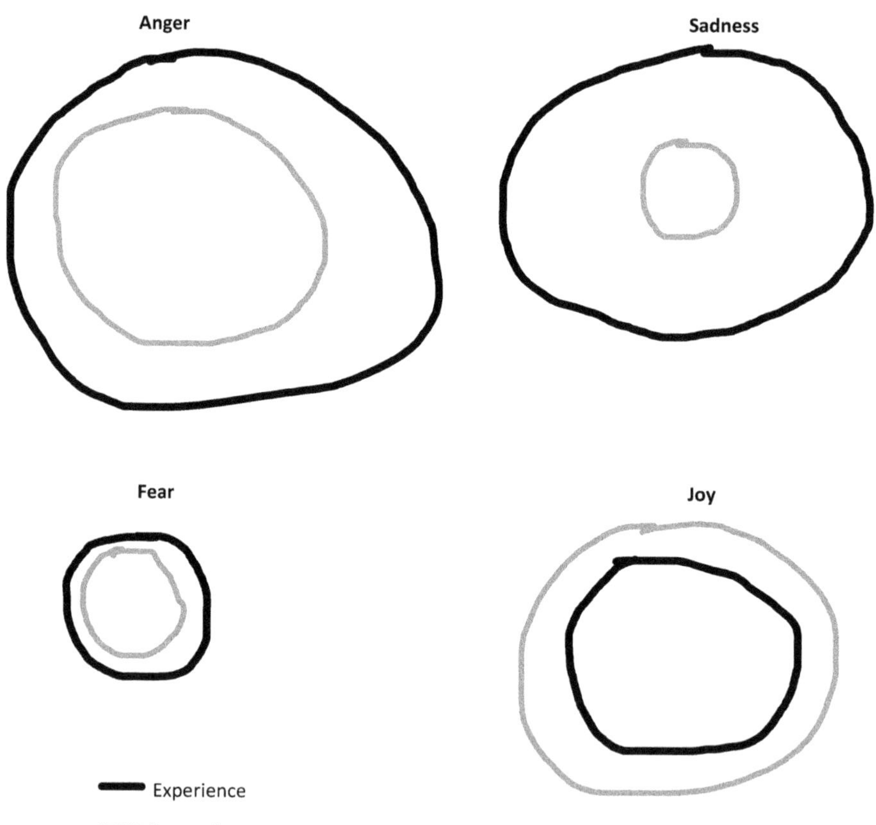

Figure 7.1 Harry's Circles

Facilitator Examples:

My experience of anger is my biggest circle. I like to think I have a strong sense of natural justice but, in honesty, it's more about my own stubborn views of how life should be and how people should treat me. Both at work and at home, I can feel let down and think that I would have treated others better. I don't always express my anger, but I have no trouble doing so, which is why my expression circle is a pretty good size.

My experience of sadness circle has been bigger over the past months. There has been a lot of loss. My expression of sadness circle, however, remains fairly small. I am quick to be there for others who have shared these losses, but it is hard for me to open my own sadness. It takes a lot of persistence by others to get me to talk about these losses, or my sadness in general.

My experience of fear circle is quite small. I am not fully sure what this means. I have a sinking feeling that it probably means I have constructed a life that doesn't push or challenge me so much. I think I express most of the fear that does emerge.

My joy circle is a reasonably big one. I do enjoy messing and joking, and there are things and people that I get a kick out of. But I often put on an even sunnier face than I feel, and use humour at times to mask other emotions. So my expression of joy is a larger circle than I actually experience.

The other facilitator explains to the group that she is going to ask him a few questions. She wants to keep her enquiry as open as possible. She does not want to make interpretations or make comparisons with her own profile – she is there to let him reflect on what he has drawn. Her aim is to arouse his curiosity rather than satisfy her own.

She will start by asking something quite general like "what strikes you when you see these eight circles?" or "are there any surprises?" Next, she might ask him to comment on the emotion in which there is the largest discrepancy between what is felt and what is expressed. She may probe a little deeper, looking for him to verbalise what might happen if a particular circle was bigger or smaller.

It is often reassuring for the participants to see that the facilitators have their own struggles and contradictions, and they may want to ask questions too. What would it look like if your expressed sadness was larger, and what impact might that have on some of the other circles? And so, it takes off!

When the group have grasped the form and potential of the exercise, we ask one of them to volunteer to bring the second facilitator through the exercise. Others can join in, but we point out that we don't want to leave anyone too long with the heat on. The questions are often challenging and insightful, but asked with kindness. We recall one asking, "would you recommend that belief

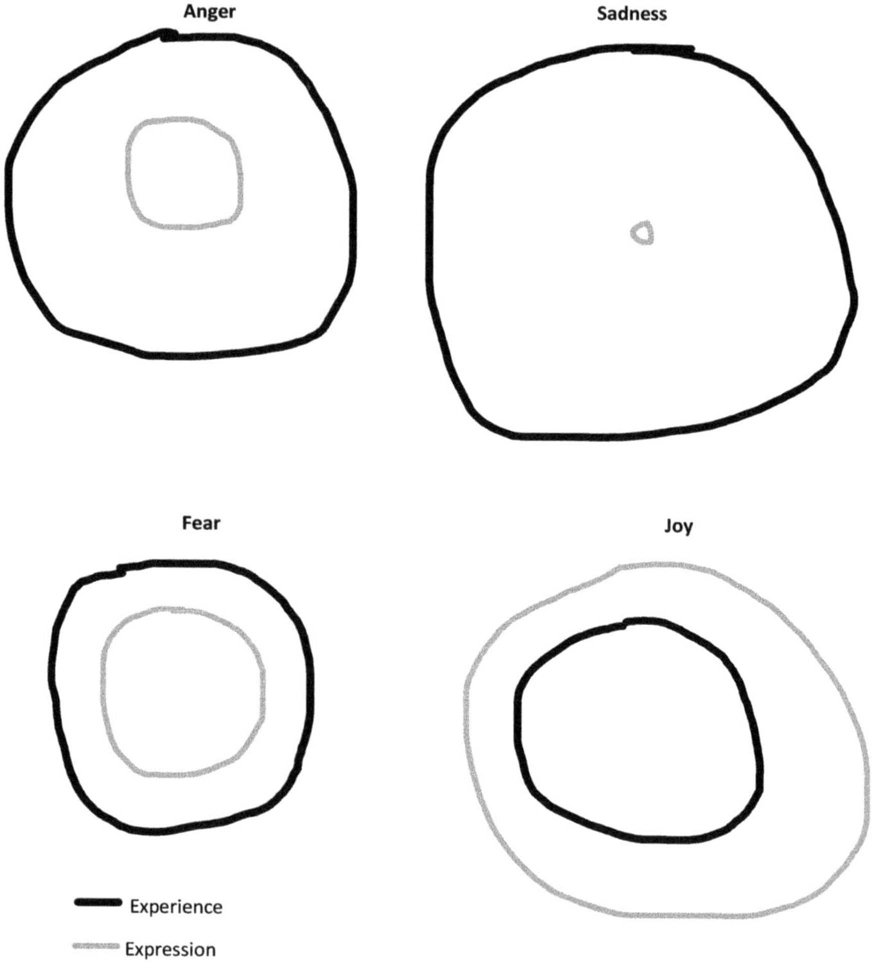

Figure 7.2 Orla's Circles

to anyone else in the group?" when they had unearthed one of our more idiosyncratic beliefs about emotional expression. The group begin to appreciate the value of their curiosity. It is then over to them to draw their circles and guide each other through the exercise (see Figure 7.2).

First Participant Example: Orla

With regards to my anger, I have huge expectations of people in my world and it infuriates me when these are not met. I try not to show it (my expression circle), but it can leak out of me at times and then my anger will be very evident. I would be holding it, holding it, holding it, and then it bursts out. I can think of times when it really rattled me. The funny thing is that I control my anger at work: it's at home when it is much more liable to show itself.

My experience of sadness is a big circle. I feel a lot of sadness. I only allow myself to go towards it when I am on my own (which I find sad in itself). The circle for how much I show sadness is minute. If I start to feel sadness in the company of others, it's like an alarm has gone off and I have to vacate the building. I would hate anyone to see my sadness. It would leave me too vulnerable.

I have always been aware of fear and it is an emotion I can see the good side to. My work is physically dangerous at times and it heightens my senses. It can be really useful. I don't always show it, and I can certainly hide it if I want to. At an early age, there was a teacher who used to terrorise and humiliate me, and I learned never to let her see that she was getting to me. It is the one emotion I have control over. I can choose to reveal it or shut it down.

I do experience joy and most times when I do, I express it. When I am with my nephews, I can really throw my head back. I love old people too. I love listening to their stories. I am also a great messer, although there are times when the joking is just there to fill the empty silences. Yes, I sometimes put on the happy face. It's like "fake it till you make it". That's why my expression circle is bigger than my experience one.

Second Participant Example: Nicola (see Figure 7.3)

I think people would be very surprised to hear that my experience of anger is quite big. I am usually seen as placid and tame, but that is not what I am experiencing. Anger is in my head so much of the time but I don't show it. I swallow hard and it festers inside. The only person I ever turn it against is myself. I have a lot of inward anger. I wonder if all my angry thoughts protect me from my sadness. In terms of expression, I have only ever rarely expressed it. it's only in this group that I have realised anger could be about more than just lashing out.

There is sadness in my life but I keep it under lock and key. I tell my partner which is why the inner (expression) circle is there at all. But she is the only one who ever sees it. I almost have a terror of breaking down in front of others, because I think they would judge me very negatively (as my parents did). The bottom line is that I learned that sadness shouldn't exist.

The experience of fear is huge in my life and that is why it is my biggest experience circle. I have a lot of social fear and I worry a lot, mostly about things that

Figure 7.3 Nicola's Circles

would never happen in a thousand years. I might not talk about it but I think people notice it, so I must be expressing it in some ways.

I hardly know what joy is. I put on a brave face, can even seem cheery but it is a total mask. Part of the reasons is that I feel I don't deserve joy, so I don't label it. Part of it is shame that my emotions are so messed up: when I cut myself, that split second of physical pain, I would call that joy. That's my expression circle. That is upsetting to tell you. This lack of joy is such a strong symbol of my not living. I don't live, I survive. It's only at this point in my life that all this hiding of emotions is catching up with me, although I have no idea how it could be any different.

In guiding each other through this exercise, they start with a general enquiry as to what it is like for the person looking at their own circles. Further probing is more fluid. They may ask about the emotion where there is the biggest difference between the experienced and expressed circles. For example, they may query the experience of that emotion earlier in life. They might ask if the emotions change in different contexts (such as work as opposed to home), or if one emotion is likely to be masking another. A particularly creative way to go further is to push for "third circles". Examples of these would be a third circle to represent anger towards self, or a circle representing the degree to which an emotion is avoided. By this point, they are more prepared to risk feedback. For example, if someone is evidently quite angry in the room but draws a very small circle to represent this, the group may gently reflect that this is not how they experience the person. They help them to see how their expression of emotion may be slightly different from how they think they are behaving. This ties in nicely to signalling, as sometimes group members will state things like, "I know you say you don't experience any sadness, but I have often felt it when you have been giving your self-enquiry".

Drawing the relative size exercise will take more than one session to complete, especially with groups of eight or more people. You do not want to rush this exercise.

CHECK OUT

We finish with a check out, ensuring to hear from everyone about how they are as they leave the group.

Self-Enquiry 13 and 14: Reflections on Drawing the Relative Size

For these self-enquiries, we ask them to continue to reflect on their circles – both those who have taken their turn, and those who have yet to. Encourage them to foster curiosity about what emotions they least experience and express, and in what contexts. These are likely to be the emotions they will be working on as the group progresses. These reflections are generally quite brief until everyone has had the chance to draw their circles.

Session 15: Taking the Role of an Emotion

Aims of Session 15

- Continue exploring the experience and expression of emotion
- Engage in an exercise that facilitates embodied experience of an emotion
- Begin to notice how expressing emotion helps others get into ventral

Session Plan: Session 15

If everyone has finished drawing their emotion circles, we begin session 15 with a brief warm-up exercise followed by a check in. We invite the group to reflect and take stock, both on what it was like to take part in the exercise, and what it was like witnessing others. Some talk about how it moved them to ventral seeing others' circles. Others may reflect what it was like to talk about an emotion that has been long absent from their lives. This leads us in to the next exercise.

INTERVIEWING MY EMOTION

Taking the role of an emotion is a powerful embodied psychodrama technique that helps individuals sit into and truly experience an emotion. The facilitators first model the exercise before asking the group to try it. Explain that one facilitator is going to explore one of their emotions in more depth. They are going to *be* this emotion and speak from this emotion's perspective. Explain that the other facilitator will be like an investigative interviewer, trying to find out information about this emotion. They will seek to understand the role the emotion plays in the individual's life, rather than identify with it or soothe it.

INSTRUCTIONS FOR TAKING THE ROLE OF AN EMOTION

- Pick and name one emotion to work on.
- Before sitting into the chair, try to imagine bringing this emotion to the forefront. You may want to remember a specific time when you felt this emotion, to help you embody and lean into it. Note what it feels like in your body.
- You will be allowing this emotion a voice for a brief period of time. You will be speaking from the emotion's point of view.
- If you notice judgements coming in, try acknowledging them and letting them go. Continue to speak from the emotion's perspective.

- After you finish answering the questions, be sure to de-role by standing up, taking a few deep breaths, and shaking off the emotion. Then sit back in the seat as your whole self.

To demonstrate to the group, one facilitator states the emotion they wish to explore. They spend a moment allowing themselves to think of a recent time when this emotion was present, so that they can better feel it. They then sit into a chair as this emotion. The other facilitator interviews the emotion, using the following questions which are written on the board. We are careful not to deviate from the questions.

- When do you show up in X's life? Give me examples.
- What do you do when you show up?
- When does X block you?
- How does X feel about you?
- What would it be like if you were more present?
- What would happen if you weren't in X's life at all?
- What message would you give X?

Facilitator Example: Anger

- When do you show up in Ellie's life? Give me examples.

Interestingly, I think I am more present than she likes to admit. I am always there lurking in the background, but she doesn't allow me to show myself. I do, however, come out when she feels really used by others, and at the end of her tether with people. I often show up when she is on her own and remind her of how people have hurt her, how they take her for granted and treat her like a doormat. I tend to make her ruminate on these events and leave her feeling really exhausted by it all.

- What do you do when you show up?

I fixate on what has happened and I tell her how pathetic she is to let people treat her this way. I will go round and round in circles replaying what has happened and putting my own spin on things. I berate her, but I also think up dark vengeance fantasies of how she could get her own back, or what she would say to those who have hurt her. Sometimes I tell her to just block everyone out, shut them all out. That will teach them!

- When does Ellie block you?

Pretty much all the time. She likes others to think she is calm and easy-going. This matters to Ellie because she has always been praised for being calm. She sees me as aggressive and not appropriate. She is also a little scared of me. She will allow me out the odd time, in arguments with her partner, but even at that, it is usually after a big build-up and then, when I come out, it can seem like she is reacting disproportionately to whatever has just happened.

- How does Ellie feel about you?

She is a little scared of me. She knows on some level that she needs me, as otherwise people will shit on her, and continue to shit on her. But she doesn't want to show me in case others leave her, or reject her. She's had a couple of bad experiences with me in the past, and I know that has made her suppress me more.

- What would it be like if you were more present?

I think she would learn that I am actually trying to help her, help her see that she deserves to have her needs met. She doesn't have to be a doormat for others or their emotional punch bag. I think she would be less afraid of me and feel more empowered if she allowed me some space.

- What would happen if you weren't in Ellie's life at all?

That would be a disaster. She really would be a complete pushover and I think she could actually become quite depressed. She wouldn't ever stand up for herself and others would take advantage and lose respect for her.

- What message would you give Ellie?

Listen to me and let me surface a little. I promise I won't hurt you. I am actually trying to protect you. You can trust me. I am part of you.

The facilitators swap roles. We spend a moment checking in with both, asking how they found the experience, what they noticed, and if anything surprised them. We also check in with the group about how they found observing this exercise and what came up for them.

We split the group into pairs so that they can experience taking the role of one of their emotions. Highlight that it may feel unusual and a little strange initially, but encourage an open curiosity towards the exercise. Instruct those who are carrying out the interview to stick to the questions and format outlined. After everyone has had a chance to go through the process, come back to whole group and get feedback on what it was like participating in both sides of the exercise.

FINAL REFLECTIONS

Many emotions will have been triggered during the last exercise, and so we allow time for broader discussion. The group often talk about noticing the physical expression of emotions and their urges to move away from the experience. They reflect on surprising moments, usually the message from the emotion. They are also curious as to what happens after they expressed the emotion. Some find that they berate themselves, while others describe a sense of relief and empowerment.

Self-enquiry is to review all handouts and reflect on their work to date. We have now completed the first phase of GRO and will break for the individual reflection sessions, before moving on to the latter phase of the programme.

Chapter 8

The GROhari Exercise

The opening 15 sessions constitute the first phase of the programme and contain the bulk of the taught material. Once the group have grasped the language and concepts of GRO, it is time to take another step forward. The second phase ups the pace. With a deepening sense of connection and safety, the group is in a good position to take more responsibility and the challenges are greater. The GROhari Exercise is the first part of call and it is introduced to group members in an individual reflection session.

It is not helpful or necessary to go into the background of the GROhari Exercise with the group, but it is useful for facilitators to understand how it evolved. In an early edition of his classic book *The Theory and Practice of Group Therapy*, Yalom reviewed the development of T-groups ("T" representing training in human relations) (Yalom, 1985). One of the cognitive aids used in these trainings was the "Johari Window" (named after Joe Luft and Harry Ingram who developed it). This is a four-box personality paradigm that clarifies the function of feedback and self-disclosure (see Figure 8.1).

Box A is "public"; it is what is known to both self and others. Box B is "secret"; what is known to self but not known to others. Box C is "blind"; what is known to others but not known to self. Finally, Box D is labelled as "unconscious", unknown to self or others. The goals of the T-group were to increase the size of Box A (public) by decreasing Box B (secret) through self-disclosure and decreasing Box C (blind spots) through feedback. Box D, the unconscious, was considered out of bounds! We have adapted the Johari Window and hence it is titled the GROhari Exercise (which participants usually shorten to GROhari, as in "I'll never forget my GROhari").

The headings of known/unknown to self/others were dropped at an early point, but we stuck with the four cells or parts with a freedom as to what we would include in each. What we envisaged was that each person would have time and space to explore four categories related to their overcontrol in front

DOI: 10.4324/9781003321576-8

	Known to others	Unknown to others
Known to self	A	B
Unknown to self	C	D

Figure 8.1 Johari Window

of the rest of the group. We didn't want to copy the Johari, but rather use it as a base from which something reflecting the essence of GRO could emerge.

The first category is straightforward. Group members are asked to talk of what the group already knows about their overcontrol. This encourages them to reflect on what they have told the group about the history and presentation of each of the three themes. It is also a chance to reflect on what has become apparent about their overcontrol that may not have been explicitly stated.

The second category relates to self-disclosure. This is an opportunity to tell the group what they have not yet revealed about their overcontrol. The timing of this invitation is important. Earlier in the programme, participants are cautioned about revealing too much too soon. It is explained in terms of a Connect + 8 (see Chapter 5) in that not only can a person feel too exposed, but others might not be ready to reciprocate. Now, however, after 15 sessions there is a strong sense of safety and cohesion. Indeed, many group members have commented at the end of the programme about how well GROhari is timed. A vulnerable disclosure at this point is an expression of trust, a gift to the group. It is unhurried. It is a chance to go into more detail about their overcontrol and to risk going further than on previous occasions. It provides time and space to fill in facets that they have not yet had the opportunity to share.

The third category is closely tied to the second; it is a response to what they have just declared. Disclosure is a vulnerable act. If it is followed by acceptance and support, then a deep sense of connection and feeling understood is the outcome. Participants refer to the feeling of being met and heard. One member who had been involved in a well-publicised trauma that had resulted in her telling and retelling what had happened on multiple occasions told the group that this was the first time she had felt truly heard. Further, participants often comment on how reassuring it is to hear others identify with what they have disclosed; it's very soothing to hear that they are not alone. They may well hold feared calamitous outcomes that do not materialise. The fears of rejection and disgust fade away when they look around at a sea of accepting faces. This is neuroception in action!

The fourth category relates to what a person hopes to bring to their life outside the group. They will have watched and heard others in group, and will know from what they have seen that change is possible. They are usually surprised that they, too, will have moved up the continuum of all three themes. This is the chance to reflect on the sort of changes they now hope to bring to their lives outside of group. They realise that this is not about tearing down protectors in some unsustainable way, but having better access to a sense of safety in which social engagement becomes easier. This category is not so much a statement of intent as a statement of hope for their future, a direction in which support from the group is elicited.

The GROhari Exercise is a powerful tool that achieves a number of aims. It is sufficiently demanding that it is almost akin to a tribal initiation, and therefore brings a new level of connection and cohesion. It helps the group to further explore the relationship between life experiences and the development of overcontrol. It promotes sharing and disclosing of experiences that may be shameful and holding the person back; disclosure is the antidote to shame. It allows the group to respond to such revelations with support and non-judgement so that co-regulation is activated. It is a clear declaration of care and commitment to themselves as to what they will work on as they progress through the latter part of the programme. It is also a signal of purpose both to themselves and to the group: "I am committing to working on my overcontrol *and* your overcontrol; we are in this together", thus centrally representing a key aspect of what the group therapy is about.

Finally, our expectation of what can be done in the GROhari Exercise is a crucial element in how it is carried out. We expect that carrying out the exercise will be an act of Radical Openness!

Individual Reflection Session

As a way of transition to the second phase of the programme, each participant is invited to a one-to-one reflection session with one of the facilitators. This usually lasts between 60 and 90 minutes. This meeting used to be termed a review, but some group members said this sounded very corporate. Others felt that it sounded like an appraisal, which seemed a bit intimidating. We have settled on "reflection". We usually build in a break in group sessions for at least a week so that we have time to meet everyone. Facilitators schedule times anonymously and participants sign their name on the slot that suits them. This means that allocation is random. This is important in a group where dynamics are easily interpreted or misinterpreted.

Aims of Individual Reflection Session

- Extended reflection of their journey so far
- Understand the four distinct parts of the GROhari Exercise
- Grasp the work that will be required before the next group

Session Plan

Feedback on the First 15 Groups

The prospect of spending more than an hour with one of us on their own can be a little anxiety-provoking for some. However, most relax into chatting about the group, how they have found growing closer to others, which theme seems most pertinent for them, and changes that perhaps we have not heard about. This is important. There may be much we have not picked up about their struggles, their triumphs, and the impact of the group dynamic.

The Four Parts

As the session develops, we move to preparing them for the GROhari Exercise. We give them a blank page divided in four. They are encouraged to write initial responses in each of the quadrants, so that they have a reminder of what is required in each category. They are going to have time to mull over how they respond, and we don't want them to have any doubts as to what each entails. At the end of the individual session, we give them a handout as a further aid (see Appendix A).

Reflecting

We explain that they are initially invited to consider what is known to the group about their overcontrol (both in how they have behaved and what they have shared). It is helpful to acknowledge that many aspects of their overcontrol are apparent and for all to see in the group. These may be small declarations but, nevertheless, they are significant. This category can be approached in different ways. Some understand immediately and appreciate that their overcontrol has been evident. Others need to be guided through what has been observed of their overcontrol. They may find the discussion of each of the three themes in turn a helpful stimulus. "How do you think the other participants would describe how you connect with them, or indeed yourself?" "Which of your rigid patterns would have become apparent to them?" "How would they have seen you relate to your emotions?" This requires reflection and self-awareness. We see it as an opportunity to consolidate what is recognisable about their overcontrol.

Sharing

The second category provides an opportunity to talk in more detail about aspects of their overcontrol that they have not yet disclosed. The notion of revealing such vulnerable information may come as a jolt (though sometimes a relief). There may be some material that they have not got around to discussing, but this is more of an invitation to share personal information that would not usually be discussed with others. It is rare that they bring something up in this session that they do not disclose to the group afterwards. In that sense, this is an important trial run. They can try out how much detail to include. They get to see our supportive reaction and to test out some deeply held personal fears about what is likely to happen when they take such a risk. It is important that they see this as challenging but safe. This is an opportunity for them to get a sense of how it would be to talk about events in their lives, some of which have felt too toxic to share. This category has such potential for de-shaming as their vulnerability meets authentic and warm acceptance. They should not feel that material is being wrenched from them or that their privacy is being invaded. This is a huge step towards greater engagement with the group process.

Some people get stuck into this straight away and others seem flummoxed by the idea, as if there is a suggestion that they have been holding back. We gently explain that we have not previously invited such information and that there has been limited scope for this type of personal revelation. Some find it helpful to hear examples of the type of information that can come up here. Go gently through the usual suspects. Material generally comes in two categories. The first is broadly referring to how their overcontrol came about. Reference can be made to their childhood, their family, and their early experiences. Some refer to major experiences that shattered their sense of safety and trust. Others refer to a succession of experiences, such as a focus on achievement or comparison with siblings, that similarly fostered a more extreme presentation of overcontrol. It is important that the latter are not seen as less significant. We need to lead the way in acknowledging the impact of neglect or a lack of nurturing of their emotional life. These experiences result in the same path of feeling unaccompanied. The second category tends to be more about the expression and cost of overcontrol. This is often hard to acknowledge: the loneliness, the sense of being different, the grudges, the confusion about being so lost even from themselves.

Accompanying

The third category involves "accompanying" the person who is disclosing to the group. The group reaction comes at a sensitive and vulnerable moment. What each person needs most is to feel that they were heard, that they are still accepted, that they are somehow still being held. A cornerstone of GRO is that over the course of their life, those who attend will have received no shortage of advice. What will be rare or foreign is to feel truly accepted, particularly in the face of revealing their vulnerability. This involves two sides. Each person has the chance to show up for their comrades. More challenging for many is that they also have to be open to that support. For many this is new territory and requires a greater leap of faith.

Moving Forward

This fourth category is forward-looking. It asks about the future each group member wants to build. It is helpful to review the three themes with them so that there is a chance to reflect on changes they have seen in themselves and in others. This is a good starting point because any meaningful change usually occurs first in the group. It is as if the person is saying "let me tell me what I am working on, let me set out the path of change that I am embarking on". They have laid out the costs of their overcontrol and this is not how they want their life to continue. Some find it frightening to state such intent because it implies a commitment. But what is sought is something we can support and rally behind.

The risk here is that the responses are too ambitious, too general, or too reliant on others. We are all for generalising outside the group, but such changes may prove difficult to set up (e.g., if they involve others) and they are not observable by the group. It is consistent with the group process that we would all see the steps being taken, and be in a position to provide feedback and support along the way. It is easier, too, within the group to ensure that such steps are realistic. It is best to see the response here as a personal declaration of intent.

It is important that they leave this individual session knowing that the four parts of the GROhari Exercise will be the focus of the next few group sessions. It is equally important that they leave the session feeling supported, nurtured, and hopeful. This gives them a sense of agency about what is to come and a confidence that they can rise to the challenges involved.

Sessions 16–18: The GROhari Exercise

Aims of Sessions 16–18

- Openly explore the nature and expression of their overcontrol with the group
- Experience being accompanied
- Declare hope and intent for the second phase of the programme

Session Plan: Session 16–18

Check In

The group have not seen each other for a period of time, and so it is important that everyone has a chance to check in. This is welcomed. We ask them where they are on their ladder coming into group today, and for any reflections on their experience of the individual session.

Explaining the GROhari Exercise

We then move on to the GROhari Exercise. The hope is that group members will have given thought to this after their individual reflection session. It is usually a task they take very seriously. We start by drawing the four quadrants on our whiteboard and give each its heading. We detail what is involved in each category. It is useful for them to hear this again. It helps set the tone and allows space to reflect on what they are about to embark on. We highlight that this is not about four sets of lists but four communications. It is best that they do not read out what they have prepared, but talk directly to us all. It doesn't matter if they fumble on some points; it is more important that we feel their emotion. In the third category, we highlight the importance of our full and authentic presence and participation. Accompaniment is the lifeblood of GRO.

The GROhari Exercise

As they digest the upcoming task, we place four chairs at the front of the group to represent each of the four categories of the GROhari Exercise. Using chairs highlights the importance of the exercise. The person sitting at the front of the group is centre stage. It is their time and we are giving utmost respect and attention to this. Sitting into the chairs also helps to embody and be fully present in the four areas, in contrast to speaking from their usual seat in the group.

This is the only exercise we do not model. Our invitation for the first to step up is not usually met with a clamour of volunteers. But somebody will volunteer. It can be tempting to choose someone whom you expect might find the right level of vulnerability, but we need to go with the process. From this point, there is much more trust in the group. There is much less therapist involvement other than our attentive signalling. It is a self-directed process, each individual judging their own disclosures and their own pacing. This may be the first time that we, the facilitators, are "sitting under the participants". We join in the third category but keep our contribution short, personal, and authentic. It can be hard for participants to remember all that was said to them in the third category (accompanying), and so one of us will write these down so that they can reflect on them at a later point.

It is helpful to advise each person to take a moment and a few deep breaths as they move from one chair to the next.

Getting a Sense of a GROhari Exercise

Here are two examples of this exercise.

First is John's GROhari.

I am going to start with what you know about my overcontrol. To be accepted, I worked really hard at achieving in sports. That is what I put my energy into. I had unrelenting standards for myself that had to be met. I judged others whom I felt were not working hard enough on the teams I was on. The sports success led to success in business. I have told you a bit about that because it is part of my life, but I feel this gives off such a false impression of who I truly am. That's the easy bit.

Emotions are just a no-go area as I have told you. They feel too dangerous to go near. You have seen how closed I am emotionally, and that I struggle with sadness especially. I developed this protective shield that you will now be familiar with. You have told me that it can be intimidating. This was one of my ways of keeping people at a distance. I think I also mentioned that I had a lot of responsibility from a young age. I don't remember much fun or laughter. There was work that needed to be done at home. I think you have seen the judgemental, critical, serious person who emerged from all this.

I developed a set of rules to get me through from the start to the end of the day. If I go outside that formula, I spin out of control. It runs with military precision and, like most military things, it is as likely to lead to disaster as success. Most of the time, what I do is very carefully planned. This is such a contrast to my dorsal side that I am at last understanding. For long periods, I just resort to shutting down the system. I think you saw glimpses of that in some of the early groups.

John moves chair and informs us that there is much he hasn't yet told us about his overcontrol.

OK … (John takes a deep breath and his hands start to shake) I haven't given much detail about how bad things were at home, notably my Dad's mental health difficulties. I was ashamed of conditions at home, and I don't recall ever bringing someone back there when I was younger. In fact, I was terrified that someone might call to my house.

I think one of the reasons I am so scared of anger was that there was so much violence at home. I have been frightened of my own anger. As a child, I had to be pulled off other people when I lost it. I have a terror of that happening again.

I had a speech impediment and I was mocked viciously at school because of it. I became expert at not drawing attention to myself. I felt I was different and somehow at risk, and so I cut myself off from people. I kept everyone firmly at a distance.

What I find very hard to tell you is that when I was about 12, I was flattered by the interest of a teacher. He spent time with me, took an interest in me that I was not getting at home. I had no idea that he was grooming me. The abuse started when I was 13. He had befriended my Dad and there was no way I could say a word about him. He carried out small acts of power and humiliation all through my teens. He had photos that he threatened to share. Even over long periods when he didn't touch me, he would indicate to me that he could any time he wanted. I think from that point, I shut down all emotion. I found it hard even to stay present. The concept of Dorsal has made so much sense to me. That is something I learned to do so well, to shut down completely. My whole life was a big shameful secret that nobody could ever find out about. From the age of 13 I had two lives, one I could share, and one I could never talk about to anyone. It led me down a road of telling lies to cover myself.

My personal life has been a shambles. I have never really known how to be myself or how to express myself. I have never really opened up to others with the result that I don't have close friends. I was married to someone I loved and she grew lonely. In the end, she couldn't bear it anymore and left. This is a terrible loss for me that was entirely my fault. My coldness and distance drove her away. I had no idea how to be intimate on any level. It really is as simple as that (quiet crying). She hadn't signed up for this.

I have had this veneer of confidence but it's just a show. My whole life seems a lie. I am just a misfit. All relationships have ended badly.

John moves chair and invites accompaniment from the group:

My heart aches for you, John. I have been incredibly moved by what you said today. You said that your wife didn't sign up for this, but you didn't sign up for this either. You didn't sign up to be bullied and then abused and to have to live this secret life. What struck me was not just that you told us more of what has happened to you, but you are now telling it with emotion. It makes me feel so close to you, so protective of you. You are working so hard in this group. I feel inspired by you. You are a warrior and you will get there. We will get you there, and you will get us there. Thank you so much for trusting us today. You may have arrived distant and closed at the start of this programme, but you are neither of those things now.

I think it was brave of you to go first, but braver still to open yourself up. I didn't see it coming. I thought that you would hide from us today, but you did the opposite. You said all your relationships end badly, but I don't think that is going to be the case with this group.

It's a harrowing picture of this vulnerable boy being lured by this new person in his life whom he thinks he can trust. It's very sad to hear of all that resulting isolation and withdrawal. I identified with so much of what you shared with us, and I think you have opened the door for me to go further.

I feel so moved by what you just told us. I feel so much more connected to you and so glad you have shared that with us. I was going to say that I wanted to hear more about you, the inner you, and get to know your emotions more. I think what you have done today is an amazing step towards that.

I feel so sad and angry at all that you have been through. It makes total sense now why you strive to achieve so much and be better than everyone else. I used to feel a little threatened and intimidated by your successes, but now I see the vulnerable human behind that. I think you are really courageous and I hope that you will continue to trust us.

I would never have known you suffered so much. I weep for the teenager who was snared in something he couldn't get out of or even tell others about. I feel so connected to you. You have hidden your pain for so long and it makes total sense why you shut others out, but you don't need to do that anymore. I hope that you feel proud of what you have done today. You are making a new beginning. We're rooting for you.

John moves chair for the last time to state some of his immediate aims and goals within the group.

Thank you, what you have said means so much to me.

I want to start feeling and expressing my sadness more. I know I mentioned in the circles exercise that sadness terrifies me, but I know I need to start to get to know it better. I have this terror that it will bring me down a path I will not be able to come back from. I need to experience it in here with you all, to know that I can handle it and that I am safe.

I want to open up to the few close people I have left in my life. I feel like they are all slowly drifting through my fingers. I know what I need to do. I just need to let them in a little more and show my vulnerability.

I want to experience life, to feel the wind in my face. I'm fed up switching off when others are talking, tuning out, planning what I am going to say. I want to start living my life.

This is John's GROhari. The written word only catches some of what happened, and doesn't do any justice to the depth of the connection felt in the room. It turns out that John is a highly emotional person, which had not been evident to this point. It was evident now. How the rest of the group responded was also significant. At the start of the group their social signalling was poor. Now, in a ventral state, it is clear that they are listening with their hearts. Their eye contact remains firm. The tone of their voice is soft. Not one of these things has been coached. They have been liberated as their social engagement system kicks in.

Here is Susan's GROhari:

I thought I wouldn't be nervous starting this, but my palms are sweating and I feel that I can barely look at you all – and this is only the first category. (Long pause) This is what I think you already know about my overcontrol.

I have shared that I grew up in a home where all my physical needs were met. We were never left wanting, which often leaves me feeling guilty as to why I struggle. We were brought on holidays and had lots of toys, but it always felt so silent. There were unwritten rules that I must be a good child, I must never make a fuss, I must never let the family down. I was never allowed have friends over because I knew, in my parents' eyes, that none of the neighbourhood kids were "good enough". I think my parents' notions made me feel like an outsider from quite a young age. I always felt different and struggled to make friends in school. I was told be grateful that I was being taken off to some museum. It was awful. I always felt so deeply lonely. You will have seen that I am still hesitant about connecting. I am uneasy when the group spends time with me as I feel other people are more important and more deserving.

The family atmosphere fed into my rigidity too. I had to be good at school, at music lessons, at everything that they decided I should do. If I got 90% in tests or exams, I would be asked what happened to that last 10%. Nothing was ever good enough. We were not punished physically, but there was something unsafe in the air. There was an absence of praise, an absence of being seen. My mother was fixated on appearances. As I mentioned to you guys, I have struggled with an eating disorder for years. She didn't regularly "fat shame" me, but she would pinch at my little skin when I was small and say "ooh, we need to watch that doesn't get any bigger". You have seen some of my set habits that resulted from this.

I think I have told you of my struggle with emotions. It's like they never existed. Very often I truly do not know how I am feeling. I have all these rules in my head such as that crying is weak, and anger is a disgusting emotion that must never be shown. My parents never fought, they never argued, but we knew when they were upset because the silence was even more deafening. Emotions just didn't exist.

Susan takes a breath and looks up at everyone.

Now this is the really tough part. While I feel I have shared lots with you all, there are things I have never mentioned. In fact, I have never told anyone some of these things. I made a list because I was afraid I would freeze and go into shutdown. I know you can be a bit wary of my lists but I promise I will only look down at it the odd time.

I haven't told you the true extent of my loneliness and disconnection from others. When I went away to college, I struggled even more to fit in. I started drinking to give myself courage to attend events and nights out. This quickly escalated, and I found myself not being able to get through a day without a bottle of wine or vodka to help me sleep. Even though I was successful in college and indeed had a successful career, I was drinking my way through most of it. It got to a point though where people in work started to notice. I hadn't let anyone close enough to have a friend who could have pulled me aside. Instead, one day I was called into the CEO's office and simply told to pack my stuff and leave. I feel immense shame over that. Even now, when I see anyone from that company, I cross the street to avoid them.

I also haven't been honest about the extent of my eating disorder. When I used to feel upset or I wasn't living up to my standards, I would set crazy goals for exercise and work out until I was in so much pain that my body was about to collapse. I used to punish myself by not letting myself eat, sometimes for a few days. I know I am saying all this like I am reading a script about someone else, and it is hard to feel it. But it is there, deep in my body.

I have never had any romantic relationships because I have never known how. I feel so sad about that. I have no idea what it would feel like to be in a partnership with anyone, and I would be terrified they would get one glimpse of the real me and run a mile. On the outside, I know I appear like a cold, harsh person who has no interest in others. The awful part is that I actually do like people. I want people in my life. I can't continue as lonely as I have been.

Susan is encouraged to take a few deep breaths and allow herself to settle as she invites reflections from the other group members.

I experience you as someone who is very composed. You have used the word reserved and I do get that sense. You always have our back and we are just getting to hear of your suffering and sadness. I think it's a huge step for you to start looking after yourself, to start being honest as to what has been happening. I trust you and I feel so much more connected to you now.

I have always admired you. But I am usually watching you comforting us or being wise to us. What I heard just now gave me an insight into your soul. For the first time, I could see how you needed to protect yourself and I felt I got you. I found it strangely comforting, and it put me straight me into ventral to hear you talk with such openness. Real, deep ventral sadness. The most use you could be to us would be to keep digging deeper, so don't feel this is selfish work.

I think I've always been drawn to you. I can see a lot of me in you and you in me. I know you're quiet and reserved. I was always very curious to see what's going on underneath. I saw you holding back. I can now see why. I see a lot of sadness in you. We are truly lucky to have you in our group. I admire your courage. This isn't easy, but it's safe here.

I am so moved after what you described. You have always minimised your neglect and I can see why. You think that you didn't have it as bad as others just because you had toys and went on holidays. But what happened to you was also traumatic. Your childhood was so empty and sad, and of course there was pain when your emotional life was not recognised. I can feel that pain. I am with you in it. It's going to hurt as you open all that up as you did today. We can hold that pain with you. When you are ready, it's OK to start feeling.

I felt your sadness and could see that little girl making herself small. I would love for you to make yourself big here in group, take up more space. We are here for you.

After a few gentle tears ran down her face, Susan thanked the group and took a moment before moving into the fourth chair. Here is what she said.

I want to lean into my emotions so that I feel them in my body, rather than have them in my head. I am beginning to see that they are there and that I just need to let them come. I felt emotion just now when you were giving me your reflections and I shed some tears. It's a small start, but a huge moment for me. I want to experience joy and feel that I am worth it. I know I need to figure out my boundaries. This means that there will be moments when I have to feel and show gentle anger to communicate when some lines are being overstepped. I feel utterly terrified even saying this. I can't believe I am putting this out there.

I want to make more connections with others, even just acquaintances. You all accept me here and I know I can connect and co-regulate once I feel safe. I guess I need to find other places and other ways where I can feel that safety. Because I have heard loud and clear from you that you don't want that false me who is always trying to fit in with what everybody else wants. I don't have to be the perfect little girl anymore who is suffering in silence and appeasing everyone else. I am excited about finding my own voice.

I want to work on challenging some of the unrelenting standards in my head, especially the ones that lead me to punish myself severely when I feel I haven't achieved them. Thank you so much for hearing me.

Finally, Mary was one of the first to do a GROhari and her reflection of it still lingers with us.

The GROhari was so significant. We all shared our hidden struggles and it was eye-opening. It is hard to put into words how difficult I found it. When I sat in the first chair and saw the whole group looking at me, I just froze. But, somehow, I started and went through what had become obvious, all my overcontrolled ways. I had to push myself so hard in the second chair. I couldn't believe I was sharing so much. I had to draw breath after that. Then the third chair was indescribably reassuring. I really needed that. In the fourth chair, I went through how I needed to do some work around connection, but the real challenges would be around emotion, particularly anger and joy. And I gave examples of things that I felt might be within my grasp, and then went back to my seat. I think the terror increased initially which is not what I expected. The thoughts came flooding in. What if they hated me now? What if they thought I was an attention-seeker? What if they thought I was weak? What if they used what they knew against me? But I just felt these reassuring squeezes from the two people either side of me. I managed to look up and see the reaction of others – two were crying and one of the older guys gestured he was so proud of me and I knew, incredibly, I was still accepted.

Check Out

At the end of these sessions, we finish by taking the emotional temperature of the room. We ask everyone to take a moment and tune into themselves: what are they feeling in their bodies, what is staying with them. This is shared. For all concerned, it is likely to have been a powerful experience that will leave them emotionally exhausted but, hopefully, more connected and more energised for the tasks ahead.

Chapter 9

The Tracker

Coming out of the GROhari exercise, the group is more cohesive, more trusting, and more compassionate towards each other. There is a deeper understanding of the factors that have contributed to the development of overcontrol strategies. Such awareness offers a strong foundation for change to occur. So much has been achieved by this stage in the programme. Many new experiences have been created and bonds have been strengthened within the group. Now is the time to focus on the fourth category of the GROhari: moving forward. In these sessions, the emphasis is on exploring attempts at Radical Openness, both inside and outside the group. The tool to capture these efforts is called The Tracker.

The Tracker has evolved over several years. In its simplest form, it consists of a single line. An X below the line represents a habitual, overcontrolled style. An X above the line represents engagement with life (in terms of demonstrating connection, flexibility, and emotional experiencing and expression), a moment that is often bypassed or avoided. The Xs are used to give a visual representation to the group.

The Tracker performs many functions. It is primarily a way for each individual to reflect on their own attempts at change and to better understand the role and origin of their protectors that may make change difficult. It is carried out in front of the group and so it is a social exercise: the others question, reflect, give feedback, and support throughout this process. The Tracker feeds on the group's energy and takes advantage of the different roles and contributions each member brings. It offers opportunity for further support. It is the focal point for celebrating achievement. It strengthens the bonds between group members. It helps to gently explore and understand the fears that keep them from moving above the line to a more engaged life.

The Tracker is a means to catch a short period of time, perhaps just ten minutes, in which there has been a purposeful effort to engage more fully with life. One of the first realisations it brings about is that there are multiple daily opportunities to engage in connection, to show flexibility, to feel and express emotion. This is a vital first step; whatever other obstacles may be

DOI: 10.4324/9781003321576-9

in the way, a lack of opportunity is not one of them. Each person must then select one attempt that they will bring back to the group. It makes most sense that they would choose one that is meaningful for them. The Tracker allows them to slow down what happened and increase awareness. It allows them to explore their experience through a series of questions that are designed to enhance their understanding of the event. What did it feel like to make a move towards this engagement? Did any protectors kick in? Were they aware of old fears showing up? Were they able to dust themselves down and try again if they found themselves returning to old ways? What have they learned from this Tracker, and how can they incorporate that learning into their next effort? Trackers are a means to feel supported as efforts are made to soften overcontrol; they are a further means of increasing attunement and the tribal bond.

It is worth noting four points. First, we are establishing a routine for the next seven sessions, rather than this being a one-off exercise. Second, the Tracker is integral to the group process. Trackers are explored in front of the group. Within this safe and accepting environment, each person can speak about what it was like to move towards more engagement. There is no judgement in what might come up as obstacles or blocks. The motivation for change is increased because of the sense that every person is being willed on by the group. Third, Trackers could become a pressure to change, another demand, another avenue for self-criticism, but they are as much about curiosity as they are about change. A Tracker should stretch and gently challenge, but not stress and overwhelm. Fourth, while its basis is straightforward, it is evident from an early point that the Tracker is more than a description of a stand-alone event. It does not take long before it becomes clear that what starts off as a description of a simple incident represents a broader picture of ingrained habits, deep fears, and courageous efforts to overcome costly overcontrol. The Tracker provides the opportunity for a set of seemingly small changes to build into something life-changing.

A thorough description of The Tracker can be found in the handout in Appendix B. If you are not familiar with the Tracker, we strongly recommend that you read the handout and then proceed with this chapter.

Sessions 19–25 The Tracker

Aims of Session 19: Introducing the Tracker

- See a few Trackers live in action
- Grasp that Trackers offer a way to explore efforts at being more radically open

Session Plan: Session 19

Introduce the Tracker

We start with a pairs exercise to reflect further on the fourth area of the GROhari Exercise. This is another chance to discuss hopes, goals, and aspirations for the remainder of the group. This should be supportive and encouraging, while also acknowledging inevitable fears and ambivalence. This sets up the Tracker as something that is purposeful and planned, while also recognising the importance of starting small.

We explain that we are now moving on to the Tracker, a way of tracking our overcontrol and recording efforts to be more radically open. The Tracker generates motivation for creating moments of fuller engagement with life that may not otherwise happen. It is a tool that can enable fundamental, durable changes in relation to the three themes. It is a means to share that journey with the group.

We give an introduction, explaining the concept of crossing a single line as it is laid out at the beginning of the handout. We briefly describe the five numbers, giving an overview of what each represents. Without further ado, we start with a personal example. One of us goes to the board and draws the Tracker lines. We put in our Xs relating to a recent example which, without any explanation, is likely to be mystifying to the group.

The second facilitator then asks the core seven questions verbatim. While the example is not going to be dissected at length, it needs to be personal, with a level of vulnerability. It is important to model that we are always working with examples that have personal meaning. The group members also find it riveting when we are talking about our own struggles.

Tracker Questions

Which of the themes are you working on here?

After a few Trackers, they are likely to start by writing the theme on the board but, early on, it is important to foster the habit. Before writing any Xs, the theme should be declared. It focuses everyone on what to look out for. If someone chooses the theme of Inhibited Emotion, one emotion should be stated as this allows for a much clearer Tracker.

Tell us why you have chosen this example

It is important that we all know the relevance of the example. What is the person working on, and how does this example fit in to that aim? Don't continue if this is not clear. This question prevents going down a road that may be confusing, and sometimes shaming, if it appears that they are losing their way. Rather than go straight into the context of the particular event, we want to know why they have chosen this example and why is it important to them.

Give us a brief context for this Tracker (and then mark your Xs or tell us where to place them)

The Trackers cover a very short time period (typically no more than ten minutes), and it is crucial to describe the context in which this time is set. As they are describing what happened, encourage them to place where each X occurs. It needs to be brief so that we do not get caught up in the story or the other people who may be involved.

What strikes you when you see this Tracker?

This question encourages the person to reflect on what is significant for them in this specific Tracker. The aim is to aid and stir reflection, not to come up with solutions. Significant moments may involve a point at which a line has been crossed. However, sometimes a significant moment is the repetition of the same number – a second or third 2 may be different from the first; staying with a 4 may represent a critical triumph.

Choose a point where you crossed a line. How did you know you crossed that line?

This question explores the embodied sense of crossing the lines. It asks the person to reflect on how they knew they crossed a specific line by thinking about how it felt in their bodies, what thoughts and urges they noticed. It deepens their understanding of what it takes to move between the lines.

What are your take-home messages?

This is a key reflective point. The take-home messages are not a rambling philosophical position. They should set out what a person has learned from their Tracker. In the context of fear and ambivalence, they can be powerful statements.

What would you like to do next?

This question can help set up further Trackers. It often bears repeating if something is proposed that is very general, or set a long time into the future. However, if the person is genuinely unclear as to what they would like to do next, there is still the option of becoming more curious as to what is happening. We have seen how much someone gains from noticing how challenging they find something, how certain connections may not be helpful for them, or how quickly their rigid protectors swoop in.

At this first exposure to a Tracker, it is helpful for the group to try and develop further meaning of what each number may represent. It is highly probable that our example will include some combination of 2s, 3s, and 4s. As they work out what these numbers represent, they are learning in a deeper, more meaningful way than being given a lecture on the subject. We clarify the interpretation of each number and point out that they will need to hear and see a few Trackers before each level is fully grasped. The best thing they can do is to keep telling us what they don't understand. After further clarification, we invite them to watch the second facilitator go to the board to do their Tracker (illustrating a different theme). This time one of the group is invited to ask the questions.

When this example has concluded, we invite volunteers to "accompany" the facilitator. This is very much in the vein of accompanying in the GROhari exercise. Carrying out a Tracker is an act of vulnerability and it is reassuring and helpful, on so many levels, when several others offer words of support, or describe the impact of what has just been shared. Such accompaniment is an important last act of the Tracker.

With the facilitator examples now completed, one of the group is invited to describe a recent experience that could form the base of a Tracker. They may not have set out with change in mind, but the format of the Tracker allows them to observe and reflect on their own behaviours. Sometimes a facilitator will ask the questions so that all see the model of questioning again. At other times, another group member takes up the challenge readily, and the facilitators take a secondary tole, just checking that the questions are adhered to.

After a couple of people have accompanied the group member, we split the participants into smaller groups of pairs to see what they have grasped so far. We start a list titled "What we know about the Tracker". We add to the list each session, as it grows from their observations and uncertainties. Where possible, we use their language.

What We Know About the Tracker

- Trackers relate to a brief period of time.
- Each number has its own meaning, and these meanings differ slightly for each of the three themes.
- Don't get too caught up in the story.
- A Tracker often brings up fears and contradictions.
- A Tracker aids deeper understanding of the power and role of protectors.
- A good Take-Home Message can be helpful in setting up what might be done next.
- Advice and problem-solving are not helpful.
- Stick to the big emotions where possible like anger, shame, fear, sadness, and joy (which can be diluted by terms such as "disappointed" or "frustrated").

What We Know About Asking Tracker Questions

- Stick to the questions. This is especially important for early Trackers.
- Keep moving – the more you have to dig, the more likely digging is not going to help. You want to be helpful and encouraging and avoid labouring on one question that may feel shaming or suggestive that the person is not getting it "right".
- Take time to pause for accompanying at the end.

Self-Enquiry

Their task for the next session is to bring in a Tracker. They are asked to read the handout and they are cautioned that, unlike the other handouts, it is not short. They are alerted to the "tips and tricks" section. It is made clear that we welcome confusion, as that is often a first step towards real clarity. If they are not sure whether they have chosen an appropriate example or whether the Xs are in the right position, then these will provide opportunities for learning. However, we emphasise that the best way to hasten our understanding of the Tracker is for everyone to arrive with an attempt at a worked example. The possibilities for Radical Openness are beckoning.

Clinician Note

The strongest contribution a facilitator can make in this session is to have a ready, authentic example. Seeing is believing. If you get into the Tracker without personal experience, the train will come off the tracks very quickly. Use consult to know the intricacies of Trackers inside and out. The group needs to know that you are on top of this!

Inhibited emotion is a particularly important theme to demonstrate as it can be more difficult to understand. A 4 is not a reduction of emotion and may in fact be uncomfortable or distressing; a 5 is not a higher intensity of emotion, it is a feared (and usually improbable) catastrophe that feels very real, such as "If I start crying, I will never be able to stop".

Session Plan: Sessions 20 and 21

Aims of Sessions 20 and 21: The Early Trackers

- Experience sharing a Tracker
- Take a turn questioning another group member
- Accompany others after their Trackers
- Build a list of learning and reflection points

The First Tracker

The important thing is that everyone should get the opportunity to do a couple of Trackers over the next two or three sessions. At the beginning, there needs to be a sense of movement. When one person has finished, another goes to the board to wipe off their Xs and clears the way for the next person. We try and keep these early Trackers short and, as much as possible, let them flow. The participants need to feel that they can do this, that their seemingly small, everyday examples provide great learning points (for themselves and the others). They also need to become more confident in their ability to question others in a constructive and supportive manner. Keep the "accompanying" to just two or three individuals each time. There needs to be a lightness to these sessions, applauding what is being grasped, rather than getting bogged down in any confusion. Encourage and validate and don't leave the heat on too long.

Here are three typical early examples starting with Emer's Tracker (Figure 9.1).

Which of the themes are you working on here?

Rigidity.

Tell us why you have chosen this example

Well, it's no surprise that I am choosing Rigidity. I have to be productive from dawn till dusk. I am a stickler for what all of us in the family need to be doing.

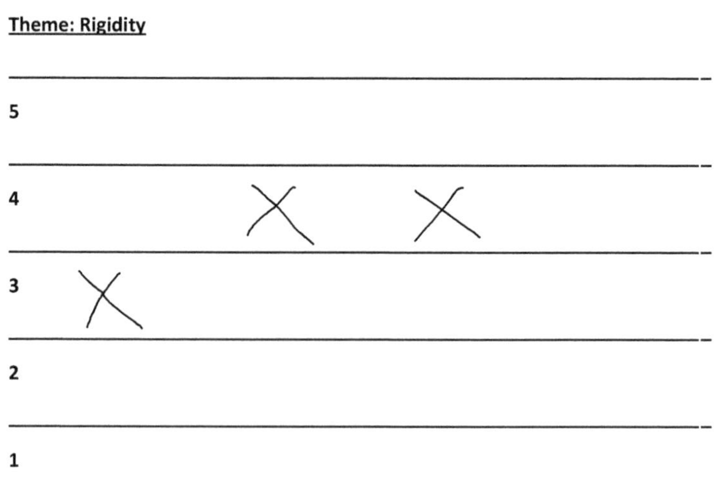

Figure 9.1 Emer's Tracker

My infinite lists mean I have something I can turn to whenever I want to beat myself up about what a lousy mum and wife I am.

Give us a brief context for this Tracker (and then mark your Xs or tell us where to place them).

On Tuesday, I saw in the local paper that the cinema was doing morning showings at 10:00 am. They were showing La La Land the following day, which I had missed the first time around. I never thought it was a serious option for me but, when I left the kids to school yesterday, I just found myself parking the car at the cinema.

That first 3 is me sitting in the car just thinking that this is possible. The 4 is me heading to the door, expecting a hand on my shoulder any second saying, "Madam, will you step this way, what on earth were you thinking". My heart wouldn't have been racing faster if I'd been a drug mule going through customs. The second 4 is me settling down, eating popcorn, and relaxing as the trailers started. I loved it, and I could never have dragged Don (my husband) to it. I didn't tell anyone when I got home, and I couldn't tell anyone other than you guys, but it is a step … and I didn't get busted!

What strikes you when you see this Tracker?

The fact that I did it. I still can't quite believe that I made it to a 4.

Choose a point where you crossed a line. How did you know you crossed that line?

When I crossed from the 3 to the 4, I felt a lightness in my body, almost a giddiness. I felt free for those few moments. It was as if all the tension lifted and eased within me. My mind even slowed down.

What are your take-home messages?

That flexibility and spontaneity are hard for me, but they are so worthwhile.

What would you like to do next?

Well, one step at a time … I will go to the cinema again, that's for sure.

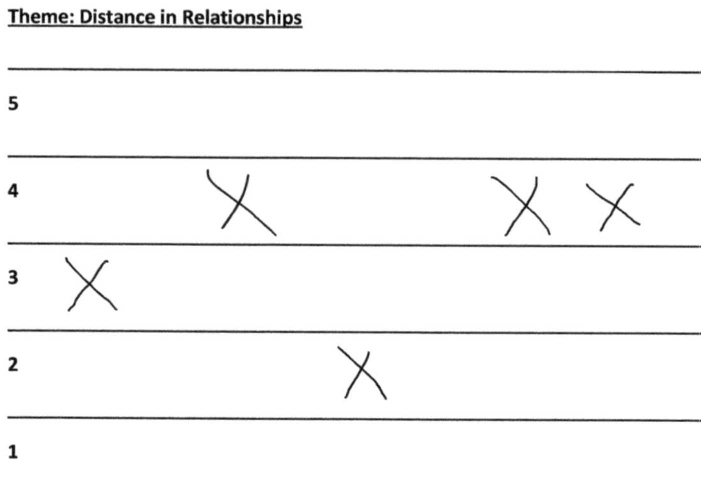

Figure 9.2 Mike's Tracker

The second example is from Mike (see Figure 9.2).

Which of the themes are you working on here?

Distance in Relationships.

Tell us why you have chosen this example

I wanted to work on better connection with my ex-wife with whom I still need to have contact. I tend to be judgemental in relationships in general, but particularly with her. In her company, I can easily get triggered into what I call my "bubble", a state of angry distance. We were due to meet and I saw this as a chance to practise remaining open.

Give us a brief context for this Tracker (and then mark your Xs or tell us where to place them)

I arrived a few minutes early and she was late. That might have been enough to set me off before this programme, but I was fine about it. I was early, she was late, that's just how it is! I was still in a 3 when she arrived. I took my space and shared as much as she did (4), which would previously been unheard of. We were high on the closeness scale when she took a work call. That triggered old memories of how she used to do this, and I shot back down to a 2, the righteous anger simmering away merrily. "What the hell is she doing prioritising some work call over time we agreed to spend together!" I flicked through my phone just to steady myself. I was very aware that this was my Tracker and I saw the stark choice. I could go into my righteous bubble, or I could push myself to be ready for her when she had finished.

Which I did! I re-engaged with her warmly and she remarked on it, without any prompt. She said there must be something or someone good happening in my life! That's my last two 4s. I stayed there for a while.

What strikes you when you see this Tracker?

The 4s really strike me. I actually can't believe I managed to reach a 4 and stay open and engaged.

Choose a point where you crossed a line. How did you know you crossed that line?

Oh, definitely the first 4 back to the 2. I could feel it in my body. I tensed up and I could feel all my muscles tightening and my jaw too.

What are your take-home messages?

I do care about this relationship and it is one that I can work on safely because she knows me so well. I can learn a lot here about relating to others, as well as getting on better with her.

What would you like to do next?

I have already done it. I messaged her after that lunch and thanked her, and asked to meet up again soon. I would never normally do that. She usually reaches out to me first. We have another lunch booked in, and I intend to have even more 4s.

The third example is from Jenny (see Figure 9.3).

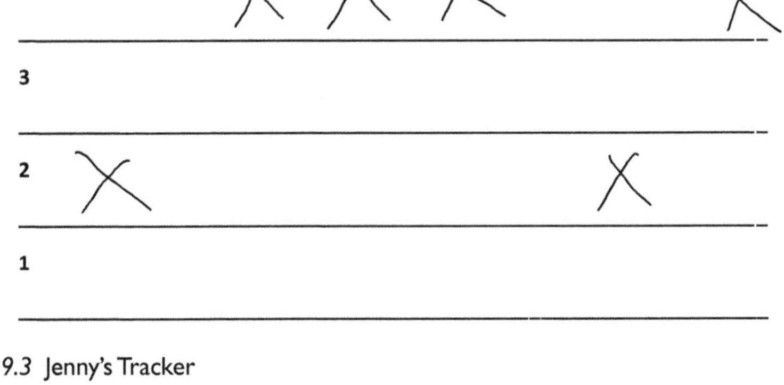

Figure 9.3 Jenny's Tracker

Which of the themes are you working on here?

Inhibited Emotion and the emotion is sadness.

Tell us why you have chosen this example

I run a mile before I let emotion in. I just don't go there. I use humour, I leave, I deflect, I put on a mask, anything but let anyone see my sadness. I don't touch sadness and it doesn't touch me. It has been that way since the evil of my childhood.

Give us a brief context for this Tracker (and then mark your Xs or tell us where to place them)

My dog Zeke lived with my father for the last year. Zeke died two months ago, and part of me has been aching to tell my new partner but I have been terrified of getting upset. When the opportunity came up, I was aware of my sadness rising. I told her I was going for a shower, which I knew was avoidance. I said to myself, "this is my tracker and I am in a 2". I sat down in the shower and just let my sadness pour out. I sobbed for a few minutes which is unheard of for me. That's definitely a 4. A few 4s. When I heard her come towards the bathroom, I just switched it off like a light. I quickly got up and turned my back before she could see me. She asked if I was ok. And though I wanted her to hear my sadness, I was terrified of letting her in. I said I'm fine. That's my second 2. At the door she asked again and I said: "Actually, I'm not OK". That's my last 4 on the Tracker. I let her hold me and I wept.

What strikes you when you see this Tracker?

What strikes me most is that I got back to a 4, and that I let her hold me in my sadness.

Choose a point where you crossed a line. How did you know you crossed that line?

I think that drop from the 4 back down to the 2 really hit me. In that moment, it was like a cascade in my body. It's like I could physically feel myself pushing the sadness back down and feel every fibre of my body freezing up again.

What are your take-home messages?

I find this question really hard. I know I should say that it is good to feel sad but it is bloody tough. I guess a take-home message for me is that sharing my emotion brings me and my partner much closer together in that moment.

What would you like to do next?

It's interesting because I feel sad right now having told you this. I feel sad about my dog and sad for me. I am telling you this, and I am staying with it, which feels like I am in a 4 now. I need to do more of this.

Accompanying

After each Tracker, we invite some words of accompaniment from two or three people.

Emer had been slow to commit in the early part of the programme, and so the group felt that this was a big step. She had chosen the theme that was most challenging for her. None of us was the least bit worried that she had crept in to the cinema and had not told a soul when she got home. The group reflected that she was on the way to Radical Openness. Their confidence in their relationship with her was revealed after the break when one of them arrived back, coat on, hood up, sun glasses covering her face, checking if she was being followed. We all guessed correctly – she was pretending to be Emer going to the cinema!

Mike felt that his was a small example, but the group weren't buying this! They said that it really captured his increased openness that they were witness to. When reflecting, he acknowledged that he was most likely to go down to a 2 if he perceived rejection in any form. And he perceived rejection very easily. The group commented on Mike's capacity to keep coming back from his 2s. They noted how he stood taller as he described this Tracker, reflecting his confidence that he could get back to 4s.

Jenny's example catches that it was not that she lacked the skills to touch her own sadness. The group reflected this to her, and they commented on how powerful it was to see her stay with her emotion. They said that they did not feel burdened by her sadness, but rather they went up a few rungs on their own Polyvagal ladder.

Hopefully this gives some sense of the atmosphere of the early Trackers where the group give and feel real support. These are all examples where there was movement. However, we can learn as much from a succession of 2s or the zigzag of moving rapidly up and down between a 2 and a 4. We focus on a strong learning point from each, so that they feel pride in their efforts. At the end of the session, we all join together and start pooling what we now know about doing a Tracker, adding to the list already started.

Clinician Note

Trackers are complex at first. There is confusion as to what the numbers represent. However, each number has a reason for being there, and it is well worth persisting, despite any initial uncertainty. It is amazing how quickly participants adopt the language of the Tracker once they get the hang of it, and how deeply it allows them to examine their overcontrol. It is important that they seek out Trackers rather than waiting for them to happen. Trackers need to be deliberate and purposeful. It is also important that participants use the wisdom of the group as a resource, for example, in working out what to do next. We introduce occasional pairs exercises to discuss reactions and key learnings from Trackers, which can provide a change of energy and pace.

Session Plan: Sessions 22–25

Trackers are now well under way. As they progress, there are some variants that we set up, which foster deeper reflection. Before these are outlined, we want to draw your attention to two types of Trackers that tend to come up naturally in every programme. The first is an "unsuccessful Tracker" and the second we term a "rare Tracker".

"Unsuccessful" Trackers

The value of a Tracker is not just solely in eliciting change, but also in deepening an understanding of an individual's overcontrol and acknowledging their protectors. We go to some lengths to convey that Trackers are primarily a vehicle for respectful curiosity. Often, Trackers that are viewed as "failures" provide the greatest insight and understanding. An "unsuccessful" tracker helps to give greater clarity into fears, often through a better understanding of what would constitute a 5. A tracker that never reaches a 3 invites some thoughts as to why this might be. Do they know how to get to a 3 and then a 4? Would this feel safe or what protectors might be kicking in? A tracker consisting only of 1s invites reflection on a tendency to go to dorsal and why this might be. A personal discussion often broadens to the whole group exploring why change is so much easier in ventral, and why this can be a hard state to reach.

An example of an unsuccessful Tracker is presented here (see Figure 9.4).

Which of the themes are you working on here?

Distance in Relationships.

Tell us why you have chosen this example

I chose it because I am so careful to avoid any situation that might involve discomfort or conflict. But, to be honest, I don't think that there is anything of value in this Tracker.

Give us a brief context for this Tracker (and then mark your Xs or tell us where to place them)

The context is that my sister had left a message saying that she was going to drop in a present for one of our kids. I was happy about that but, as the time drew near, I started to worry that she might be coming over to blame me for not

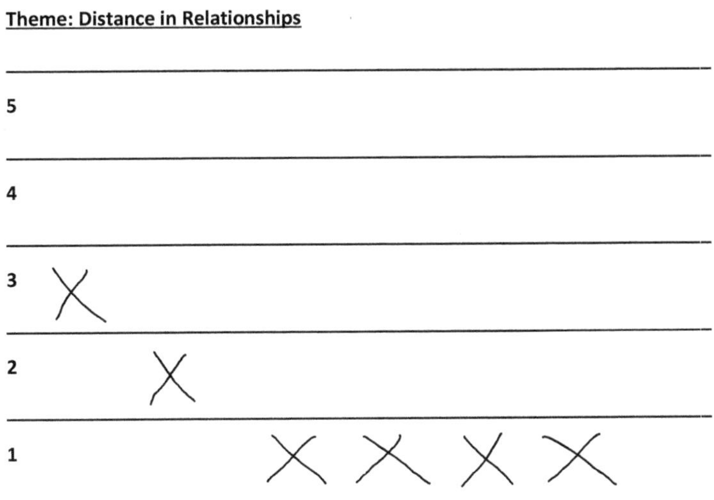

Figure 9.4 Paul's Tracker

taking her side in an argument she was having with my brother. This is where the Tracker starts. Initially, I was open to the idea of being around to talk to her when she called over. So, I started at a 3. But as I heard her car approaching, I found my mind racing and I crept upstairs, leaving my wife to talk to her. I knew exactly what I was doing, and so I am giving that a 2. I was shutting down completely. From that point, I could draw in as many 1s as you have room for. When I am like that, I don't feel any connection with anyone at all.

What strikes you when you see this Tracker?

How pathetic I am. I just cannot seem to lift myself out of my 2s when I fall into them.

At this point, the group member who was guiding Paul decided to go rogue and not continue with the set questions. Instead, he enquired gently about what was behind the descent into a series of 1s by asking Paul if he was aware of his 5s. The reply was interesting.

I was thinking, what if she wants me to side with her against my brother? What if she wants me to stand up to him? My whole being was telling me not to go anywhere near that. I think I can piece together why this is the case. When we were growing up, there was no space for ups and downs. If we were not getting on, there was hell to pay. We were terrified of falling out with each other. So even the thought of getting into anything like this with my sister brings up these old memories. There is little six-year-old me panicking about how my parents will react. The 5 is this terror of their reaction, and of what happens to me if I were to get this vulnerable. The 5s drive me upstairs to avoid such a conversation at all costs.

The group members showed great compassion towards the child who needed this protector in his life, and the adult who became this frightened so easily. This allowed Paul the space to appreciate the history of his fears and how avoidance has become a default safe route. However, even from this example, the current costs are stark. His wife, once again, is left to face his challenges and his sister is confused and hurt by his reluctance to engage with her. He told the group that his "valid reasons are invalid" as he talked about hurting those he cares about most. He agreed with the group that there was much to learn from this Tracker.

"Rare" Trackers

Infrequently, and yet at least once in every cycle, someone moves from the everyday small examples to a greater event in their lives. The results can be uplifting for the whole group. The following example is not something we seek specifically from participants, but demonstrates the power of the process (see Figure 9.5).

Tom's Tracker was on engaging with his emotions. He had been "inspired" by another participant's example in which she had stayed with an emotion, though she had clearly found this very challenging. His aim was to stay with

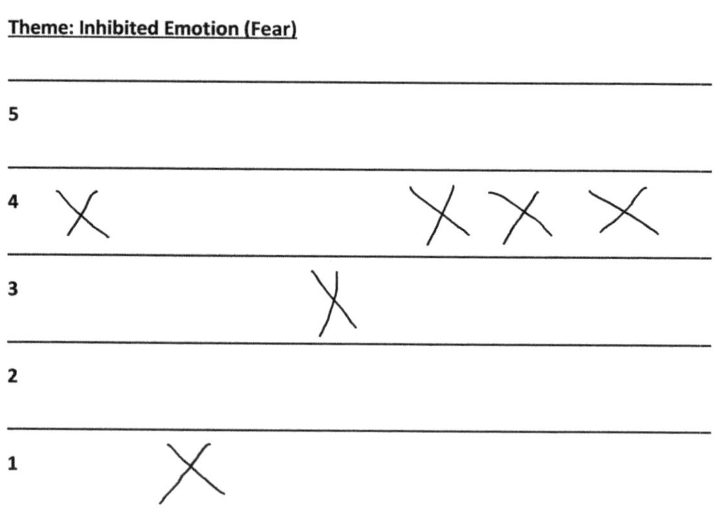

Figure 9.5 Tom's Tracker

whatever emotion might come up as he reflected on his childhood trauma. He had told us in his GROhari that he had been abused by a sports coach from the age of seven. The abuse occurred in a local sports hall. Tom now lived far from that area and had no desire to return to his home place where the abuse had taken place. After the previous group, he had the idea of asking his sister, who still lives locally, to take photos of the inside and the outside of the building. He described how the memories of one room still gripped him and impacted his life all these years later. Even asking for the photos brought on surges of panic. He explained to the group he had to keep telling himself that going towards his fear couldn't kill him, that he wouldn't die, even though he might get very upset. He said this to himself over and over again – that he could survive sitting with his fear.

The following day his sister sent photos of the inside and the outside of the building. He started the Tracker from the moment he opened the file on his phone. He was aware of his terror, which he felt was an opening 4. He felt physically sick and realised he was shaking. He talked encouragingly to himself. He had lived with the memories of what happened there for over 25 years. It was time to let himself feel the emotion that would come up. When he saw the first photo, he shot down to a 1, overwhelmed by his reaction. It occurred to him later that this state of "freeze" was exactly what the perpetrator (long since dead) forced him into every Saturday. After realising this, he felt himself become more open to experiencing the fear again without shutting down, and he moved to a 3 and then a 4. He stayed with his emotion and recorded a series of 4s on the Tracker, all of which were different. At first, he was pushing himself to stay with the terror. After a while, he felt the fear weaken, which was still a 4 as far as he was concerned (he was right!). As the fear lessened, he stayed open to his emotions and realised that the fear was being replaced by a deep sense of pride. He could hear his self-critic mocking him, but this familiar voice was unusually weak and distant. His final 4 was an image of his adult self, going into the changing room and taking his younger child self out by the hand and reassuring him that this would never happen again. He felt utterly liberated by what he had done.

Tom had expected that there would be a feeling of relief in the group. In fact, his Tracker had triggered a whole range of emotions. There was a lot of anger and sadness in others who had also been abused. There was anger not just towards Tom's perpetrator but towards abusive figures in their own lives. Several felt overwhelmed by a sense of unfairness. The sadness was at both Tom's loss and their own. Tom apologised for bringing down the mood in the group but they assured him that no apology was due – he had set off a whole series of potential Trackers! He had led them to open themselves to their own emotions. "I am crying in ventral", as one reassured him. Some stayed with their emotions and realised that they could have moved from one emotional response to another; it was possible they could have a range of reactions to the same event. Others realised they too had a 'room', a place or a memory they had shut off, that still had a hold on their life and was now something that they wanted to face. Their feedback to him was that they were truly inspired by his courage.

Over the coming sessions, we begin to introduce variations in Trackers. These include the options of Live Trackers, Walking the Tracker, and Longer Trackers.

Live Trackers

If someone does not have a Tracker or does not feel it is a strong one, there is the option of a "live" Tracker. For this, we would often not go to the board, because this could take away from the person getting into the present moment and noticing what is happening, particularly in their body. Here is an example.

Grace was finding it difficult to get into her emotions and the group asked her how she was feeling at this moment. She said that she was starting at a 3, open to checking in with her emotions. They pushed for a little more and she mentioned feeling some sadness. She then noticed that it was hard to focus and stay present, which she named as 2s. They asked what image or memory was coming to her mind as she felt the tug of her sadness. This is what she said:

It's my birthday tomorrow but, due to Covid restrictions, I can't go and see anyone. I rang my mother this morning and was trying to connect with her. I said that for my birthday I wanted her to do an online lesson with me, and teach me how to bake a madeira cake. And she just dismissed me. It didn't hurt at the time but thinking about it now … (a tear runs down her face), I can feel it. This is a 4. (Long pause). This is my sadness. It reminds me of an incident when I was a child. I remember giving her a birthday present, it was sweets which I had spent ages wrapping. I was so excited to give them to her. And she dismissed me in much the same way. I was no more than six years old. She said you couldn't give someone sweets as a present, that wouldn't be a present at all. I am still sad as I think about that. I find this level of 4 almost physically painful.

One group member drew the Tracker on the board for Grace. When she had finished answering the Tracker questions, another accompanied her. He acknowledged the hurt this must have caused her on both occasions, as a child and as an adult. This validation seemed to support Grace in leaning further into her emotion. Her head was now supported by her hand as if it was the only thing that could keep her upright. She grew quiet. Then she looked at each member of the group and said how profound it was to see them upset for her, and how their reaction allowed her to stay with her emotion. Over and over again, she said, "so this is 4 in sadness". When asked what she was going to do next, she stated that she felt she needed to talk to her mother.

Live Trackers seem to work particularly well on the theme of emotion. It is generally easier to get into an emotion in the group, taking advantage of the connection that has evolved. As in Grace's example, it is helpful to ask what they are feeling now, what they notice as they tune in. From there, the 'live' part consists of the person openly speaking about what they are feeling, no holds barred, and noticing any movement away from the emotion. We often gently encourage them to look around at the faces of the other group members to help them stay with the emotion and to feel the group's presence. Some people have opted to close their eyes which can also work well.

Walking the Tracker

We call this "walking the walk", and it is a powerful way of embodying the experience of the Tracker as opposed to staying in their head. We have the numbers 1–5 laminated on A4 size sheets. These are placed on the floor near the board, and the group member is asked to walk their Tracker and talk us through, step by step. They are asked to open themselves to the physical sensations and urges of their Xs, and to show us in their movement and gestures what each X feels like.

We have seen many powerful examples of each number, such as curling up in a 2 or growing taller in a 4. The point of movement is also telling, with one jumping confidently on to his 4 while another could only dip a toe, his other foot still firmly on a 2. It is helpful when the group pick up on other changes such as facial signalling, about which the active participant may be unaware.

Without fail, the group will initially dread the idea of walking the Tracker and there may be some reluctance. However, feedback from group members finishing the programme suggest that we should persist. They appreciate heightening their physical awareness. This often yields new insights into what keeps them stuck, and how they could better reach or hold a 4 when they know what one feels like.

Longer Trackers

When they have experienced a number of Trackers, the option of a longer Tracker provides further integration and learning. The core set of questions are still asked, but additional enquiries deepen the reflection. Here are some examples.

The first and most common thing to look for is recurring **patterns.** "We have seen and heard three or four of your Trackers now. Do you see any pattern to your 2s?" A recent example was a participant who described his 2s as "living my life with my thumb permanently on the ejector seat". He found this such an important observation, and he was determined to do something about it.

Similarly, it is interesting to look for a pattern in the feared 5s. A good starting point can be to listen carefully to the 5s of others. Our own 5s may sound so reasonable while the 5s of others seem so improbable or even bizarre. It is a helpful way of realising that although 5s seem real, they are emotional representations from the past, a signal from our brains not to tread on territory where we have previously been hurt. The more we put words on them, the more we see how unlikely they are to happen at this point in our lives.

Sometimes it is interesting to enquire about the **hypothetical.** "I know you didn't reach a 4 on this Tracker, but I am interested as to what it would have looked like and felt like if you had reached one". "Can you describe what your thoughts, feelings, and urges would be if you had made it to that 4?"

Sometimes a person may be invited to write up **two sets of "X"s**. The obvious example is to have one set of Xs for how an emotion *felt* and another (in a different colour) for how the emotion was *expressed.* There are other ways in which two sets of Xs can be used to highlight a distinction such as how something was experienced internally, and how it might have looked to others. This can be a good way to explore signalling.

Crossing the Bridge

At this point, everyone has completed a number of Trackers, and there has been much learning and accompanying. As we start to bring the Tracker sessions to a close, we introduce the concept of the bridge.

The metaphor of crossing a bridge is one we like to use. We explain that our tribe has lived for a long time on the "overcontrolled" side of the river where their needs are not being fully met. By now, after several months of hard work, they have built a bridge (using the three themes) to the far bank, "the land of Radical Openness". This far side of the river may offer a more fulfilling life. We ask them to review the Trackers as efforts to cross the bridge and see what life is like there. They may feel that in terms of their goals, they have not yet got on the bridge. They may feel that though they did not do enough to cross to the other side, their Trackers show that they are on the bridge. Or they may feel that, on certain Trackers, they reached the other side.

To begin exploring what constitutes reaching the other side, we ask for some volunteers to put forward a recent example for the group's consideration. Eva had carried out a Tracker on her Rigidity. She told us that she would spend hours on end writing reports for work. She would write a report in an hour and then spend five or six hours editing it and checking it, without being able to press the send button. Her Tracker described a recent report where she completed it and sent it off without checking. She initially felt some elation doing this, but soon the fears of mistakes crept in. She gave herself 4s in her Tracker that represented the ten minutes when she sent the report. She asked the group had she crossed the bridge. They reflected that they felt she was on the bridge and commended her for being there, and yet they did not feel deep conviction behind her efforts. It felt like something she "should" be doing, perhaps for our benefit, rather than something she had committed to do for herself. They were all concerned that she would be back to her old ways the next week. It was powerful feedback for Eva to digest and it turned out to be crucially helpful.

Let's look in more detail at Lorna's Tracker below for a different group response (see Figure 9.6).

Which of the themes are you working on here?

Distance in Relationships.

Tell us why you have chosen this example

As you know, this theme is the hardest for me. I really struggle with letting anyone in, including my husband. It is hurting him, hurting me, and hurting our marriage.

Give a brief context for this Tracker (and then mark your Xs or tell us where to place them)

My husband asked how my day was and I chose to be truthful. I felt overwhelmed with despair and I told him that. That was my first 4. I told him that I was frightened of what my sister will need from me. I could feel my embarrassment and I was sweating. I shut down briefly and went to a 2, because I thought

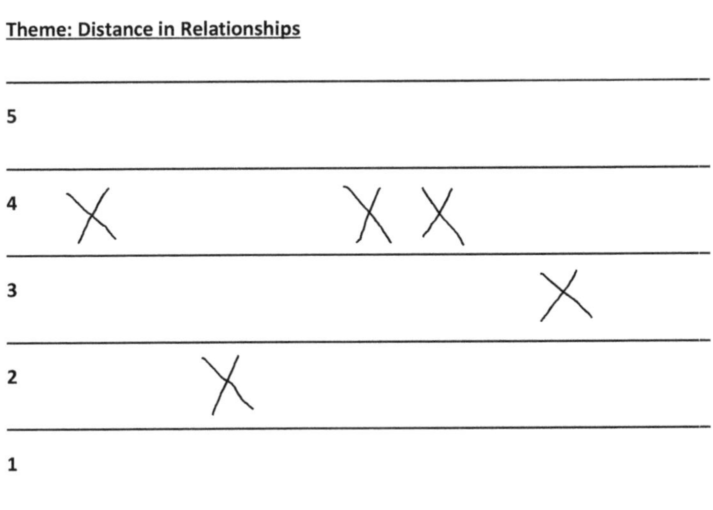

Figure 9.6 Lorna's Tracker

I was being selfish. Then I said pull yourself together, Lorna, this man has had a year of it. I sat with that. I hauled myself back to a 4. I told him that I was embarrassed to say it, but that I was really struggling with my own stuff. He was so supportive. I stayed in the 4's then. There were no words for a long while, but it was a quiet comfort, and so that was still a 4 in my books. After a few minutes that felt like an age, I broke the silence and said that I was having thoughts of self-harm. Neither of us said anything. I don't know if he realised that by saying it out loud I wouldn't do it. No way. I ended in a 3 and was still open to it all.

What strikes you when you see this Tracker?

It's the dance. That's what I call it, the hopping from a 4 to a 2 and back again. I am only now starting to see it clearly.

Choose a point where you crossed a line. How did you know you crossed that line?

I think that last 4 to a 3 felt so different. I felt at ease in my body. I didn't need to do or say anything. There was just a sense of peace and safety. I had been open and it was OK, I wasn't going to lose it.

What are your take-home messages?

So much of my life has been lived on the inside, but it is healthy for us when I connect with him, be real about myself rather than focusing on what's going on around me. I need to be honest with the people who love me and not worry about their reaction.

What are you going to do next?

I'm going to keep doing what I'm doing and telling him how I truly feel.

There were some gulps for air as people gave Lorna the feedback that, without doubt, she had crossed the bridge. One lovely bonus from such moments is how others feel energised to go further across the bridge themselves; it becomes easier to get to the other side when you see others reach the far bank.

Obstacles on the Bridge

Having established what constitutes crossing the bridge with a Tracker, it is time for each person to take stock of their progress. Are they working in the area they think is most important for them? Are they making the progress they want? Have they been able to consistently cross the bridge with their Trackers? If not, their task is to reflect on what stops them from crossing the bridge. There are three options that we encourage them to consider, options that are well described in CFT (e.g., see Gilbert & Mascaro, 2017; Gilbert et al., 2011; Steindl et al., 2022).

"I Don't Know How to Cross the Bridge"

This is an alluring belief: "I would like to be more connected, flexible, and emotionally expressive but I just don't know how". It is certainly possible that they will need the help and wisdom of the group to see what can be done, and they may genuinely feel they don't know how to take the next step. However, feedback from the group is usually that if a person is committed to engagement, it is more about dropping long-held habits than actually learning a particular new set of skills.

"I Am Terrified of Crossing the Bridge"

These fears can be understood as beliefs as to what might happen if there was full commitment to a 4. These thoughts may be terrifying, even catastrophic, and may be based in past hurts and experiences. As a person gets closer to the land of Radical Openness, they may be faced with strong fears of what might happen if they were to venture any further (examples might be "I will be overwhelmed"; "they will reject me"). If a person struggles to go deep into their 4s, they may not find out what these fears are. The group encourages each person to go close enough to the far side to engage with and articulate these fears. It is easier to decide what to do when you know what you are afraid of.

"I Am Not Sure I Want to Cross the Bridge"

This ambivalence about crossing the bridge is not so much a fear of taking the next step, or not knowing how to, but more a doubt that such a move would be of value. It could be that getting to the other side of the bridge is seen as a sign of weakness, of losing independence, or not fully reflecting their own goals. It may be seen as unhelpful. For whatever reason, if there is not the committed motivation or drive to get to the other side, then progress is going to be more difficult.

It is helpful to remind the group about honouring their protectors. Their systems learned to survive and thrive as best they could. Given what they have been carrying all these years, it makes sense that there will be formidable obstacles to crossing the bridge. The task of the group is not to tear their protectors down, or make shaming demands, but to bring a gentle curiosity. Exploring their ambivalence is a rich journey.

The group has one final challenge. We must prepare to finish.

Chapter 10

Ending

One of the strengths and costs of a closed group is that there is no choice when it comes to the timing of the ending. The ending date is set and we must all face that together. It is tempting to arrange further contact. Indeed, it is common that participants swap details and keep in touch, at least for a period of time. One of our previous cohorts even went on a day trip together! However, we must be clear that this particular group, meeting when and as we have done, is coming to a close.

Endings and goodbyes are part of life. Those who struggle with overcontrol often find them challenging. Typical responses include avoiding them altogether, being physically present but emotionally checking out, feeling angry or resentful, or numbing any emotional response to what is going on. A sense of healthy closure is invaluable. Participants may feel like all the progress they made was possible only in this setting, with this group of people. It is important they know that they can take all the good stuff with them. They are transitioning, but they are not losing all they have achieved together. This is a chance to do something different, to take ownership of this ending and honour its importance. We have chosen exercises that aid this process, and keep a focus on their emotional reaction to the group coming to a close. Our hope is to build the experience of the group closing in a healthy, ventral way, and to celebrate what they have achieved. This is a chance to face an ending and in doing so, is one last force in the instigation of change.

The end of therapy is different for each member of the group. For some, it might be the end of the closest connection they have ever felt. For others, they might be chafing at the bit to get to the next phase of their lives; they may feel proud of what they have achieved and ready to move on. And for others again, they may feel regret that they are not where they hoped they would be by the end of the group. Whatever the differences, there is likely to be a shared mourning because we came to matter to each other. Our own research shows clearly how the group comes to be embodied for so many as a durable resource, an internalised experience of co-regulation (O'Sullivan, 2021). Participants talk of important moments in the group still impacting

DOI: 10.4324/9781003321576-10

them months later and holding a felt sense of the group in their hearts. 'What would the group think' is a phrase that often comes to them.

Finally, we must acknowledge that as facilitators we too will miss the group. Not only have we been witness to the anguish and pain, but have felt our own. We have been inspired by the courage and kindness. As Yalom comments, "some of life's truest and most poignant moments occur in the small and limitless microcosm of the therapy group" (Yalom, 1985, p. 374). We must face this ending together.

Session 26: Penultimate Session: Moving Forward and Endings

Aims of Session 26

- Reflect on their journeys through GRO
- Highlight areas of change to each other
- Explore how they typically face endings
- Embrace this ending

Session Plan: Session 26

Brief Check In

The penultimate session always seems to come around faster than we or the group expect. The ending will have been referenced, but it is in these next two sessions that we spend time honouring it. Open the session with a gentle warm up. As we are on weekly sessions now, it is particularly important to spend a few minutes allowing the group to settle. We ask people to take a moment and tune into what they are bringing into group today, or where they are on their Polyvagal ladders.

My Journey and Moving Forward

After the previous session, we send them a handout titled "My Journey". This invites them to reflect on their journey through GRO. They are encouraged to be creative and flexible in how this might be done, but we offer suggestions. They may look at each theme in turn, write about their 2s and 4s both inside and outside of group, or think about key turning points and significant moments in the programme. An interesting category is one that asks them what they are doing now that they couldn't have imagined themselves doing prior to group. Finally, they look at their next steps moving forward. Each group member will have had a week to think about this exercise.

We explain that this is not about huge moments, but more about catching those small points that turned out to be personally impactful. We want them to engage in this exercise in ventral and so we divide them into pairs to support each other and to suggest further areas that may have been overlooked. This is kept quite short (perhaps a quarter of an hour), because we want the whole group to hear what each has to say. There is always so much to be learned from hearing others. Here are three examples of "My Journey" work.

Robert has been keeping notes during the week:

This has been an extraordinary journey. It's hard for me to see it as a single journey, because it has been made up of so many treks along the way. GROhari was big for me. There was stuff there that I had never spoken about. I almost can't believe that I expressed deep-rooted things to you that I hardly even acknowledged to myself. I feel a weight of shame lifted. I am becoming more accepting of the impact of my childhood. I think I did well to survive it. Many of my current costly habits helped me survive back then.

Week by week, I felt less separate and less alone. I can't tell you how much that meant, as I have always been on the outside. But not here. I came to care about your lives, I came to see what we had in common, and I came to trust. Deeply trust. I let myself be held and listened to, confident that you would not judge me.

I thought I was numb, but it turns out that I am not. I had supressed sadness for so long. Tracker after Tracker I realised that I was just good at keeping one step removed from it. Now I can go there. Feeling ventral emotion has been a life-changer.

And, finally, there is the journey with myself. I came into this group disliking myself. I am starting to want myself to be happy. I never thought I deserved that because I disliked myself so much. To want myself to be at peace is a revelation.

The path is never easy or uniform as Sarah shows:

I started the group in fear and I end it in fear. I do feel that I have been on a journey, but I am just not ready for the group to end. I am scared about the group ending. I am in sympathetic right now. I am scared of losing everyone. I do feel that I went on a journey, but I find it hard to focus on that right now. Maybe I haven't learned enough? Maybe I will collapse when the group ends?

There was a beauty to the group's reaction to Sarah's plight. They accompanied her. They cared for her. They told her that her fears were their fears. In that moment, that is what she needed. They let her come back to ventral in her own time.

Emma had started her journey with very black and white thinking, but now she was finding herself liberated, even in how she expressed herself.

This seems so unlike me but, if it feels comfortable, I am going to invite you to shut your eyes. I want you to let your imagination colour in my journey. Imagine me starting at the bottom of a very deep hole. You can feel the tightness of the space, the cold earth. There is so little light. I am there, often curled up in dorsal, but sometimes trying to motivate myself to get digging again. I pick up my spade. Surely if I dig deeper, this would have to help? But it doesn't. I just dig deeper into hopelessness. In the early weeks of this programme, I see a ladder being lowered down. I don't know whether I should dare to climb it. I couldn't bear to have my hopes dashed. It doesn't look an easy climb. It's called a Polyvagal Ladder, whatever the hell that is. But I look up, way up. Is there some more light? I think I hear voices. I put one foot on the first rung and start to climb. It feels scary. At least my dorsal pit was familiar. Now I am neither up nor down. The voices sound a little clearer. I hear a laugh (that must be Jane!). There is a smiling face leaning over, though I can't make out who it is. Now I find myself looking up, not down. By mid-programme, there are hands reaching out for me. They are your hands. There are words of support. It is you guys talking to me. As I emerge, I must look quite a sight, because I have been in that pit for a long time. I am squinting into the light and unsure of how to relate. But you don't judge me. You seem glad to see me which feels astonishing. You are putting a cover over the hole of despair so I don't fall back in. As I get stronger, I find myself offering support to others who are also struggling. That feels good too. I feel pride and happiness that we are getting used to this new world. I look out and realise that I can go further, and that there are others with whom I can connect. I notice that I still have my hand tightly gripping on my overcontrolled spade. But I have no need for it. I don't have to dig any more. I feel lighter as I lay it down. It feels time to step out further.

How We Typically Engage with Endings

Every therapeutic model stresses the importance of ending well, of clients having the experience of an ending that respects their work, and allows them to feel the bittersweet emotions that are often present. We encourage a frank discussion on our typical patterns of endings, and an acceptance that we will all have our own protective reasons for why we might want to avoid or deny endings.

We start off the discussion by outlining some of our own challenges with endings. This opens the floor to saying how difficult endings may have been earlier in our lives. It lessens the shame around certain reactions to endings. It invites everyone to state how they might want this ending to be.

Facilitator Examples:

I am not a big fan of endings at all. I will be there physically but not emotionally. I can recall being at funerals of loved ones where I just could not cry – there was nothing there. I felt really ashamed and found myself worrying about how others might be judging me. Then, much later when I am on my own, the ending and the loss will hit me like a ton of bricks.

I have avoided some endings completely. For example, I just didn't turn up for any of my graduations. More usually, I will busy myself which gets me out of having to feel the ending. I will be the one who is looking after everyone else, ensuring they are OK, cleverly avoiding having to sit with myself.

We then ask each participant to take a moment and reflect on their patterns of endings and to share this with the group.

Participant Examples:

I don't do endings well at all. I can come across as quite cold and uncaring. People don't know what they have meant to me because I don't tell them. It's protective, I suppose. I often regret it. I think my worry is that I would get emotional and that would upset others. I wouldn't want to upset anyone, and I don't like being upset myself. That's why I avoid endings. To be honest, I have wondered would this be my last session.

I do leaving and ending badly. I procrastinate so much that in the end it is all rushed and happens in a flurry. Or sometimes I stay on too long, which is equally as bad, as the ending is dragged out and becomes meaningless.

I go all philosophical. It's not an end, it's really more of a beginning! That's how I avoid them.

In the past, with friendships, I sabotage them. I jump out before they can leave me. I do it cleverly. It's a gradual thing, so it doesn't feel too bad. I just slowly reduce contact until there is no more. All this comes back to haunt me though, and I remember all the people I have pushed out of my life and I feel deep regret.

Check Out

We finish with a brief check out and we encourage the group to think over the next week about how they might like this ending to be. How could they embrace and experience this ending in a more ventral state that feels connected and safe?

We let them know that, in our final session, we will be inviting them to think about things they are leaving behind in the group, and things they are taking with them. We explain that they may wish to bring an object or symbol that represents what they are taking with them. This is something they can keep with them as a reminder of their time with this tribe.

We also invite the group to give a message to future group members. This could be in any format, a few words, a poem, a drawing, whatever they wish. We have a beautiful book in which we put all these messages. We leave it on a table for future participants to flick through at any time. This is a lovely way for the current group to feel their legacy lives on and to be held in mind. It is also a gift to future participants who are likely to start the group with plenty of doubts, and will have shaky moments along the way. There are some profound messages that are added to the book at the end of each cycle.

This poem is one example:

THE GIFT
Conversations in comfortable silence
Understanding that goes beyond its parameters, the insurance of belonging
Safety not experienced with any other being
Accepted flaws celebrated in complete unity
The smiles of reassurance that acknowledge understanding
The sense of acceptance, impossible to manufacture,
The unspoken feeling, the gift of belonging

Session 27: Final Session

Aims of Session 27

- Spend time honouring this ending
- Tell each other what they leave behind as group ends
- Tell each other what they will take forward from the group
- End with a wish for all the group members

Session Plan: Session 27

Check In

We start session 27 with a brief recap on all that we have covered in our 26 sessions to date. We highlight the areas we have covered and all that we have been through together as a tribe. The intention is to instil a deep sense of pride and achievement. It is a statement saying "look at all that we have been through and how far we have come". We don't spend long on this; it is more a summary. We then ask the group for their check in to recall any moment they were proud of. This doesn't have to be *the* moment they were most proud of, just any occasion that comes to mind. This is a gentle, encouraging way to get everyone into ventral. It also brings hope and feelings of pride for each other. They will smile and nod at each other, and there is constant signalling of yes, "you did that and so much more".

The examples they give usually include sharing parts of their lives in GROhari that they never thought they would share with another, sharing Trackers where they pushed themselves to a 4, and pride in showing up for each other and themselves each week, especially when times were tough.

Here are some examples:

I feel proud of my honesty. I felt safe and secure here, and I am proud that I grabbed that with both hands.

Pride is not an emotion I usually feel or allow myself to feel. But I am proud of myself for what I shared in my GROhari. I said things that I was sure I wasn't going to share. It was a huge relief.

I guess I am proud of finding my voice, and being authentic when I use it.

I am so proud of relationships that I've made here. I feel like we are friends. I'm here because I want your company.

I'm proud that I stayed, contributed and connected.

Janus Gate Exercise

In ancient Rome, Janus (pronounced like the name Jane: *"Jane-us"*) was the god of beginnings, gates, transitions, and endings. He was usually depicted as having two faces, since he looked both to the past and the future. He is the inspiration for our last exercise.

We get the group to form a horseshoe, with the backs of their chairs towards the door (it is helpful that they can all see each other). They write down up to three things they have decided to leave behind. We invite them to keep it simple and from the heart. Examples might include part of a rigid protector, or a belief that they should not show a certain emotion. It is important that these are personal, meaningful, and make sense to them. We invite them to imagine how we would dispose of them – perhaps make a bonfire, or put them into a large chest that will be sealed tight and buried in the ocean! Each in turn talks of what they have chosen to leave behind and why. They scrunch up the pieces of paper and hurl them away to symbolise that these are the things that are being discarded. We encourage them to support each other in this exercise. So, when one person has said what they are leaving behind, others may wish to comment or express how moved and happy they are for that person in their choice.

Examples:

I am leaving behind staying numb. It may have allowed me to survive my childhood, but I don't need it anymore. It's been a terrible way to live my life. Living is experiencing the ups and downs and knowing it's OK. And numbness isn't sustainable. If keeping myself numb means needing to stick my fingers down my throat or cutting my skin, then it's not worth it. It is not worth it. I don't need to do that. I will not punish myself for feeling. I salute the younger me who did everything in her power not to feel anything, but it is time to leave that behind.

I am leaving behind my disconnection. I am going to stop isolating myself. I am not a burden. My happiness or sadness is not a burden to others. It makes me a human being. I don't need to isolate myself if things get bad again. As someone else in group said, I may be an introvert but that does not mean that I don't need people.

I am leaving behind the idea that I don't need people, I do need people. You have shown me that. I am also leaving behind feeling scared and judgemental of sharing emotions, and always invalidating my feelings, especially anger. My anger is healthy and OK.

I want to leave behind the shame I feel over my addiction. I know now that it was a protector, trying to keep me safe. Even though it harmed me and those around me, I see now that it was hiding my sadness and keeping me in a spiral of shame and self-loathing.

I am leaving behind my constant avoiding. I'm so much more aware of it now thanks to you guys. I had such a fear of letting people in, but I let you in and that has been profound for me. I am also leaving behind trying to control and fix people, which leads to massive self-neglect. And with that I am leaving behind the thought that I deserve to be last.

I am leaving behind the idea that I am not allowed to be sad or angry, that there must be a specific reason to feel them. I am also leaving behind the idea that I can deal with everything myself, that I must show happy me and not burden others.

After everyone has shared what they are leaving behind and thrown the pieces of paper away, we turn the horseshoe so that it is now open and towards the door. We invite them to take a few deep breaths before settling into the looking-forward chairs. This is the time to say what it is that they are taking with them from the group. Many will have brought their own object to symbolise what they are taking with them. Some are small, perhaps a shell or a button. Others are elaborate, perhaps a drawing or a photograph. What is important is what each represents. This tends to be a very moving experience.

Here are some examples:

I am taking with me huge gratitude for the group. The care and support from you all allowed me to safely visit some of my emotions. I felt held, reassured, and was able to muddle forward with you by my side. I am also taking with me images of my Trackers, especially the emotion ones. I realised the biggest step for me is from 2 to a 3, after that, a 4 is not so hard. I am going to remind myself of that. I am also taking with me the image of the bridge. Life is much better in the land of Radical Openness. I will keep moving along that bridge and I now have the courage to fight for myself. My object is a picture of an elephant that my niece drew for me. It symbolises strength, wisdom, and dignity. You showed me that I have these qualities, and I will be forever grateful for that.

I have found my voice and I am taking that with me. I am going to encourage myself more and loosen up a little. I am also bringing my Polyvagal ladder with me. I spent so many years in sympathetic, but now I know what ventral looks and feels like. I am more aware of how to get there, and I know that I can do it. I love candles and this candle will be my symbol of the warmth and affection I felt here every session.

You have all given me the gift of peace. I am bringing that with me. I now have some peace to move forward. I am also bringing with me a deeper awareness of the cost of my overcontrol and how I was pretending to everyone. My object is a picture of a hand. I felt each of your hands on my back many times throughout this group.

I am bringing with me the bravery of everyone in this group. That has been very reassuring. I am also bringing with me the awareness that there is no danger in connection, no danger in being more flexible, and no danger in going towards my emotions. I feel so privileged to have been part of this group. I have a little keyring that is chipped and broken, but it comes everywhere with me because it is on my car keys. It will forever remind me of how you accepted my brokenness and gave me a home.

I am bringing the feeling of this group, this tribe with me. The essence of group. I feel like I have sense of people and their heart and their struggles. I'm very proud of us all, and the authentic connections we made. I know that once you get it you can get it again. I am also taking our shared purpose. I'm not alone. Being vulnerable is not a weakness, it's a strength. I can ask for what I need: a hug, a cup of tea, a walk, someone to cook dinner for me, or simply to leave me alone. It's OK to be me and tell myself I am good enough.

I am bringing the growth that has happened here. I love growing seeds. Nature teaches me so much. But not every seed will just grow. Specific seeds need particular soil. The soil I grew up in didn't work for me. But I have learned that you can rescue a plant by putting it in a different soil, with the correct amount of light and nutrients plus lots of TLC. This group has been my soil and I have flourished here with you. My symbol is this tulip. It reminds me of us. The tulip strikes through the cold earth in a spear like fashion in February. It has the most beautiful flower, but its strength is its greatest asset. Watch a tulip in high wind: it will bend with the wind, almost dance, and later stand tall undefeated because of the cellulose in the stem. I learn a lot from tulips. Flexibility is core to life.

Final Check Out: Wishes for the Group

We bring our final session to a close with a check out. Each person is invited to give a wish to the whole group. There will be some tears (ventral tears) and deeply moving sentiments. For a group who were strangers five months ago, and had difficulties with connection, flexibility, and emotion, these final moments catch how far they have travelled, not just in what they say, but in how they convey it.

Our concluding task is to present each participant with a certificate of completion. This symbolises their commitment and engagement. We express our honest and authentic gratitude for being witness to their journeys and our admiration for their courage. We wish them peace, contentment, and, most of all, flexibility to live a more radically open life.

References

American Psychiatric Association (2022). *Diagnostic and statistical manual of mental disorders* (DSM-5-TR). Washington, DC: Author.

Badenoch, B. (2018a). *The heart of trauma: Healing the embodied brain in the context of relationships*. New York: W.W. Norton.

Badenoch, B. (2018b). Safety is the treatment. In S. Porges & D. Dana (Eds), *Clinical applications of the Polyvagal Theory* (pp. 73–88). New York: W.W. Norton.

Bain, C., Brookes, S., & Mountford, A. (2002). *The Geese Theatre handbook: Drama with offenders and people at risk*. Winchester: Waterside Press.

Baudinet, J., Stewart, C., Bennett, E., Konstantellou, A., Parham, R., Smith, K., Hunt, K., Eisler, I., & Simic, M. (2021). *Radically open dialectical behaviour therapy adapted for adolescents: A case series. BMC Psychiatry*, *21*, 462. https://doi.org/10.1186/s12888-021-03460-3

Beckes, L., & Coan, J.A. (2011). Social baseline theory: The role of social proximity in emotion and economy of action. *Social and Personality Psychology Compass*, *5*, 976–988. doi:10.1080/10926771.2013.813882

Block, J.H., & Block, J. (1980). The role of ego-control and ego-resiliency in the organization of behavior. Development of cognition, affect and social relations. *The Minnesota Symposia on Child Psychology, 13,* 39–101.

Block, J.H., & Block, J. (2006). Venturing a 30-year longitudinal study. *American Psychologist*, *61*, 315–327.

Bohane, L., Maguire, N., & Richardson, T. (2017). Resilients, overcontrollers and undercontrollers: A systematic review of the utility of a personality typology method in understanding adult mental health problems. *Clinical Psychology Review*, *57*, 75–92. https://doi:10.1016/j.cpr.2017.07.005

Booth, R., Egan, R., & Gibson, J. (2018). Group radical openness. *The Behavior Therapist, 41*, 154–156.

Booth, R., Keogh, K., Doyle, J., & Owens, T. (2014). Living through distress: A skills training group for reducing deliberate self-harm. *Behavioural and Cognitive Psychotherapy, 42*(2), 156–165.

Brooks, J.L. (Director) (1997). *As good as it gets*. TriStar Pictures.

Caspi, A. (2000). The child is father of the man: Personality continuities from childhood to adulthood. *Journal of Personality and Social Psychology*, *78*, 158–172.

Coan, J.A. & Sbarra, D.A. (2015). Social baseline theory: The social regulation of risk and effort. *Current Opinion in Psychology*, *1,* 87–91. doi:10.1016/j.coppsyc.2014.12.021

Collins, N.L. (1996). Working models of attachment: Implications for explanation, emotion, and behavior. *Journal of Personality and Social Psychology, 71*, 810–832. https://doi.org/10.1037//0022-3514.71.4.810

Dana, D. (2018). *The Polyvagal Theory in therapy: Engaging the rhythm of regulation*. New York: W.W. Norton.

Dana, D. (2020). *Polyvagal exercises for safety and connection*. New York: W.W. Norton.

Dana, D. (2021). *Anchored: How to befriend your nervous system using Polyvagal Theory*. Boulder, CO: Sounds True.

Derogatis, L.R., & Melisaratos, N. (1983). The brief symptom inventory: An introductory report. *Psychological Medicine, 13,* 595–605. http://dx.doi.org/10.1017/S0033291700048017

Egan, R., Long, E., McElvaney, J., & Booth, R. (2021). Group radical openness: A feasibility study. *Counselling and Psychotherapy Research*, 00, 1–12. doi:10.1002/capr.12480

Elliott, R., & Rodgers, B. (2008). *Client change interview schedule*. Unpublished research instrument, University of Strathclyde, Glasgow.

Fay, D. (2021). *Becoming safely embodied*. New York: Morgan James Publishing.

Flores, P.J., & Porges, S.W. (2017). Group psychotherapy as a neural exercise: Bridging Polyvagal Theory and attachment theory. *International Journal of Group Psychotherapy, 67,* 202–222.

Fox, L. (2008). *The essential Moreno. Writings on psychodrama, group method, and spontaneity*. New Paltz, NY: Tusitala Publishing.

Geller, S.M. (2020). Cultivating online therapeutic presence: Strengthening therapeutic relationships in teletherapy sessions. *Counselling Psychology Quarterly*, *34*(1), 1–17. doi:10.1080/09515070.2020.1787348

Geller, S.M., & Porges, S.W. (2014). Therapeutic presence: Neurophysiological mechanisms mediating feeling safe in therapeutic relationships. *Journal of Psychotherapy Integration, 24*(3), 178–192.

Gibson, J., Booth, R., Davenport, J., Keogh, K., & Owens, T. (2014). Dialectical behaviour therapy-informed skills training for deliberate self-harm: A controlled trial with 3-month follow-up. *Behaviour Research & Therapy,* 60, 8–14.

Gilbert, P., & Mascaro, J. (2017). Compassion: Fears, blocks, resistances: An evolutionary investigation. In E.M. Seppala, E. Simon-Thomas, S.L. Brown, M.C. Worline, L. Cameron, & J.R. Doty (Eds), *The Oxford handbook of compassion science* (pp. 399–420). Oxford University Press.

Gilbert, P., McEwan, K., Matos, M., & Rivis, A. (2011). Fears of compassion: Development of three self-report measures. *Psychology and Psychotherapy: Theory, Research and Practice*, *84*, 239–255. http://doi.org/10.1348/147608310X526511

Gilbert, P., McEwan, K., Mitra, R., Franks, L., Richter, A., & Rockliff, H. (2008). Feeling safe and content: A specific affect regulation system? Relationship to depression, anxiety, stress and self-criticism. *The Journal of Positive Psychology, 3*, 182–191.

Gross, J.J., & John, O.P. (2003). Individual differences in two emotion regulation processes: Implications for affect, relationships, and well-being. *Journal of Personality and Social Psychology*, *85*, 348–362.

Grossman, P., & Taylor, E.W. (2007). Towards understanding respiratory sinus arrhythmia: Relations to cardiac vagal tone, evolution, and biobehavioural functions. *Journal of Biological Psychology, 74,* 263–285. doi:10.1016/j.biopsycho.2005.11.014

Hempel, R.J., Rushbrook, S.C., O'Mahen, H.A., & Lynch, T.R. (2018). How to differentiate overcontrol from undercontrol: Findings from the RefraMED study and guidelines from clinical practice. *The Behaviour Therapist, 41*(3), 132–141.

Junger, S. (2016). *Tribe: On homecoming and belonging*. London: 4th Estate.

Keane, R. (2016). Emotional under and overcontrol: Exploring the underdeveloped dialectic. Unpublished doctoral dissertation. National University of Ireland, Dublin.

Keogh, K., Booth, R., Baird, K., Gibson, J., & Davenport, J. (2016). The radical openness group: A controlled trial with a 3-month follow-up. *Practice Innovations, 1*(2), 129–143.

King, L.A., & Emmons, R.A. (1990). Conflict over emotional expression: Psychological and physical correlates. *Journal of Personality and Social Psychology, 58*(5), 864–877.

Lee, R.M., Draper, M., & Lee, S. (2001). Social connectedness, dysfunctional interpersonal behaviors, and psychological distress: Testing a mediator model. *Journal of Counselling Psychology, 48*(3), 310–318. https://doi.org/10.1037/0022-0167.48.3.310

Linehan, M. (1993). *Cognitive behavioral treatment of borderline personality disorder.* New York: Guilford Press.

Lucre, K., & Clapton, N. (2020) The compassionate kitbag: A creative and integrative approach to compassion-focused therapy. *Psychology & Psychotherapy: Theory Research & Practice, 94*(1), 1–20. doi:10.1111/papt.12291

Lynch, T.R. (2018a). *Radically open dialectical behavior therapy: Theory and practice for treating disorders of overcontrol.* Oakland, CA: Context Press.

Lynch, T.R. (2018b). *The skills manual for radically open dialectical behavior therapy.* Oakland, CA: Context Press.

Lynch, T.R. (2018c). Tribe matters: An introduction to radically open dialectical behavior therapy. *The Behavior Therapist, 41*(3), 116–125.

Lynch, T.R., Hempel, R.J., Whalley, B., Byford, S., Chamba, R., Clarke, P., Clarke, S., Kingdon, D., O'Mahen, H., Remington, B., Rushbrook, S.C., Shearer, J., Stanton, M., Swales, M., Watkins, A., & Russell, I.T. (2020). Refractory depression – Mechanisms and efficacy of radically open dialectical behaviour therapy (RefraMED): Findings of a randomised trial on benefits and harms. British Journal of Psychiatry, *216*(4), 204–212. doi:https://doi.org/10.1192/bjp.2019.53

Miller, M.W., Kaloupek, D.G., Dillon, A.L., & Keane, T.M. (2004). Externalizing and internalizing subtypes of combat-related PTSD: A replication and extension using the PSY-5 scales. *Journal of Abnormal Psychology, 113*, 636–645.

Mischel, W. (1968). *Personality and assessment.* New York: Wiley.

Mischel, W., & Ebbesen, E.B. (1970). Attention in delay of gratification. *Journal of Personality and Social Psychology, 16*(2), 329–337. doi:10.1037/h0029815

Mischel, W., Ebbesen, E.B., & Raskoff Zeiss, A. (1972). Cognitive and attentional mechanisms in delay of gratification. *Journal of Personality and Social Psychology, 21*(2), 204–218. https://doi.org/10.1037/h0032198

Neuberg, S.L., & Newsom, J.T. (1993). Personal need for structure: Individual differences in the desire for simpler structure. *Journal of Personality and Social Psychology, 65*(1), 113–131. https://doi.org/10.1037/0022-3514.65.1.113

Orsmond, G., & Cohn, E. (2015). The distinctive features of a feasibility study: Objectives and guiding questions. *OTJR: Occupation, Participation & Health, 35*(3), 160–177. doi:10.1177/1539449215578649

O'Sullivan, C. (2021). *Exploring overcontrol: From evidence to experiences.* Unpublished doctoral dissertation. National University of Ireland, Dublin.

Panksepp, J., & Biven, L. (2012) *The archaeology of mind: Neuroevolutionary origins of human Emotion.* New York: W.W. Norton.

Porges, S.W. (2011). *The Polyvagal Theory: Neurophysiological foundations of emotions, attachment, communication, and self-regulation.* New York: W.W. Norton.

Porges, S.W. (2018). Polyvagal Theory: A primer. In S. Porges & D. Dana (Eds), *Clinical applications of the Polyvagal Theory* (pp. 50–72). New York: W.W. Norton.

Porges, S.W. (2021, August). Response to criticisms of the Polyvagal Theory. www.polyvagalinstitute.org/background

Sackett, D.L., Rosenberg, W.M., Gray, J.A., & Haynes, R.B. (1996). Evidence based medicine: What it is and what it isn't. *British Medical Journal*, 13(312) (7023), 71–72. doi:10.1136/bmj.312.7023.71

Samuel, D.B., Riddell, A., Lynam, D.R., Miller, J.D., & Widiger, T.A. (2012). A five-factor measure of obsessive–compulsive personality traits. *Journal of Personality Assessment, 94*(5), 456–465. doi:10.1080/00223891.2012.677885

Steindl, S., Bell, T., Dixon, A., & Kirby, J.N. (2022). Therapist perspectives on working with fears, blocks and resistances to compassion in compassion focused therapy. *Counselling and Psychotherapy Research, 00*, 1–14. https://doi.org/10.1002/capr.12530

Swales, M. (2018). Dialectical behaviour therapy: Development and distinctive features. In M. Swales (Ed.), *The Oxford handbook of dialectical behaviour therapy.* Oxford: Oxford University Press. doi: 10.1093/oxfordhb/9780198758723.001.0001

Thompson, M.M., Naccarati, M.E., Parker, K.C.H., & Moskowitz, G.B. (2001). The personal need for structure and personal fear of invalidity measures; Historical perspectives, current applications and future directions. In G.B. Moskowitz (Ed.), *Cognitive social psychology: The Princeton symposium on the legacy and future of social cognition* (pp. 19–39). Mahwah, NJ: Lawrence Erlbaum.

White, L. (2002). *The action manual: Techniques for enlivening group process and individual counselling.* Self-published.

Wildes, J.E., Marcus, M.D., Crosby, R.D., Ringham, R.M., Dapelo, M.M., Gaskill, J.A., & Forbush, K.T. (2011). The clinical utility of personality subtypes in patients with anorexia nervosa. *Journal of Consulting and Clinical Psychology, 79,* 665–674. doi:10.1037/a0024597

Yalom, I.D. (1985). *The theory and practice of group psychotherapy* (4th ed.). New York: Basic Books.

Yalom, I.D., & Leszcz, M. (2020). *The theory and practice of group psychotherapy* (6th ed.). New York: Basic Books.

Appendix A

The GROhari Exercise Handout

Much of your time in the individual reflection session will have been spent discussing the categories of the GROhari Exercise. The name comes from a training aid used to teach group therapy called the Johari Window. This has been modified for GRO and so it has been named the GROhari Exercise. Yes, we know it's not that funny!

The GROhari Exercise helps you to plot four aspects of your overcontrol which are explained here:

REFLECTING	**SHARING**
ACCOMPANYING	**MOVING FORWARD**

Reflecting

This is a gentle start in the sense that you are being asked to say what the group have come to know about your overcontrol. For example, you may outline aspects of your overcontrol that you have discussed in group, or you can point out what the group are likely to have noticed. These are the obvious signs of your overcontrol. You know them. We know them. It can be helpful to think about the three themes and how they show up.

Sharing

This can feel scary at first to consider further sharing, but it is important that you control the pace and what you want to share. This category is an invitation to talk about aspects of your overcontrol that you haven't yet disclosed to the group. What you talk about here may take many forms (not all listed here):

- How early experiences have influenced your overcontrol (perhaps an emphasis on achievement, perhaps how early experiences encouraged you to close down)
- Ways in which your overcontrol is currently expressed (this may include many things like self-harm)
- How those close to you have been negatively impacted
- How you have held on to grudges from the past
- The cost of burying so much emotion or getting stuck on the edge of your own life.

This involves trusting the group with material that may be truly challenging to share. There is often an element of shame attached to what is disclosed. This is material that may have never or rarely been shared with others for fear of rejection. Can you take the risk that this tribe will continue to accept you and listen to you without judgement?

Accompanying

This is about inviting the other group members to respond to what you have just said, as well as to what they have noticed about your journey to this point. They will tell you what it has been like to listen to what you have just disclosed and to have travelled this journey with you. We encourage you to try and be open to what they are saying (which can be more challenging than it sounds).

The other side of this coin is that in addition to letting them accompany you, there is the opportunity for you to accompany them. This means neither bland validation ("you're a lovely person...") or advice ("what you need to do is..."). What is most useful is to honour what they have just disclosed, show acceptance and support, and let them know how their journey is connecting with you. This is not just in what you say, but in how your signalling, even your tone of voice, can help them to reach ventral. This is a time to contribute to deep, safe connection.

Moving Forward

This final category is a declaration of hope and intent. This presents the opportunity to lay down a marker as to what you want to focus on for the rest of the programme. Are you going to work on all three themes or is there one that stands out as being particularly important for you? This is also a chance to reflect on the changes you are already noticing in group and consider how you want to bring these to your life outside the group. It is often best to think small, with the group as the starting place. Give this some serious thought. It is not for anyone else to choose the direction you decide to take.

A Few Suggestions

- **Don't leave this until the last minute**. GROhari is an important step in the programme. Have something to hand you can scribble on because some points are so uncomfortable that they could easily be forgotten. Write down headings – but don't overthink things! This may seem contradictory but the GROhari Exercise should be done from the heart, not the head. You want to tap into some emotion. That is more important than an overrehearsed, exhaustive list.
- **Take the plunge**. Particularly in the second category of further sharing, you may be drawn to holding back and coming up with reasons as to why sharing might not be such a good idea. If in doubt, be courageous. Don't think about it, justify it, reason with it. Just go for it.
- **Think tribal.** GROhari needs your active participation with others as they take their steps. In the third category, you will be asked to authentically honour each member of the group for what they have just disclosed. You may tie this to other things you have learned about them on their journey. A premise of GRO is that the others in the group would profit more from your listening, your authentic signalling, your acceptance of their story than your advice. Can you accompany them and let yourself be accompanied?
- **Think about what is important for you.** It is too easy to hide behind some very broad or vague aims. What is it you want to bring from the group to your life outside?

Appendix B

The Tracker Handout

The Tracker is a core component of the final sessions of GRO. It is a way for you to record and track your efforts to be more radically open. It helps to create experiences that may not otherwise happen, moments when you engage more fully with life. It is a tool that enables you to gently push yourself to make fundamental, durable changes in relation to the three themes. It is a way to share these with the group so that everyone understands each other's struggles and triumphs.

Key features of overcontrol are avoidance, vigilance, and caution. You will have learned during the GROhari Exercise that, due to different experiences, some people feel that connection, flexibility, and emotional experience and expression are fraught with danger. That is why you have learned to prioritise trying to feel safe over active participation. Therefore, any new engagement with life is going to be anything but straightforward, since it will set off alarm bells. Engagement with the Tracker is going to highlight many well-worn paths and flush out the fears that keep them in place. From the Tracker, it will also become apparent that opportunities for engagement are far more common than you might have imagined.

How Do I Grasp the Tracker?

The best way to grasp the Tracker is to observe a few in action. The facilitators will demonstrate some of their recent examples. Trackers generally begin to make sense after you have seen them. Trying them out will highlight the parts you understand and the parts you don't. The questions you may have after early attempts will help build a fuller understanding. This handout, alongside what is shown in group, will help you learn how the Tracker can be used.

A good way to start understanding the Tracker is by reflecting on a recent moment when you "crossed a line" in relation to one of the three themes (distance in relationships, rigidity, inhibited emotion).

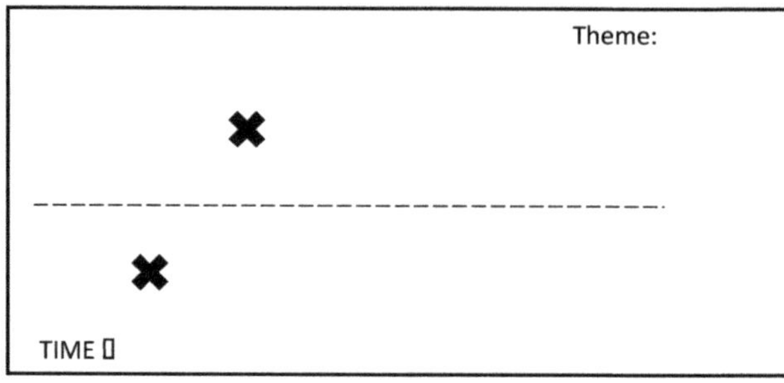

An X below the line represents your usual, habitual overcontrolled style. While there is nothing wrong with being below the line (indeed, it is necessary in some circumstances), a life spent largely below the line is likely to incur heavy costs over time (such as loneliness). Thus, catching this moment where you sought to engage with life, either through connection, flexibility, or emotional expression is important. You are representing this with an X above the line so that this moment can be discussed with the group.

Unsuccessful attempts to "cross the line" turn out to be just as interesting. They provide us with important information about the protectors that act as blocks and obstacles to change. So, don't rule out Xs below the line as being of no value.

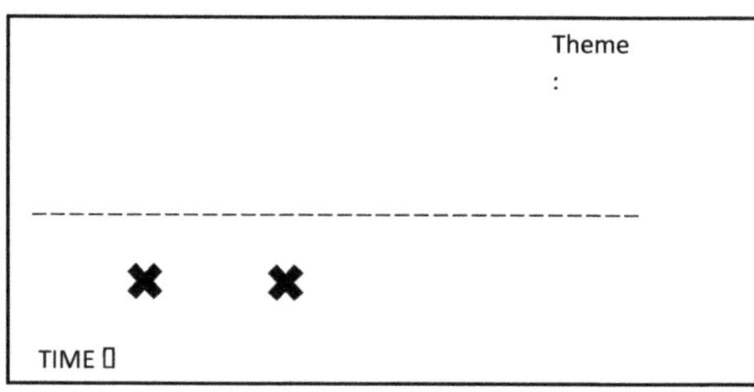

However, the single line does not catch enough aspects of what would be helpful to know. There may be moments when you are open to engagement, but an opportunity does not present itself. For example, you may have contacted a friend with the intent of improving connection, but the friend might not have been available or keen to connect at that time. In this case there was an openness to change, but there was no opportunity to follow it through.

This now gives us three categories: reluctance to engage with an opportunity of connection, flexibility, emotion; being open to such an experience; actual engagement with the experience.

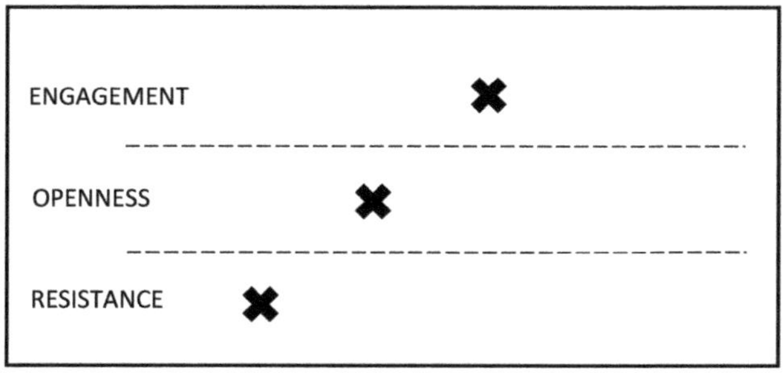

The majority of Xs are in one of these three categories, but it has been helpful to include two more. Many people talk of an unwillingness to risk engaging with change because of their fears of what might happen if they fully committed to a new path. To give an example from the GROhari Exercise, you may have been reluctant to share vulnerable information about yourself because you had strong images of the group rejecting you when they got to know the "real you". It is such catastrophic fears that often encourage our persisting with avoidance and staying on the edge of life. Even if these fears rarely materialise, they need to be placed somewhere so that they can be referred to, named, and validated.

Finally, there is a state that seems more "tuned out and shut down" than reluctant. People refer to lying in bed, feeling numb, or being dissociated in a way that seems much less active. You need to be able to record if sometimes you have felt too overwhelmed to function. This "shutdown" dorsal state is the final category of the Tracker.

This gives us the five levels of the Tracker that we use in GRO. It may be useful to use these terms mentioned here to give a rough sense of the five levels.

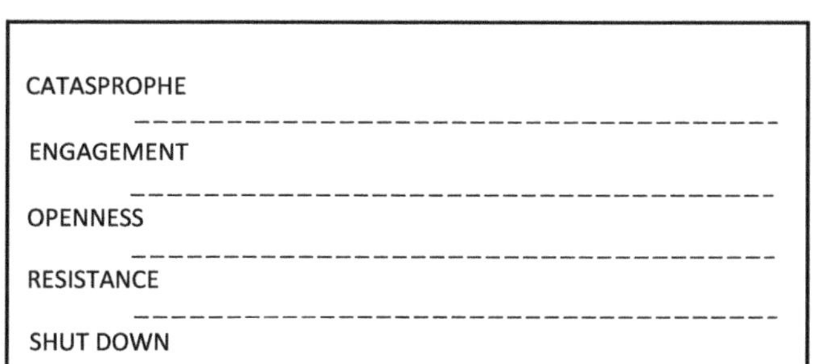

Since the terms vary depending on the theme, we refer to the five levels by number. This may seem odd at first, but it is amazing how quickly the numbers become a shared language. Presented here are the Tracker numbers in relation to the three themes.

Theme 1: Distance in Relationships	
5	Feared catastrophic outcome.
4	Connecting or engaging with others in an authentic way.
3	Open to connection.
2	Avoiding, deflecting, distancing. Not sharing. Not trusting.
1	Completely disconnected.

Theme 2: Rigidity	
5	Feared catastrophic outcome.
4	Actively flexible, spontaneous, embracing novelty, ambiguity, or other perspectives.
3	Open to flexibility.
2	Wilfully rigid, opting for tight control. Perfectionistic or overly judgmental. Overly cautious. Inhibiting spontaneity or joy. Locked in own perspective.
1	Mindlessly rigid.

Theme 3: Inhibited Emotion	
5	Feared catastrophic outcome.
4	Feeling emotions on the one hand and expressing them on the other, experiencing their ebb and flow. (Strong or distressing emotions are still a 4, not a 5.)
3	Open to emotion but none present.
2	Suppressing, purposefully shutting down emotion or its expression.
1	Numb.

As you can see, the numbers have different meanings for each theme.

It is important to note that the Tracker numbers are not progressive. One is not better than another, nor does a higher number represent more of anything. Each number has its own meaning.

As a general rule, overcontrol will result in too many 2s in your life. Growth will come from trying to include more 4s. What you will also find is that the more you commit to a 4, the more you expose your 5s (the feared outcome in your mind as to what is the worst that could happen).

Tips and Tricks for Doing Trackers

Here are six tips you may find useful when you are carrying out a Tracker:

1 **Create a habit of being Radically Open.** This is what the Tracker should capture. It doesn't matter whether the example is a success or not; the aim is to attempt to be more radically open. Remember that Radical Openness is focused on the three themes – you need to be clear which one is under investigation. Your Tracker should fit with what you prioritised in the final category of your GROhari Exercise.
2 **Choose short and recent.** Stick to an example that lasted no more than 10 or 15 minutes in real time. It is fine to consider something longer in describing the overall context, but when it comes to doing a Tracker, it needs to refer to a brief period of time. The event should also have occurred within the last couple of days.
3 **Examples should be meaningful and activating.** It is important you do not describe something just because it happened. Most of your Trackers should get your heart rate going a little, both because they matter and because they touch areas that are not comfortable. There will usually be a physical response to a meaningful Tracker that we encourage you to catch.
4 **Aim small.** Change comes from a series of small, everyday examples that build into something significant, rather than through some dramatic moment of resolution. Something small can also symbolise something much bigger. Don't apologise for your example appearing trivial – because it probably isn't!
5 **Chase your 5s.** If you don't know what your 5s are, then you are not going deep enough into your 4s. Those 5s are long established fears. They need to be exposed so that you can decide if you want to leave them in the driving seat, silently dictating your life of 2s.
6 **Always finish with a take-home message.** Ideally, this will be specific and important to you – something you have learned about yourself from this Tracker. The aim is to build momentum. Saying aloud what you have learned from one Tracker often helps to set up the next.

Tips and Tricks for Questioning Trackers

Unstructured questions about an individual's Tracker can easily wander off target, and so it is proposed that the questioner stick to a specific set of enquiries. Here are seven that help a person reflect on their Tracker.

- **Which of the themes are you working on here?**
- **Tell us why you have chosen this example.**
- **Give us a brief context for this Tracker and then mark your Xs.**
- **What strikes you when you see this Tracker?**
- **Choose a point where you crossed a line. How did you know that you had crossed that line?**
- **What are your take-home messages?**
- **What would you like to do next?**

These questions allow space to reflect on the Tracker and to work out the next steps to be taken on the Radically Open journey.

In relation to questioning someone about their Tracker, here are some points that might prove helpful.

1 Stick to the questions on the list. It can feel a bit inhibiting to read out a prepared set of questions, but this is the best thing to do. Resist the temptation to be creative, particularly in the early days of Trackers. There will still be much for you to do.

2 Listen to the answers. Sometimes your responsibility will be to slow things down rather than let someone march on without direction. Is it clear which theme they have chosen? If they are uncertain which one they are exploring, the example will be harder to follow (they can always do a second Tracker on the same material using a different theme). Is it clear that they have a short (no more than 10–15 minutes), recent (within the last day or two) example? Some examples have enough material for more than one Tracker (which is great), but they can only do one Tracker at a time. If it is the inhibited emotion theme, is it clear which emotion they are tracking? Sometimes they can drift in to other emotions or indeed the emotions of other people. Finally, it is worth asking yourself whether you feel a question has been really answered. If not, repeat it. Maybe we should say that again. Sometimes the most helpful thing you can do is to repeat the question!

3 Tread lightly. This is tricky because, as far as possible, you want the person doing the Tracker to get lost in their own thoughts and have some uninterrupted time to reflect. But, on the other hand, you don't want them to get lost in a wider story that becomes distracting. We can help you with this one.

4 Check the Xs. You may need to question the position of some Xs. You don't want to be undermining if a pattern makes sense to someone, but an occasional gentle query can help. For example, some people are reluctant to give themselves a 4 when it is clearly warranted. They may need a little cheerleading.
5 Get them to reflect. The reflections are not on life – they are specific to the Tracker. Your reflections are only likely to distract, so probe for their own.
6 Make sure they finish with a take-home message. It is important that they state something they have learned about themselves from this specific Tracker and commit to some specific actions. It can be a telling end.

One Event – Three Themes

Here is an example of a brief event with material for a Tracker.

Last night I was thinking about phoning my sister and then I thought why bother. It's only going to be hassle and I'll feel put upon. The next thing she'll be dumping her kids with me and heading off, and I'll really go off the edge. And then I thought, but I do actually want to phone her and so I did. We started chatting. It turns out that we are both really concerned about how Mum has been. I told her I had been over the previous morning and Mum was just staring into space. When I had got back into the car, I felt the tears stream down my face. I told my sister this and she was so supportive. I talked more than I usually do, and I checked in with her. I said if she and the kids were in the area tomorrow to make sure to drop in.

The person now has to choose the theme under which this will be explored. To illustrate this point, the same event is explored under each of the themes. Here are the three Trackers:

Tracker on Distance in Relationships

Which of the themes are you working on here?

Distance in Relationships.

Tell us why you have chosen this example.

I have always had a difficult relationship with my sister, partly because she is very undercontrolled in contrast to my overcontrol. I would like to spend more time with her. I also need to spend more time with her as there are things we have to attend to together (such as looking after our elderly mother). I tend to enjoy being with her more than I think I will, and so the challenge for me is to call in or pick up the phone. I am very good at dissuading myself when the thought or opportunity of contact presents itself.

Give us a brief context for this Tracker and then mark your Xs.

This was a moment yesterday evening when I was wondering whether to phone her or not. On the one hand, I had an urge to phone her. On the other hand, I had worries as to what this might open up. Anyway, I did phone her and this is what happened. My first 2 is me telling myself that no good can come from the contact. I stay in that reluctant zone for a bit longer. Then I feel a certain openness, a 3, which I close down, back to a 2. And then, I just pick up the phone and stay engaged with her when we are talking, the two 4s.

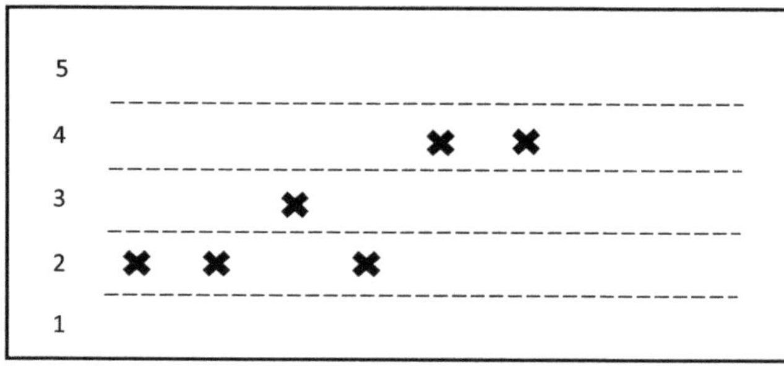

What strikes you when you see this Tracker?

I think that first 3 and then the jump from a 2 to a 4 are significant. I can go to a 3 but that is inevitably followed by a 2, which I am great at justifying to myself. As I moved to that first 4, I had 5s ringing in my ears ("you will pay for this; she is going to take such advantage of you"). But I just said, "sod it, phone her". I didn't delay, which would have given time for all the doubts to really get going. I think that is key. Then I was pleased that when I did connect, I stayed with the 4s. I didn't go down to the beckoning 2. I opened up with her about my feelings whereas I would usually stay interrogating her.

Choose a point where you crossed a line. How did you know that you had crossed that line?

To be honest, I think it's the first 3. I was saying to myself that I did want to phone her. There was probably no going back from then. I felt a sort of openness in my heart, in place of my usual gut-churning 2s.

What are your take-home messages?

I think this Tracker is highly relevant. I don't think I am bad at connecting. I think I am good at not bothering. I am not sure I would have connected with her, other than I knew I was due a Tracker today. That really motivated me to push ahead. This applies to so many people in my life. I know the reclusive me is an easy option, and one that drags me down over time. I hate to see this side of me, so it's a word I should be using to bring it home to me – I am too reclusive.

What would you like to do next?

I don't like to quote NIKE but "JUST DO IT" does come to mind. I have too many ways of feeling good about not doing. I need to see making that connection as really important. So, I am going to keep saying if in doubt, opt in rather than out – with my sister, but also right across the board. I know my life is better when there are more people in it, and I am connecting authentically with them. So, you are going to see many more connections over the next while.

Tracker on Rigidity

Here is a Tracker from the same event on the second theme.

Which of the themes are you working on here?

Rigidity.

Tell us why you have chosen this example.

I am highly judgemental. I go to contempt very easily – towards myself as well as others. I have what I term "standards". These are very tight rules and boundaries that I believe the world should operate within. I love my sister, but I hate the way she does things. I have this constant criticism of her going on my head when I am with her. I like to control my contact with her.

Give us a brief context for this Tracker and then mark your Xs

This Tracker was an opportunity for me to loosen up on my judgement of her, and an opportunity for me to open myself to her kids. I start in my usual 2. Then I feel that I could do something different. Before I get a chance to go back down again, I open myself to her view, my first 4, and then to a spontaneous suggestion, my second 4.

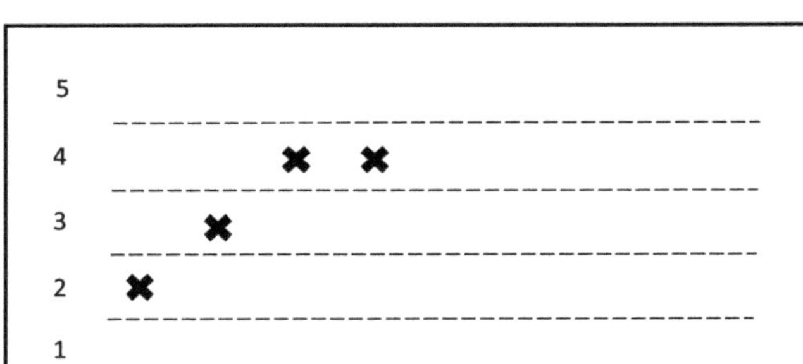

What strikes you when you see this Tracker?
I think it's probably staying with the second 4. It's too easy for me to go to a 4 and then go straight back to that critical, rigid 2. Here in this second 4, I engage with her on her terms and I told her to pop over with her kids which is a crazily spontaneous suggestion ... well for me anyway!

Choose a point where you crossed a line. How did you know that you had crossed that line?

It's the move from the 3 to the 4. I felt grounded, quiet. I was listening to her, not jumping ahead in my own mind. I was engaging her instead of being in my own head.

What are your take-home messages?

I think there are two things going on here. The first is that there is a moment after I open up to her that I really try and get inside her head, get her perspective. That is very, very unusual for me because when you know the answer to everything, there is no need for another viewpoint! I think the second thing is that I don't need to relate to my nieces so rigidly. Of course they should be dropping in. I am their uncle, for God's sake.

I do think life would be easier if I was less certain, less inflexible, less rule-bound. Other people in my life would undoubtedly gain from less rigid expectation, but maybe I would too. It's not just others who fail me, perhaps most of all it is me that fails me.

What would you like to do next?

I am going to bring you examples next time of me easing up, letting go a little with myself and with others.

Tracker on Inhibited Emotion

Here is a Tracker from the same event on the third theme.

Which of the themes are you working on here?

Inhibited Emotion. And the emotion is sadness

Tell us why you have chosen this example

I remember doing the "circles" exercise earlier in the programme and two things stuck out. One was the big angry expressive circle that dominated the board. The other was the contrast between my experienced sadness (quite big), and the little dot that represented my expressed sadness. I know my anger is a way for me to mask my sadness, and I am beginning to understand the reasons for this. It is time to lean into my sadness.

Give us a brief context for this Tracker and then mark your Xs

This catches a moment when I had left my Mum. I noticed just how old she has suddenly become and I let myself feel that when I was back in my car. I started off in a 2, which is all very practical and focusing on what needs to be done. There was another minute of that. And then I just asked myself what I was feeling. No action. No focus on anyone else. I just asked myself, how am I doing? And that's my 3. The 4 is some gentle crying that I let happen before I "pulled myself together", back to a 2.

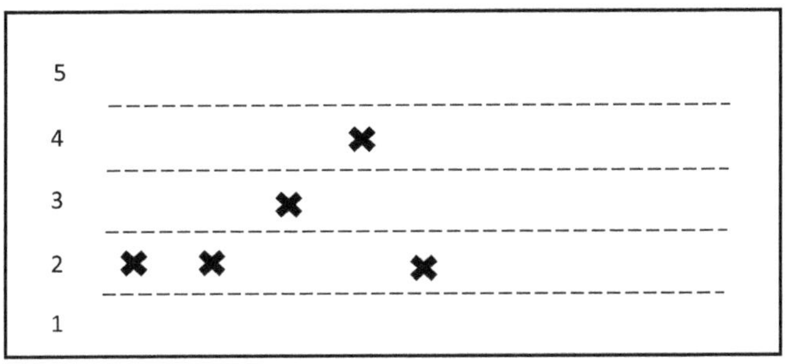

What strikes you when you see this Tracker?

I think it's that moment in the car going from a 3 to a 4 when I felt the tears trickling down my face and I stayed with it. I could say that I shut it down quick enough (which I did) and that it's typical that I didn't let anyone hear or see my sadness (which I didn't), but actually it's huge for me to let the sadness come at all. It's been a very long time since a tear of sadness rolled down my cheek.

Choose a point where you crossed a line. How did you know that you had crossed that line?

It's that moment when I crossed into a 4. I am well pleased that I got into sadness, even if it was brief. I felt the weight of it, I felt it heaving through my body. And I was able to move away from it when I needed. That's important because one of my real terrors is that if I open it up, I won't be able to put the cork back in again. I'll be left crying and shuddering for days. That's one of my feared 5s, which of course didn't happen.

What are your take-home messages?

Keep at this. It's OK. I can survive my emotions, and I may actually feel better afterwards.

What would you like to do next?

The next step is truly scary because I know that it's not a true 4 until I let my sadness come when I am with someone. That terrifies me saying that out loud because there is no logical reason not to do this, and yet the prospect fills me with a physical dread. That must be the next step.

Appendix C

Frequently Asked Questions

1 Is there an evidence base for GRO?

The answer is yes. To understand the status of the evidence base requires an understanding of how GRO has been developed. In its development, we followed the principles of "evidence-based practice" which were first set out by Sackett in the field of medicine, and later applied to many other disciplines (Sackett et al, 1996). This comprises three elements: our own clinical observations, the preferences and views of those who have participated in the programme, and formal evaluation of our outcome measures. Each of these is outlined here.

First, our clinical observations motivated our interest in whether overcontrol might underlie many treatment-resistant forms of psychopathology. The journey from there to the final GRO model has been outlined in Chapter 1. Although that covers the formal steps along the way, it catches less of how we integrated our clinical observations at each step. At GRO consult meetings, at team meetings, and informally, we were constantly posing questions. We wanted to work out how best to create a structure that would allow participants to become more curious about their overcontrol, more accepting of how it developed, and more open to ways of softening it. We were always trying out options with GRO colleagues, asking them for their ideas, seeing how an exercise could be refined. In the eight years building GRO with this population, our clinical observations continuously grew, and this accumulating body of knowledge greatly informed the development of the programme over time.

Second, in respect of the importance of adapting to clinical need and participant preferences, we met every participant at the end of treatment. This now amounts to over 300 people. The negligible attrition levels for a treatment spanning five months are remarkable, but we wanted to know what kept them attending. When they described the differences the intervention had made, we wanted to understand their perspective. What did they feel had been the contributory factors? We listened to their responses, trying to set aside our preconceived ideas. To further minimise our influence or their potential wish to please us, we enlisted the help of a graduate student who was not part of the programme to carry out further interviews. Some of her findings have been outlined in Chapter 1 (O'Sullivan, 2021). This feedback influenced certain practices within the model. For example, participants reported how much they valued breaking into pairs (particularly in online groups) and so we have made that a feature of many sessions. They talked about the importance of having space for their own work. Thus, we expanded the time spent on GROhari and Trackers so that they could follow their own goals at their own pace. These are some examples of participant preferences that we integrated.

The third element of our approach is our formal assessment of outcome. This is in line with the value we place on scientific evidence in improving the quality of GRO. Each participant is given a battery of questionnaires at the start and end of every programme. This allowed us chart how GRO was superior to our early skills group. It has also informed us that our online groups have been effective, but not quite as effective as those held in person (see question 7). It has provided the opportunity to trial measures for a more formal study. Our feasibility study, again detailed in Chapter 1, not only shows very promising results but is a crucial step required before the gold standard of a randomised control trial (Egan et al., 2021). The constant expansion of our evidence base is central to our work.

2 Is the model still developing?

The model has been fully developed. We are not anticipating that any of the core elements of this group therapy are likely to change. There are variants in practice however, notably in the length of sessions and the spacing between them. Our colleagues in Inverness run one GRO group per week, while in Westgate, the sessions are shorter but more frequent. In supervising these two teams, we have seen that there is plenty of room for individual style, and one of the joys is that the sessions are not too tightly scripted. However, the group is essentially the same and the outcomes and feedback are very similar.

The one area in which there may be future modification is the use of the Polyvagal ladder and its accompanying language and constructs. Polyvagal Theory has been adopted by many therapists. It is an accessible, stimulating, and awareness-enhancing model to use. We have tried other lenses but this is the one that our participants have found most helpful. It adds greatly to all three themes. The science behind the theory is not without its critics (see, e.g., Grossman & Taylor, 2007). Porges has made serious efforts to refute these criticisms but, without question, there is room for further research to test out the central hypotheses (Porges, 2021).

3 What happens when the programme has finished?

At some point, two or three weeks after the end of the programme, the facilitators meet the same individuals they met for the mid-way reflection session. This is a chance to discuss together our ideas for a report or letter to their referring agent. We like to detail their journey, not only so that others involved in their treatment are aware of their progress, but also so that each person feels that their efforts were recognised. We read them an early draft of the letter so that they have an opportunity to provide input. They are often moved by hearing how carefully we have followed their journey and valued their contribution. The letter is addressed to them and copied to the referring agent. It aims to capture their progress in a thoughtful manner, including their courage, strength, and struggles over the five months. This letter also provides the opportunity to make any onward recommendations.

The meeting is also a chance to catch up. It is always interesting to see what they have found most valuable, what they miss now that the group has ended, and the challenges they face in bringing its benefits to their life outside group. They generally appreciate the chance to discuss this transition. It is important for them to hear that in our longer-term research, many describe more change in the six months after treatment. The end of the programme does not mean that their progress is halted.

4 Is GRO a specific trauma treatment?

No. Many people who come to GRO have a history of trauma. It is likely that they will progress to a trauma programme (we happen to have a very good one in our hospital!). They will be in an immeasurably stronger position to benefit. They will have experienced trusting others and connecting with them. They will have worked on being more open. They will understand their protectors and ambivalence. They will also have a deeper and more compassionate sense of their history. Their emotions will be far more easily accessed. For those who are overcontrolled, GRO offers a strong foundation to take on the challenges of trauma work.

5 Should someone participating in a GRO group read this book?

This is a book to aid people running a GRO programme. It may be of interest for participants to read after they have completed GRO. However, we would foresee problems with someone reading the book at the same time as participating in a programme. Our concern is that it may foster too much thinking, too many comparisons, too many views on how the facilitator is doing their job, all of which are likely to prove distracting. Further, the readers may be set apart from others in the group, and their spontaneity may be dampened as they know what lies ahead. This not a psycho-educational group in which new information is the way forward. GRO benefits from getting away from the cerebral to the experiential, and that is not likely to be enhanced keeping one chapter ahead.

6 What about handouts?

In our first GRO group, the participants arrived armed with notebooks and pens. They liked taking notes and discussing the finer points of what was being covered. While it may have suited them to maintain some distance in this way, it did not suit the purpose of the group. When we started providing handouts, it was easier for us to discourage note-taking. The sessions on the three themes, on the Polyvagal ladder, on the GROhari, and on the Tracker, all benefit from some clearly presented information that they can read again. However, the handouts are not set in stone. To the contrary, they evolve and change with each group to reflect the particular dynamic and specific discussions within that group. We would be happy to support you in building your own set of handouts for your population.

7 Can GRO be offered online?

Yes, GRO has been shown to work very well online with certain minor adaptations. It is not something we planned; we had only ever envisaged offering GRO face-to-face. In March 2020, however, the arrival of Covid brought our hospital-based groups to a halt. In a predicament faced by so many, we found the option of face-to-face work suddenly taken from us. We were fortunate that the hospital responded rapidly. Our two GRO groups operating at the time were functioning online within a week. There were some technological challenges and glitches, but there was great relief and good humour from us all, as we muddled through the early challenges. We researched best practice in delivering therapy and cultivating therapeutic presence online. We found articles to help support this transition (e.g., Geller, 2020).

We were unsure how it would be starting with groups that had never met face-to-face. We put great effort into the early preparations, doing test calls in the week before the group started. This provided the opportunity to give feedback on distance from the camera and even lighting (it sometimes helped to move the angle or position of the laptop). Our group agreements included additional points such as ensuring to keep cameras on, having a confidential space when taking part in the group, ensuring no interruptions, and not looking at phone or emails during sessions.

For the check in and check out, as well as for many of the key exercises, we advised the group to name the person they were passing on to, so as to minimise people talking over each other. We put them in breakout rooms when they were working in pairs. This occasionally led to delays when participants were booted into cyberspace and we could not find them. However, for the most part, it worked well.

There were particular challenges around facilitating the Drawing the Relative Size exercise and the Trackers. We needed to be confident about drawing and marking to their instruction. We shared our screen and then drew on their behalf, checking with them as they went through each exercise to ensure we were capturing their experience correctly. This demanded practice so that we could carry out the tasks smoothly. For GROhari, participants needed to lean towards their camera and show their accompanying both verbally and non-verbally. It was touching how well this worked. Certain variations such as Walking the Tracker had to be omitted. Play was also a challenge as most of our games require physical movement. We went back to the Geese Theatre for recommendations for online play, and they did not disappoint.

We have completed ten cycles of GRO online. We sought feedback as we went along and have been delighted with the results. Overall, the measures and participant feedback showed that GRO continues to be an effective intervention, even when facilitated online. The hybrid group (the first group in 2020) and the face-to-face groups had slightly better outcomes than the online groups which is, perhaps, not surprising. Our aim for the present is to have two face-to-face groups and one online so that we can meet the needs of participants who live far from the hospital or have other obstacles to attending in person.

Index

For Product Safety Concerns and Information please contact our EU representative GPSR@taylorandfrancis.com
Taylor & Francis Verlag GmbH, Kaufingerstraße 24, 80331 München, Germany

www.ingramcontent.com/pod-product-compliance
Ingram Content Group UK Ltd.
Pitfield, Milton Keynes, MK11 3LW, UK
UKHW020140200926
475702UK00005B/843
9781032343358